THE SEASONS OF
RICK RODERICK

THE SEASONS OF RICK RODERICK

A Memoir by **THOMAS ZIGAL**

★ TEXAS WRITERS SERIES

TCU PRESS
Fort Worth, Texas

Cover and title page portrait: Rick Roderick, November 1993. Photo courtesy of Kim Vrungos.

Library of Congress Control Number: 2025049920

TCU PRESS

TCU Box 298300
Fort Worth, Texas 76129
www.tcupress.com

For the boys

Marshall, Travis, Taylor, Max,

Danny, Owen, Willie, Arend

CONTENTS

"We have two or three great moving experiences in our lives—experiences so great and moving that it doesn't seem at the time that anyone else has been so caught up and pounded and dazzled and astonished and beaten and broken and rescued and illuminated and rewarded and humbled in just that way ever before."

F. SCOTT FITZGERALD
"One Hundred False Starts"
The Saturday Evening Post, 1933

HEY, MISTER, CAN YA TELL ME WHERE A MAN MIGHT FIND A BED?

IN THE FALL OF 1969, when I was more or less a senior in college, I lived in Brackenridge dormitory on the University of Texas campus. The illustrious writer and *Harper's* editor Willie Morris had lived in the same dorm seventeen years earlier, but I didn't know who Willie Morris was at the time, and I didn't read his description in *North Toward Home* until many years later:

> Old Brackenridge Hall, a yellow-brick affair with Spanish stucco roofs, stood right at the edge of the long intramural field, only a quarter of a mile from the capitol, and just across a narrow street from a line of dingy shops and greasy cafés. We called it "The Slum Area," not only for its general dinginess but for its violence, both organized and sporadic, which erupted inevitably on the weekend nights after the beer houses across the street closed down. Brackenridge Hall was where life was, stripped of its pretenses, where one saw every day the lonely, the pathetic, the hopeless young men—often poor though sometimes not, often ignorant but not always, but never anything if not various. Here a fairly sensitive boy could not avoid a confrontation with his basic and bare-boned self, and see a big state university in its true dimensions.[1]

The beer houses and greasy cafés were gone by 1969, replaced by a nicer, more expensive dorm, but the poor boys of Brackenridge were still pathetic and hopeless, confronting their bare-boned selves, and I was one of them in good standing.

There was something providential about Rick Roderick's appearance at Brackenridge on that crisp December day at the end of the semester. I was desperate to get out of my year-long contract because I wanted to live off-campus with my girlfriend, and the only way out was to find a replacement to take my room. I had tried to reason with the starch-stiff retired army captain in charge of campus housing, but he wouldn't budge. He didn't like me or my long hair and Moroccan ring and gambler's vest and tasseled Spanish boots and cocky attitude. Everything about me reminded him of the peace pukes he saw every night on the six o'clock news. Everything about him reminded me of Nixon's henchman Bob Haldeman, right down to the waxy black crewcut. After our third and final contentious meeting in his office, he leaned forward in his chair, hands folded on his desk, and said, "Find somebody to take your place, son, or forfeit your deposit and get a bill dunning you for the spring semester, payment due in two weeks. Those are the

Tom Zigal reading in the dorm room at the University of Texas at Austin where he would meet Rick Roderick in December 1969. *Photo courtesy of Thomas Zigal*

rules, my friend. We'll send a collection agency after your parents if we have to."

I couldn't afford to eat the money, even on a generous scholarship from the oil company where my father was an electrician, and I was twenty-one and too old and embarrassed to get my parents involved. So day after day I sat pondering this sorry predicament in my dorm room, fantasizing about unbridled sexual bliss with my lovely redheaded Mississippi girlfriend with striking blue eyes. We'd already secured a place of our own, across the street from Eastwoods Park near campus, a squalid apartment my friend Bill Gallagher was bequeathing to me while he bummed around Europe for eight months. Maggie and I had already tried out the mattress in the small two-room dive and found it a much cozier place to make love than empty classrooms and the back seat of my Dodge Dart.

One afternoon, in the midst of my despair, I heard a loud drawling voice echo through the corridor outside my door. "Does anybody have a spare room around here?" the voice entreated. "Talk to me, people. Does anybody need a roommate?"

My roommate, Roy Burt, glanced up from the desk where he was working on a homework assignment. I leaped off the top bunk, where I was picking my guitar, and raced to the door.

"Hold on a minute," Roy said. We'd already discussed my plans to leave, and I'd promised I wouldn't stick him with a lunatic roommate. "Hey, Zigal, check yourself, man," he said. "Let's not rush into anything crazy, okay?"

Roy Burt was a young black man from Texarkana, a city whose name reveals its exact location on the border of two states. I never told him this, but when I filled out the student housing form, which asked, "Do you have any objections to rooming with a person of another race?" I had actually requested to live with an "Afro-American," the term of preference in those days. I was from a small refinery town on the Texas Gulf Coast, and although I'd studied in Louisiana, New Mexico, and Switzerland and I'd hitchhiked all around Europe and into Morocco by 1969, I'd never known a single black person in my life. I'd rarely even talked to one. And I thought it was time for that to change.

When I asked for a black roommate, I had envisioned Eldridge Cleaver. Instead, I got Julian Bond. Roy was suave, short-haired, clean-shaven, dapper in a sport coat and penny loafers. I liked Motown, Roy liked Miles Davis. I wanted revolution, he wanted conciliation. Roy's desire for acceptance in the mainstream white world led him to pledge a fraternity that fall. Nothing I could do or say would convince him that those rich friendly white boys were racists underneath their corduroy blazers and they would just as soon flay him with a buggy whip than dance next to him at a toga party or drink from the same punch bowl. The Greek system had been forced to integrate only four years earlier at the University of Texas, and by the time Roy arrived on campus, each fraternity had accepted a token black student or two. I couldn't understand what attracted him to that bigoted world.

"You're not dumping some redneck peckerwood on me," Roy said with a hint of genteel anger. "You gave your word."

We could hear the thick Texas drawl of that burly, bearded white boy who was wandering around in the dorm's hallway, looking for a room for the spring semester.

"Let's talk to him, Roy," I said. At that point I really didn't care who took my place. "Don't judge a man by his twang but by the content of his character."

"Correct me if I'm wrong, but did you just quote me some Martin Luther King?"

The burly white boy walked into our room and looked around. He seemed pleased with what he saw in the simple confines—bunk beds, a desk shared by two, a rickety bookcase, peeling green paint on the plaster walls. He was about five feet eight inches tall and weighed two hundred pounds. His dark brown hair was long and shaggy, and he wore a beard that tried to hide the deep acne scars spread across his round cheeks. There was an unlit cigarette behind one ear, hidden in the tangle of hair. He sported scuffed cowboy boots, sagging jeans, and a T-shirt underneath a natty corduroy jacket.

"You've got the Copleston collection," he said with a pleasant laugh, studying the long row of philosophy books on my shelf. I had bought *The History of Philosophy* by Frederick Copleston, S.J. (a Jesuit priest) at the only bookstore in my hometown of Texas City, and I'd transported them to Europe and back. I still hadn't read past the third or fourth volume.

"I've got the same collection," he said. "Are you a philosophy major?"

"Minor."

He extended his hand and gave me a firm power shake. I liked the politics of that gesture. "Roderick," he said, pronouncing his name with two syllables: *Rod-rick*. "I'm a philosophy minor myself."

Arms clutched to his chest, surly and unpersuaded, Roy asked what his major was.

"Speech," Rick Roderick said, and then he laughed that growling laugh that sounded like a John Deere grader crushing gravel on a country road. "I'm from West Texas," he said, "so they're still trying to teach me how to talk."

He glanced through our book collections and our record albums, commenting on what he liked. "*Soul on Ice*," he said, turning to Roy. "Cool book. I love that sentence 'Walk, chicken, with your ass picked clean.'"

He gave the immediate impression of being intelligent, well-read, worldly, with a wicked sense of humor. Roy was put off by the accent, but I wasn't. At twenty-one, I didn't have much of a Texas accent left, but I knew plenty of fine people who did.

"My car's parked illegally down in front," Rick said. "It's full up with my stuff. I drove straight here from Abilene, and everything I own is in that car. If you need a roommate," he turned to Roy, "I need a room. You guys want to help me unload?"

Enough said. I was giddy to tell my girlfriend the great news. Roy was still unconvinced.

"Let's go see what's in his car," I said to Roy after Rick walked out of the room. "If he's got a white hood, we'll veto the idea."

"I don't know about this guy, Zigal. He's like some shitkicker version of a hippie or something. Does not compute."

Rick's dented yellow VW Beetle was crammed to the roof with clothes, books, and LPs. Russian novels, German philosophers, the Rolling Stones, and Bob Dylan.

"You're all right with me, Mr. Rod-rick," I said, grabbing an armful of worn album jackets. "There's a man named Captain Bob Haldeman I want you to meet. He's got some paperwork for you to fill out."

Roy stood next to the VW, glaring at me. "It's gonna work out, Roy," I told him quietly. "You'll like this guy. Give him a chance."

"Did you hear why he left Hardin-Simmons?" Roy asked when Rick was out of earshot. "It sounds like some serious b.s."

Rick's explanation for transferring to the University of Texas involved swarming bats, an underground newspaper, a fight with a folding chair, mandatory chapel, and other grievances. He told us that the Records Office at Hardin-Simmons University in Abilene had refused to release his transcript until he paid his parking tickets and library fines, so he physically nudged aside a couple of bureaucrats and rifled through their file drawers while they called campus security. He escaped with the transcript folder marked "Roderick, Rick" only seconds before the cops arrived.

"I wasn't sure I'd make it to Austin without a shoot-out somewhere around Goldthwaite with the Transcript Police hard on my ass," he said as he placed his Copleston collection on the empty shelf where I had just removed mine.

"You don't know how happy I am that you escaped, my friend," I told him.

Roy was sulking at his side of the desk, watching us transfer books from one box to another.

Rick grinned at me through wide-set teeth. "Over at your new digs, every time you make your girlfriend smile, you tell her she needs to thank a fat man named Rick Rod-rick."

It wouldn't be the last time I heard him refer to himself as The Fat Man.

On that cool sunny day in December 1969, as we exchanged places, loading and unloading our transient belongings contained in a few cardboard boxes, the sum total of all our possessions, I could not have predicted that this stout redneck hippie from Tuscola, Texas, would become my best friend for the next three decades. And that one day, thousands of students, fellow teachers, and a vast lay audience would acknowledge Dr. Rick Roderick as the most charismatic philosophy professor of his time.

WHAT HAPPENED TO RICK RODERICK?

RICK RODERICK IS THE MOST FAMOUS American philosophy professor you've never heard of. If you Google his name and the word *philosopher*, you'll find more than a hundred thousand hits, which is an astonishing amount of current interest in a university philosophy professor who died in 2002. American philosophy professors are as popular and well-known as American blacksmiths.

Rick has attained a cult following due almost entirely to his twenty-four videotaped philosophy lectures produced by the Teaching Company in the early 1990s. Those enlightening and entertaining lectures, which he delivered in front of small audiences in a dark, low-tech studio in the basement of the medical center at Georgetown University, have attracted tens of thousands of fans, including such unlikely admirers as filmmaker George Lucas and the late Utah Senator Orrin Hatch.

Rick's students continue to mourn his loss and honor his memory with websites dedicated solely to him, and countless others have stumbled across his lectures and writings and yearn to hear more from a brilliant thinker and performance artist whose voice was silenced at age fifty-two. One online devotee said that listening to Rick's lectures was "like you weren't listening to a college professor but a crazy buddy in a bar. The voice on the tapes is funny, self-deprecating, and spell-binding as he tries to make as clear as possible such convoluted teachings as those of Heidegger, Habermas, Foucault, and Derrida."

Rick Roderick lecturing for the Teaching Company's videotape series, early 1990s.
Photo courtesy of The Great Courses

Viewers have responded to Rick in a myriad of ways:

"What he was teaching about the way we should approach the world really spoke to me."

"As a conservative Catholic, I love to hear an intelligent, articulate, compelling challenge to my belief system. Guys like Rick Roderick stop us from becoming smug and lazy."

"I owe so many hours of deep delight and existential concern to Rick Roderick. I keep coming back to his lectures like a good piece of music."

"I came to North America from Europe and had never heard of Rick Roderick before. His lectures are probably the best thing that happened to me on this continent."

Admitting his own "pretensions and prejudices," and with a

strong dose of envy, one university philosophy professor confessed online,

> Roderick's thick West Texas accent . . . and casual references to fast-food chains, daytime talk shows, and the like proved difficult to reconcile with the fact that he was primarily talking about very dense, even abstruse critical theory—the kind that only the erudite or severely pretentious claim to meaningfully understand. Roderick, however, had an obvious gift for demystifying the most enigmatic philosophy even for a [lay] audience; and seemingly without having to dilute or misappropriate the discipline's denser elaborations. This lecturing style of nuance *sans* pontification truly was a breath of fresh air. What puzzled me most about this was how someone performing such a feat could look like, talk like, and think like a West Texan, even to the point of seeming like a caricature. My own expectations about the cultural mold that a gifted philosophical mind must fit into clearly needed sober re-evaluation, despite what that reflection might illuminate about my [own] pretentions and prejudices. A careful study of [Roderick's] treasure-trove of lectures . . . seemed to be the only way to examine these expectations and understand why someone radically folksier than I could exact much greater eloquence and efficiency of meaning.[2]

That was Rick Roderick's magic. Intellectuals aren't supposed to look and talk like he did. A German or French accent, sure, but not those boots and that cowboy twang.

At the time of the lectures (1990–93), Rick was a tenure-track philosophy professor at Duke University. His dissertation had been published by St. Martin's Press as *Habermas and the Foundations of Critical Theory* (1986). (Rick once described Jürgen Habermas humorously as "the Hubert Humphrey of the Frankfurt School.") I asked Tom Rollins, the creator of the Teaching Company and its enormously successful videotape program, why he selected Rick out of so many outstanding university philosophy teachers. Rollins explained that he chose the first dozen professors based on student evaluations. He read more than fifty university catalogs and studied ten thousand student evaluations, including those from college debate-club standouts, searching for the best teachers in America. He was looking for a philosophy lecturer who could address the classic issues dating back to the Greeks but also make timeless philosophical discourse immediately relevant to a modern audience. Rick won unanimous praise from a half-dozen Duke debaters who declared him to be their favorite professor and someone who had changed their lives.

Over the next three years, beginning with his video lecture entitled "Philosophy and Human Values" (1990), Rick delivered two dozen lectures covering everything from Socrates to the Frankfurt School, semiotics, and postmodern philosophy, all in a thick West Texas accent with irreverent humor, wisecrack political commentary, and pop culture digressions. He was funny, he was a cascading fount of knowledge, he rarely condescended to his audience. But his admiring students and faculty colleagues, and those drawn to him through his video lectures, were largely unaware of who Rick really was. They could not have imagined the harshness of his Texas upbringing and the tragedy in his early life.

Rick grew up in poverty in a cinderblock hovel on the main street of Tuscola, Texas, population five hundred, a small dusty town eighteen miles south of Abilene and very much like the town of Anarene in Larry McMurtry's *The Last Picture Show.* He was the only child of two alcoholics, and although he had genuine affection for them, his parents were polar opposites of the 1950s TV show *Leave It to Beaver*'s Ward and June Cleaver. Rick's mother gradually separated from her husband and son, even though she lived and operated a beauty parlor only a few blocks away. His father was an amusing, colorful, and irascible eccentric, chronically unemployed, who loved yet berated Rick throughout his childhood.

There was darkness in Rick's youth. He'd been behind the wheel in a car accident that had killed a teenaged girl when he was a junior in high school, and that tragedy was the defining moment in his life. The incident transformed him forever. It was why he immersed himself in philosophy, psychology, and classic literature beginning at age seventeen, and why that redneck country boy pursued the great truths and deeper meaning until his very last breath. His intellectual journey began with the ancient enigma of why a loving God would let the innocent suffer and die, and whether one's life is ruled by fate or design, or simply at the mercy of chaos and entropy.

Rick was a very popular teacher at Duke, but he'd always displayed a rebellious attitude toward authority, and he ran afoul of the administration. In many ways, he resembled another combative Texas leftist and fellow University of Texas alumnus, C. Wright Mills, a leather-jacket-wearing, motorcycle-riding intellectual who wrote the political classic *The Power Elite* and who was often credited with coining the term "the New Left." Rick was denied tenure at Duke, an oft-told tale at every university in America, and he ended up in Southern California, teaching adult education at a university in Los Angeles and lecturing at a retreat for wealthy truth-seekers farther up the coast.

By that time, in the early 1990s, his marriage had unraveled and he and his wife were juggling how to raise their four sons. Rick's difficult teaching schedule, the long hours of travel by car, and the lack of financial stability began to wear him down, and depression descended upon him like the low, stifling Pacific coastal fog he'd seen for the first time. His career was in tatters, his young sons were unhappy in California, and he was desperate to pull his life together.

He remembered Austin with absolute fondness, that alluring refuge for rads and hippies like him and me, and in the summer of 1996 he called to tell me he was thinking about returning to the city he and I loved so much. Coincidentally, my wife, son, and I were moving back to Austin after a decade of following her career in

Aspen, New Orleans, and Atlanta. The two households packed up and U-Hauled back to Austin in August 1996 from opposite sides of the country, and thus began a warm and gratifying period in our lives, jubilant but ultimately short and bittersweet.

Rick and I were ecstatic to be in Austin again after a dozen years apart, and we quickly renewed our brotherly bond and resumed those endless conversations amid gales of laughter and his clouds of cigarette smoke, this time while our sons played video games hour after hour in nearby rooms, becoming best friends as well.

Austin had always been the land of milk and honey, a lush oasis in a dry country, the Athens and Rome of a hostile world. In her memoir *A Strong West Wind*, Amarillo native and Pulitzer Prize winner Gail Caldwell perfectly described that time and place in the late 1960s and 1970s when Rick and I first arrived as students: "In Austin, where the renowned Texas sunsets oversaw dreams and delusions with nonchalant parity, it was easy to lose oneself in a sort of holy madness; all of us, in those days, were acolytes to some higher cause. . . . Most of all, for a decade or two, [Austin] had a community of creative rogues and prophets who saw each day as a rough cut for celestial bliss."[3]

My friend Joe Nick Patoski echoed that sentiment in his book *Austin to ATX: The Hippies, Pickers, Slackers and Geeks Who Transformed the Capital of Texas*: "If you were academically inclined, philosophically different, or artistically gifted growing up in Texas, the university provided options. You didn't necessarily have to leave Texas to seek whatever it was you were looking for. 'Somewhere else' could mean Austin, the one free space in an otherwise harsh, mean culture that tended to look down on education, academics, the arts, outside ideas, blacks, browns, women, and immigrants."[4]

Sadly and unexpectedly, those last five years in Austin would morph from Rick's happy return into his final descent. Toward the end, he began writing an autobiography that promised to reveal how a barefoot country boy from small-town Texas would earn a doctorate in philosophy and become recognized as one of the best teachers in his field, and whose lecture series would become the best-selling videotapes in their day. But he didn't complete the book. He managed to write only a hundred pages before he died of congestive heart failure.

All of us know a handful of people who've had a profound effect on our lives. Sometimes it's one remarkable friend with whom we share our deepest thoughts and concerns, our dreams and aspirations, someone who is a reliable, trustworthy sounding-board for our ideas and ruminations. Rick was that friend for me. He was intellectually dazzling with a razor-sharp wit: intense, passionate, wise, politically engaged and a militant activist, a sports fan and a fabulous cook, sometimes slapstick, sometimes infuriating and wrongheaded and a raving lunatic, loyal to his friends and loved ones, part Falstaff and part Hamlet, and the funniest person I've ever known. My life has been diminished by his departure, lo these many years now. I can't count how many times a week I wonder what he would think about such-and-such. My friends and I often say to one another, "Damn, I wish Rick was alive so we could hear what he has to say about this." Nothing was more hilarious and cathartic than a Rick Roderick Rave.

When Rick and I inhabited this world together, as friends, comrades, and occasional combatants, there was so much joy and laughter, so many long, ongoing screeds and heated discussions, so many strategies concocted and battles won and lost. Our modest professional triumphs were always balanced by disappointments. In our salad days we lived hard, Rick and I and dozens of our friends, the baby-boomer generation of poor and working-class Texas kids who distrusted authority and rebelled at every turn. What was our inspiration? What spurred us on? The usual things, of course—music and films and visual art and a thousand provocative books and magazine articles and underground comics, the '60s zeitgeist that nurtured and shaped us all. The same reasons that Rick explained to an interviewer in 1987 why he chose to study philosophy in college: "I was aimed toward philosophy by the cultural experiences of the late '60s: first by the Civil Rights Movement, by the various assassinations, by the experience of [having] friends that I had known coming back in body bags from the war in Vietnam, and I wanted to try to understand this situation. Philosophy was just one among many things that I read in order to do this."[5]

Like the rebel Hotspur in Shakespeare's *Henry IV, Part I*, we knew that life was short, but if we could survive whatever imminent battle lay before us—the ongoing mortal brawl against the forces of bigotry, ignorance, humorlessness, and death—we would rise triumphant and be vindicated at last. If we could hack our way past that ultimate battle, the existential struggle between darkness and light, then we just might live long enough to tread on kings.

CHILDREN OF PARADISE

WHEN RICK TRANSFERRED to the University of Texas and took over my dorm lease, Maggie and I moved into my friend Bill Gallagher's vacated two-room dump across the street from Eastwoods Park, a few blocks northeast of campus. She and I were both twenty-one years old, but we kept this arrangement from our parents. Although her father was a George Wallace-loving redneck owner of a large and successful feed and seed store in Mississippi, Maggie was a fiercely political leftist-feminist who taught me a thing or two about sex and radical politics. She was a French major who'd read the French classics and the popular books everyone was reading (*The Strawberry Statement, The Second Sex, One Flew Over the Cuckoo's Nest*) and the many alternative periodicals of our time (*The Rag, Rolling Stone*). She didn't own a bra or shave her legs and armpits, and she wore blue jeans and a T-shirt every day, except when she wore cotton granny dresses. I sometimes lay in bed and watched her straighten her long auburn hair with an iron. She spoke with a soft Southern accent and had vivid blue eyes, but as I would soon discover, those stunning eyes were the product of tinted contact lenses, a minor affectation in a young woman who was direct and authentic in every other regard.

Gallagher's garage apartment was an old and dismally maintained student rental property. The exterior gray paint was peeling in scrolls, vines grew into the notched wood siding around the sagging AC window unit, and cockroaches ruled the premises with impunity, as they did all over Student Austin. But it was ours for eight months, and it was cheap. Maggie and I lived in the back room, which also had a small kitchen area, and my brother, Frank, moved in with us at some point and occupied the tiny front room. Gallagher asked me to keep an eye on the MG sports car he'd parked under a dusty tarp in the rickety, doorless garage, and Frank and I toyed with the idea of hot-wiring it for joy rides around town, but we had no idea how to do that. A nebbishy journalism student named Todd lived upstairs and pounded on his manual typewriter day and night, and the ceaseless clacking often kept us awake. Maggie would tap the ceiling with a broom handle to let him know we were annoyed, and he always apologized the next day. I admired his articles in the university's student newspaper, *The Daily Texan*. Many years later I would read that he'd won a major national journalism award.

Eastwoods Park was small and secluded, and there was a wooded magic about its grounds. The trees were old and tall and shady, creating a few quiet acres of dark canopy even in the strong spring daylight. A quaint fairytale bridge crossed the deep mysterious creek that skirted the park. The folklorist J. Frank Dobie's home backed up to the greenery, and although the old writer was dead by then, his white-haired wife still wandered around their yard tending to plants and often waved at us with a maternal smile as we played our guitars on park benches nearby. We thought of Mrs. Dobie as Mother Nature herself, a benign, comforting presence blessing all that she observed.

Eastwoods Park was the first home of Eeyore's Birthday Party, a bacchanalian springtime festival celebrating the innocent characters from *Winnie the Pooh*. An English professor named Jim Ayers started the tradition, and within a few short years, thousands were drawn to the mischief, forcing the party to relocate to the larger Pease Park. But at the gathering in 1970, there were only a few dozen students dressed as wood nymphs, sprites, and other forest creatures of a child's imagination. Maggie, Frank, and I followed the trail of marijuana smoke to the beer kegs and guacamole tables, where a band called Ramon Ramon and the Four Daddyo's was playing cool 1950s music and the pixies and gnomes were dancing beneath the primeval trees. It was an emotional time of war and death and grand deceit, so we Austin hippies escaped into these small harmless pageants wherever we could find them.

My new life near the park felt exuberantly free from the strictures of dorm living, but I stayed in touch with my old buddies by phone, those poor imprisoned bastards. The young nihilist Al Beaty, who lived across the hall from me and often prayed to the Norse god Odin in loud incantations after a quart of Old Milwaukee, began to tell me wild tales about the crazy new guy who'd taken over my dorm lease. Rick would roam from room to room, reading aloud from passages he admired: *A Moveable Feast,* the opening pages of Roger Zelazny's *Lord of Light,* the final pages of *Armies of the Night*. He presided over all-night poker games and cutthroat bridge tournaments and chess matches that lasted days on end. A mother in New Jersey had called Rick and begged him to ban her son from their poker marathons. Apparently the foolish boy had already blown three or four hundred dollars but couldn't restrain himself from the shark pool. (Rick's first rule of poker: "Play with people who are not as good as you.") Rick obliged the mother and gave the boy his money back, but in typical high dramatic style, Rick told him, "Your money's no good here anymore, son." And then he quoted a variation of Edward G. Robinson's famous line in *The Cincinnati Kid*: "As long as I'm around, kid, you're only, uh, about tenth best. You might as well learn to live with it."

But what brought me back to Brackenridge dorm for my return engagement was word that a feud had erupted between my old dormmates and the national championship football team.

The University of Texas Longhorns had won the championship with a victory over Notre Dame in the Cotton Bowl on New Year's Day 1970. The counterculture in general avoided football, considering it an aggressive male war ritual, but we Austin hippies came out of the closet to support the Horns and celebrate their triumph in stoned mayhem, throwing one hell of a wild street party on the Drag next to campus. My old Texas City schoolmate Joe Duoto and

I watched the madness from the detached serenity of Middle Earth, a mellow second-story drug clinic for freaks on bad acid trips. We weren't tripping, but the view was terrific and we avoided the drunken frat boys puking on their tasseled loafers down on Guadalupe Street.

Our goodwill toward football heroes was destroyed when Longhorn players turned out to be the kind of schoolyard bullies we always imagined they were. Three times a day, the team walked past the backside of Brackenridge dorm on their way to and from lavish meals in the special sports dining hall reserved for them in Jester Center, and three times a day they would yell obscenities at the longhairs they saw studying and playing loud stereo music behind the dorm windows. I was told that the battle began with the simple shout, "Brack sucks!" This soon escalated to nasty comments about hippies and queers, the usual redneck chortling from good old boys with size nineteen collars. Rick dared to shout back "Kiss a fat man's ass!" at these golden Apollonian figures, and an African American dorm resident from Dallas named Bob Jones joined him, unleashing a flurry of impressive street trash-talk that triggered racist remarks from history's last all-white national championship team.

Bear in mind that the Brackenridge Boys were yelling down from the upper floors, well protected by distance and screened windows. The banter went back and forth for a couple of days, with warnings and challenges and the occasional mooning by Rick, Al Beaty, and others. Binghamton Bob Gilson bought firecrackers one afternoon, lit them with his pipe, and casually tossed them out the window at the football players. They threatened to come upstairs and annihilate him. The day I arrived to survey the situation, a crazed ROTC freshman named Tim Dodson had thrown a practice grenade out the window, and the loud boom sent the football players scrambling in every direction. This proved to be the last straw. About a dozen of them charged around to the front door of Brackenridge C wing, intent on causing serious bodily harm. They were strapping football champions from tough places like Muleshoe and Cut and Shoot, Texas, and they could've torn us mere mortals in half.

I stepped into the tenuous safety of my old dorm room, and Rick handed me a baseball bat. "You'll need that," he said, unsheathing his pool cue from its leather case. "Swing for their knees."

I gripped the bat and walked out into the hall. "They're gonna stomp a mud hole in us," I told him. "Don't you guys have an exit strategy?"

Doors were slamming shut and locking. Everyone had gone into hiding.

"Like Nixon, we have a secret strategy to end this war," Rick said, tapping the thick end of the cue against his open palm. "Gay blades on the third floor. They've agreed to be our first line of defense."

The Brackenridge third floor was as notorious in 1970 as it had been in Willie Morris's day. "The [third] floor was unquestionably the filthiest establishment I have ever seen," he wrote in *North Toward Home*, "and from it emanated the most savage and grotesque, though until now unrecorded, happenings at the University of Texas in the 1950s. . . . Old newspapers covered the floors, and two of their number slept on cots in the hall so that one room could be a combination TV room, bar, and pornography library. Every so often they had rummage sales there, and for bargain prices tried to get rid of old water-wings, empty bottles, stale socks, and water-logged baseballs."[6]

Years later, the third floor still housed a bizarre collection of low-life reprobates, but I had no idea what Rick meant by "first line of defense." I heard the rumble of footsteps in the stairwell. The football players would soon be upon us. Rick and I were the only two guys standing in the open hall. I had a baseball bat, he had a pool cue. I was certain we wouldn't be able to swing at more than one pair of knees before we were overtaken. Then suddenly the angels appeared. Three young gay men rushed down from the third floor and stood stark naked on the landing. They were prepared to meet the invaders with open arms. In some strange, possibly rehearsed chorus, the Gay Choir of Brackenridge turned and grabbed their butt cheeks, bent over, and greeted the charging football players with their hindquarters offered for penetration.

"What the *fuck*!" groaned one of the jocks. I could see the entire musclebound contingent slowing to a standstill on the stairs.

Our greeters begged them for anal sex. They pleaded.

"You faggots are fucked up beyond belief!" another jock yelled.

After a few more utterances of disgust and a confused shuffling of feet, the football players retreated down the stairs and never returned. The war was over. From that day forward, the 1969 national champions went out of their way to avoid Brackenridge dorm.

The gay guys celebrated their moral victory by filling the hallway with water from the emergency fire hose and slip-sliding fully naked on their backs and bellies while the rest of us stood around cheering them on. Rick ripped off his T-shirt, made a running start, and belly flopped into three inches of water, laughing triumphantly and skidding against a wall like a gray whale calf washed ashore on some deserted beach. Our dorm proctor had returned from his ROTC drills and stood watching the madness in army fatigues, then he shut his eyes and shook his head slowly with a weary resignation. He splashed to his room in combat boots, closed the door quietly, and didn't emerge for two days.

And so began my friendship with Rick Roderick. I liked his style. He was audacious, loud, reckless, and funny as hell, a kind of West Texas Falstaff who was always at the center of revelry and trouble. I invited him and the other dorm rats over to our place across the street from Eastwoods Park for late-night parties, promising them the company of worldly hippie women from the park and musical jams featuring Frank and me on acoustic guitars. Whenever Rick and the Brack Boys showed up, we all sat around on the floor, passing jug wine and wailing like banshees into the wee hours of the morn. I've never had more fun in this life than when those wild nights came calling.

Rick was a great storyteller and entertained us between songs with his hilarious twangy yarns. I was captivated by the weirdness of his upbringing in that dead-end hamlet of Tuscola, Texas. There would be many such nights, and many more stories, and many shared songs to bind us in friendship. We'd all come to Austin from some hopeless dead-end place, and despite how young we were, we'd arrived with road dust on our boots and a little blood on the saddle. Rick, I would discover in time, had endured more tragedy than any of us. But we'd all found one another, there in that woodland garden where innocence was almost possible, and what really mattered in paradise was the company you kept before you took the long road out.

BURY ME NOT

WHO WAS THIS CHARACTER named Rick Roderick and what was his story? In the last year of his life, when we were in our early fifties and had been best friends ever since the follies and misadventures of our college days, he began writing an autobiography he titled *Bury Me Not*, a line from the cowboy ballad: "Oh bury me not on the lone prairie / where the coyotes howl and the wind blows free." By then, I was very familiar with the details of his upbringing, and for years I'd been encouraging him to put it all down on paper. Once he began the writing project, he phoned me every morning to read what he'd hammered out on his computer overnight. The early drafts revealed his unique voice down to the gravelly drawl. The anecdotes were sometimes wise, sometimes heartbreaking. They explained his origin as a dirt-poor West Texas boy: A Portrait of the Philosopher as a Young Man. I thought the book had great promise. Here is how the manuscript begins, with excerpts from its earliest pages:

> What piece of lunacy actually convinced my old man to settle in West Texas, only God knew, and as usual, He kept very quiet about it. The story that I grew up believing was that my grandfather and my father went bust in East Texas and loaded up the wagon for Oklahoma. As they crossed the Red River, they saw a one-armed man leaning on a scrub tree on the Oklahoma side. About a mile past him, they ran into another one-armed man

driving a wagon even older and more beat up than their own. This led to the first comments between my grandfather and father about the Oklahoma one-armed factor and the possibility that many of the men of that state might be so mangled. My old man noted with some gloom that it was the right arm in both cases. My grandfather decided that if the next man they saw was missing his right arm, they would turn the wagon back to Texas as fast as possible. It took almost fifteen minutes before they saw another man, this time on horseback. They were relieved to see how well he sat his horse. From a distance, he looked to be mostly together. But as he approached, it became clear that he gripped the bridle in his one good left hand. On the right side, he not only was missing his arm, but some of his shoulder and a bit of his face, too. My grandfather turned the wagon around and drove the horses headlong back to Texas. They drove them until they dropped somewhere outside Abilene. That's where they settled and where I grew up.

The closest town to where my father left that wagon was actually Tuscola, Texas. About three hundred people lived there, and who knows how many were outcasts driven there by forces as dark as the one-armed-man factor? I guess it was most of them.

▪ ▪ ▪

My father and mother met and married in this little place and lived together for twenty years before I was born. I was an only child and the object of much concern, having barely made it into the world after fighting to stay in the womb

The Roderick cinderblock home on the main street in Tuscola, Texas, is now a nicely renovated antiques, gifts, and book store with a Texas flag mural. *Photo courtesy of Jackie Vesey*

for more than twenty hours. They dragged me out kicking and screaming, and although I'm not altogether sure, I don't think my mother ever really forgave me for the trouble. In trying times, she would often recount the story of my birth to whatever group of women had gathered in her home beauty shop, my mother chain smoking Lucky Strikes and making horrible faces to dramatize the contortions of her agony. My father would listen in with mock sympathy. Sometimes he would stick his head into the shop and remind mother that when things were very close and Dr. White had asked, he had picked her instead of me to live. He would turn to me and wink. But she was little comforted. I'm also fairly sure she never forgave him for getting her into that position in the first place.

My mother and father were old and poor for all of my childhood. I don't remember calling them mother and father or mom and dad. I always called them El (short for Elwynn) and Rod, like everyone else did. And they always called me Rick, even as a baby. Rod hardly ever worked, and he knocked back a half case of beer a day. He chewed Red Tag tobacco. Lots of it. El would find it everywhere: rolls of chewed and hardened tobacco under the bed, on the table, in the bathroom. When she would jump him about it, he would remind her of her own constant smoking. "At least," he would say, "I don't blow my tobacco juice up your nose."

I remember a favorite joke Rod used to pull on her. Since she mixed a pint or more of vodka a day with her cigarettes, she would often forget she had one burning somewhere and she would light another one. Rod would simply continue the process by lighting one Lucky after another and placing them all over the house. Stumbling upon a half dozen cigarettes she assumed she'd lit and forgotten, El couldn't help but wonder if she'd lost her mind. I remember she found one burning in the freezing compartment of the icebox once and my old man laughed until he went blue.

Our little house was made of concrete blocks with window gaps covered in large sheets of refrigerator plastic. It was square, small, and ugly, with the look of a fallout shelter. My mother's beauty shop was in the front, with our one real window facing the street, and it was by far the nicest room in the house. The only other room with an inside door was the bathroom. I slept on the couch in the tiny front walkway next to the beauty shop. Behind me was the room with the big bed, the table and chairs, the icebox, and a stove that took up most of the place.

Our house sat on Main Street a block down from the only red light in town. A block farther down, Texas Highway 83 runs right through the place without slowing down. That highway splits from Texas Highway 84 three miles or so outside of Tuscola, which makes Abilene eighteen miles away and the rest of the world considerably farther.

The house was like an oven in summer, and in winter it would get so cold that a glass of water by my couch once froze almost solid. The sidewalk was our front yard and the backyard was old cars, various broken fans, stoves, blown-out tires, and an assortment of stray dogs and cats. Across Main from our place was the old Fiesta Theater, which opened only on weekends and sometimes showed the same picture for six months. Except for the Crescent Drive-in a few miles out on Highway 84, it was our only access to the movies. Next to the Fiesta were Vaughn's grocery store and the First State Bank of Tuscola. I suppose you could say I grew up in the middle of the business district.

West Texas is a hard place for everyone. It is red clay that looks too dirty to be blood when it rains and runs. Wind marks your face, and heat makes the roads look like shimmering frying pans in summer. It's the habitat for all manner of crawly things that are odious to human beings: snakes, spiders, bobcats, Gila monsters, armadillos, stone toads. Nothing I have ever seen in the movies or on television or read about in novels really tells you how hot and dirty and uncomfortable West Texas is. I once read a line of graffiti in the men's room of an old beer joint that said,

"Everything in West Texas either bites, burns, stings, or breaks your heart."

▪▪▪

I went to school in the Jim Ned school district for twelve years. We never had more than fifteen people in our class. Never more than five of them were girls. This single fact explains much about growing up in Tuscola. School was always half a day, the rest being sports (baseball, football, basketball) and release for work on the farms.

I could read long before I got to school. El would give me the newspaper and show me what and how to read, and Rod would give me the *Sporting News* and teach me the intricate mathematics of baseball. So school never seemed much work to me. I enjoyed books, and our impossibly old English teacher, Mrs. Holliday, taught us with great enthusiasm. I remember reading the poems of Robert W. Service when I was in the first grade. I knew "The Shooting of Dan McGrew" by heart. I was enchanted by the cold lore of the Yukon and the revenge and the hint of tainted love and the blaze of gunfire.

A few years later, I won a blue ribbon for reading Robert Frost's "Stopping by Woods on a Snowy Evening" aloud. I loved the way the words made me feel, as though very simple things could be important, and I was fascinated by the secret life packed into the heart of this strange Yankee New Englander I would never know. I read all of Frost's poetry I could find.

It was not that I gave up adventures or stories of death and killing, not at all. El had read Homer's *Odyssey* to me when I was younger, and I liked it so much I read it again by myself. It was like the western stories of long cattle drives and faithful women and righteous vengeance. I was thrilled when Odysseus and his son savagely killed all the suitors in the great hall. I read this part to my best friend Mickey Sansom aloud and we would replay it as a gunfight on the dusty streets and run and yell and watch our imaginary enemies fall. Nothing on the newly arrived televisions or at the movies was as satisfying.

Reading poetry aloud in class helped me to overcome some of the strangeness of being an only child. However, it did create one problem. I was looked upon as "a reader." This aroused the suspicion that I might also be "queer." I cannot convey the horror associated with failure of manhood at that time and place. I remember my dad, who in many ways was the most reasonable person in town, telling me that it was "better to rape women than be queer." I actually wasn't queer, so all I had to do was get this "reader" thing off my back. More than the average amount of fistfights and playing every sport helped. Being friends with Mickey helped also, because for him, settling issues of manhood was a specialty.

In West Texas, being a man was not only a matter of biology, it was an achievement against long and hard odds and in the face of much pain and suffering. To tell the truth, it never made much sense at all. But sense or not, I am absolutely sure that I could not have ditched that view of manhood, totally, with any amount of reading or therapy.

▪ ▪ ▪

Not much of the outside world seemed to penetrate our little town, but the election season of 1960 changed that for a while. I was eleven years old and I had already adopted my parent's politics. They were Roosevelt Democrats—"yellow dog democrats" due to the fact (and it was a fact) that they would vote for a yellow dog rather than a Republican. To Rod and El, a poor person who voted Republican was too stupid to be helped. While not so extreme, a majority of the town agreed.

1960 was different. I understood only some of this at the time, but a theological and even a spiritual war was brewing. The Democrats had nominated a Catholic, and our overwhelmingly Protestant town was concerned that "he would have us kissing the Pope's ring," whatever that meant. My parents took this fight to the streets and argued with folks up and down the block. El would curl hair, smoke, and talk about Kennedy all day to her customers. Rod would just stroll around town and make malicious fun of people's fears. He pointed out that while the Democrats had the bad taste to nominate a Catholic, they at least did not nominate the Prince of Darkness himself. My old man hated Richard Nixon with a sure and true instinct and he was not shy about passing it along. This went on for months, and I took part as best I could by passing out buttons and voter cards.

The day of the election, my parents voted early and stayed up all night to watch the returns on our little black-and-white television with the flickering pictures and fuzzy sound. The race was very, very close, as all battles between good and evil for the soul of a great country ought to be. Come the dawn, John Kennedy had won by the slim margin of votes rounded up by gangsters in Illinois and a few of the richest and most corrupt Texans who ever lived. This, of course, was not reported on television. But even if it had been, our little family would still have enjoyed one of the best days of my childhood. We were too poor to afford morality.

■ ■ ■

Over the next three years, everyone in town started talking about "Negroes." Throughout the South, these Negroes were organizing and marching and it was on the television all the time. No black people lived in Tuscola, and only a few in all of West Texas, so we began as spectators to these events. The opinion of nearly everyone around us was that this "Negro problem" was the result of a few bad black folks and white agitators from the north. On this issue, my parents and I were alone. When I was very young, Rod told me about the lynching of a black man in Honey Grove, Texas, for the purported rape of a white woman. He described how they burned and tortured the man and hanged him in a crooked tree. He told me how they cut off his heels for souvenirs and showed them around town. Telling about it made Rod mad and he would get red as he talked. He was angry with himself, he said, because he had been too scared to say anything or do anything. He also told me not to place too much blame on the other poor, ignorant "white trash" who actually did the deed. He explained how the rich and powerful used poor whites to keep blacks down and to divide people so the rich could maintain their positions of power. I listened and observed, and as I grew up I saw the truth of it.

We felt less alone when President Kennedy came on television one evening and denounced the unequal treatment of black people in terms that were as clear then as they are now. I knew the people I had grown up with would not agree, but I was not prepared for the anger and hatred this started in our little town. Kennedy was a "nigger lover" and a traitor to his race. And by siding with him, we were little better. Such things and worse were said at church meetings and in the stores and on the farms and on Main Street. It was a hard thing for me to see the full reach of ignorance and just plain old evil.

I read Harper Lee's *To Kill A Mockingbird*, and I paid close attention to what I could make out of the speeches of Dr. Martin Luther King quoted in the local newspaper. I watched El use a kind of gentle sarcasm on her customers as she lobbied for the rights of black people. But there was nothing gentle about Rod's sarcasm. He thought racism was stupid and wrong and he used the full power of his savage rhetoric against it. He had seen the great Satchel Paige pitch once in the Negro Leagues and, he said, he would "trade the whole damn town for a pimple on Paige's ass." Even with his worn-out trousers unbuttoned and tobacco juice running down his chin, Rod simply refused to be silent. I was so young and foolish that sometimes I was embarrassed by him. And it hurts to remember such a thing because, as I now know, it was at those times that he showed me how good human beings can be, even when they're not at their best. So I joined him and many others in a fight that will likely never be over in our lifetime.

▪▪▪

It was a cold, clear day in November and I was sitting in study hall getting ready for lunch when the news came that President Kennedy had been shot as he and his lovely wife rode through downtown Dallas. I was too hurt to cry and so I just stood up. I stood there like a fool and said nothing and inside I was numb and afraid and almost sick and everyone was looking at me. I looked around at my classmates and saw the ones who'd called him a "nigger lover" and joked about shooting him and I began to turn red and the anger welled inside me. I couldn't speak and no one else could either for what seemed like a very long time. Finally, old Mrs. Holliday walked down the row of chairs to me, her wrinkled face a mask of pain and sympathy, and she put her thin brittle arms around me. She began to lead me out of the room, and at the door, she whispered, "Everything will be all right." But I knew, as young as I was, that everything would never be all right again.

When I got home, I saw something I had never seen before. Rod and El were holding each other and crying. I joined them and I let go and cried too. The only other sound was the background hum of Dallas radio and the national television networks giving out maddening and conflicting details. We followed it all in silence: the lone assassin, the three shots, the Texas School Book Depository, the strange activity at the grassy knoll, and the arrest of Lee Harvey Oswald at the movie theater. We believed none of the official story, even then. It was a very long afternoon filled with the workings of secret little men and petty officials and the bland repetition of carefully constructed facts. Then night fell all over Texas.

FEARLESS IGNORANCE

READERS MAY FIND that *Bury Me Not* covers some of the same physical and emotional terrain of Larry McMurtry's early novels, but I would argue that Rick's depiction of his own small-town Texas childhood and teen years is just as soul-baring and subtly comic as McMurtry's. One summer he and his best friend, Mickey Sansom, decided to restore a '57 Chevy with a blown-out engine, a "cherry red beauty" that Rick says "looked like reckless speed and long highways and midnight cafés." They yearned for a cool car because "a young man needed a way to take a girl to the drive-in movies and play slap-and-tickle with her all night or just to thunder up and

Rick and his friend Mickey Sansom in their freshman yearbook, Jim Ned High School, 1963–64. *Photos courtesy of Debbie Stewart*

down the town's empty streets or even venture to Abilene for a hamburger or a bowl of chili." But when they began their freshman year of high school in the fall,

> The guys in the senior class took one look at Mickey and me and our car and our arrogant, smirking faces and proceeded to beat the hell out of us every day after school for what seemed like a month. I know now that nothing they did could have showed us more respect, but at the time, I feared that final school bell. Mickey did not. He didn't flinch or run. Instead, he would take on the biggest senior around and start slugging. I was too timid to do anything but follow his lead. We never won. But the day finally came when we walked out of class and found Buddy Miller, the toughest and biggest senior in school, handing us a very cold Lone Star beer and shaking our hands like we were long lost relatives from out of town. To be very clear, I thought Buddy was clinically insane. But although I was stomped from time to time thereafter, that was the last of the regular beatings.

Of course there was the usual high school angst over the "adolescent hunger" of dating girls:

> Being a freshman in a small Texas high school was the kind of humbling experience that led one later in life to be grateful for an assistant manager's job at Piggly-Wiggly in Abilene. I was not a good-looking kid and that didn't help. I already had a junior version of Rod's potbelly and enough pimples to support an acne clinic. The only girl in our class who would even speak

to me was Sharon. I would share my troubles with her. She was a bright and beautiful Texas blonde packed as tight as the wheel bearings on our Chevy. She was so far beyond me and the other guys in our high school that no one even thought to ask her out. She dated older Abilene boys from the country club families that were in the banking business with her dad or had oil or cattle. I'm not sure every small town in Texas had a Sharon, but every town should have. Someone you could lust after secretly and safely and think of when Gentleman Jim Reeves sang, "Put your sweet lips a little closer to the phone."

Sharon would give me advice about dressing (loose white shirts and Levi's) and talking to the girls (look them sweetly in the eyes) and aftershave (Old Spice). She was always eager to improve my position with the other girls and defend what she saw as my positive points. It didn't help much, but I appreciated it beyond anything I said at the time or can say now. Mickey was not much better off, and Sharon played a similar role with him.

Saturday night would roll around and Mickey and I would have no dates and sometimes the country club would have no parties, so Sharon would join us. We would sneak beer out of the house and drive fast in the Chevy up and down the dark country roads while the radio played Hank Williams and Patsy Cline. These trips were not dates and we all knew it because we talked freely with each other and said things that boys and girls didn't say, and finally the three of us were at ease with each other and we were friends.

But even the friendship of the best-looking girl in town wasn't going to satisfy the growing curiosity and adolescent hunger that Mickey and I were saddled with. In some ways, it made it worse. Mickey would glumly remind me that even the "dumb and ugly girls" wouldn't go near us, even with our cherry red '57 Chevy and Sharon as our chaperone. We suspected it would take years before we would get one of those girls drunk enough to actually have sex. I felt sometimes that it would never happen at all. I'm not sure what I thought the hurry was. Perhaps I was just anxious to solve the mystery of it, to get it off my mind, and to harden my young heart against the pain that came with romance. Whatever it was, I managed to get through the first year of high school on sports and cold beer and fantasies of Sharon naked in the hot West Texas sun.

I went out with a few of the fine young women of Tuscola and Buffalo Gap before finding my first real girlfriend. I picked the meanest, ugliest, nastiest girl in town, based on what I thought a worthless little punk like me deserved. It made the same kind of twisted sense it would make later in my life.

Peggy was a kind of blonde, short and large, with a small rat-like face that looked like it was scowling even when she smiled. She had false teeth in front from a childhood accident, but you couldn't really notice them unless you already knew. She always smelled of too much Shalimar, troweled on too much makeup, and wore her hair in that windproof West Texas style that was so hard and pointed it could cut your face. She would go to the Crescent Drive-in with me and let me touch her breasts while she ate popcorn and watched the movie. We would practice kissing and wrestle around. Sometimes we would mimic the motion of making love, what we used to call "dry humping," until I was raw and almost bleeding. Whenever I tried to touch her below the waist, she would stiffen and tell me *that* had to wait until we were married. I felt sure I could wear her down before then, and I found the struggle itself fascinating. In fact, it was Peggy's lack of emotion and passion that attracted me. I wanted to fill her with the life inside me and make her smile and laugh. After three months of dating, I finally talked myself into really liking her. I began to project all my youthful fantasies of romance onto this unlikely girl. But she felt smothered and began to hate me for it. I didn't understand this at the time and I still don't fully understand it, but sometimes it seems that the most irritating thing you can do to someone is try to love them.

It was Christmas season when she finally gave in and we struggled to make love in the back of the Chevy. We were both very drunk and it was almost three o'clock in the morning and we were parked on a lonely back road. The wind was blowing hard, it was cold, and I was so numb I didn't feel like moving at all. She used her hand to make me hard, but she approached the task like someone packing sausage, and after months of waiting, I was surprised that all I really wanted was for her to stop and never mention it again. Still, I didn't give up. It was West Texas, after all, and

I had a job to do. I tried to relax and think of the bra ads in the Sears catalogs, but she kept saying, "Hurry up, Rick, hurry up." It made me angry and finally, after an hour of trying, I said, "I just can't." She looked at me with a cold hatred and said, "I knew there was something wrong with you."

I drove her home in silence. I thought I would be happy to never see her again.

A couple of weeks after our ill-fated date, Tommy Sims walked up to me outside the grocery store and began taunting me about the size and power of my, well, manhood. Peggy had told him all about my failure and he found it amusing. Tommy informed me that he'd been having sex with her the entire time we dated, and she was saving very little for marriage. All of this actually hurt me very much and I did something insane. I hit Tommy in the face.

Tommy Sims was as mean as a wolverine and almost as cunning. He had a metal plate in his skull from a football injury, and he claimed he could occasionally pick up radio stations from as far away as Chicago. He was huge and older and very strong, capable of lifting an eighteen-pound sledgehammer by the handle end with one hand. Once, when he was drunk, he bent a stop sign flat to the ground. So he barely noticed my punch and quickly proceeded to beat the hell out of me. I tried to cover up, but he slugged through my arms and broke my nose. Blood was running everywhere when Mr. Vaughn came out of his store with a large broomstick and stopped the slaughter. It took me several weeks to heal.

What a twisted thing the human heart is. All I wanted to do during every second of that healing time was to see Peggy again and win her back. When I recovered, I tried everything I knew to persuade her to go out with me again, but she refused. The more she refused, the more I wanted her. And the more I wanted her, the more final and irrevocable her refusals became. As usual, I undermined myself with every move I made. This should've taught me a valuable lesson about courting while I was still young, but I would need more than one lesson. And I would get more than one.

BASEBALL WITH A VENGEANCE

EARLY IN OUR FRIENDSHIP, Rick and I discovered that we'd both played countless hours of baseball when we were growing up. After all, it was "The National Pastime." We were better-than-average players, but I became obsessed with the game, starting at age nine, and I was determined to be a future Mickey Mantle. Rick played baseball because Rod insisted that he play, and he developed into an all-star catcher because Rod trained him hard and with relentless drive. Later in life, Rick followed Major League and college baseball the way a divorced husband follows his ex-wife, from a distance but with some strange vestigial connection that's not easily severed.

In *Bury Me Not*, he describes playing on a racially integrated baseball team in the summer of 1964, when he was turning fifteen. At that time in Texas, white kids playing any sport with black kids was unusual and a very courageous decision for everyone involved. That bold baseball season taught Rick unforgettable lessons about bigotry and tolerance on America's field of dreams.

> My father had been a baseball player, even a kind of local legend. At eighteen, Rod had a moving fastball in the ninety-miles-per-hour range and excellent control. He knew the game well and realized that the genetic dice had rolled him an arm with a future none of the other poor boys in West Texas could imagine. He must have been filled with youthful hope at the idea of pitching in Chicago or New York, staying in grand hotels,

and having dinner with beautiful, stylish women in fine restaurants.

He didn't take his gift for granted. He worked hard at baseball, the only thing he ever worked hard at in his life. In the middle of the Great Depression, he pitched one season in the Texas League and was a consistent winner, and he made some extra money playing in the Texas oil field games. He would pitch one of those games for ten dollars and earn another ten if he won. The promoters were gamblers, of course, and they rewarded the ringers who helped them know the outcome before the games were played.

Rod hated the oil field games. They weren't real baseball. But that extra twenty dollars was real money, and so he played and waited for the call that was sure to come from one of the Major League teams. And it did. When he was twenty years old, the St. Louis Cardinals offered him a tryout and (if all went well) a trip to spring training. I think he must have seen his life like one of those baseball movies with the crowds screaming and him getting the last out in the last inning of the World Series with a fastball so tough that even Lou Gehrig couldn't get a piece of it. But late one night in Monahans, Texas, amid the stink of oil wells and only a week before the big tryout, Rod threw his arm out for tens dollars, losing a thirteen inning game 1-0. Baseball was over for him, and the only cheering came from the handful of gamblers who won a few bucks on the game.

Years later, Rod taught me baseball with a vengeance. He decided early on that I would be a catcher because I could use my brains behind the plate. Although quick with my hands and feet, I was never a fast runner. But I was able to keep my eyes open through the swing and see the field well.

Rod would load a bucket with old baseballs and I would throw to a spot marked off as second base on the brick wall next to our house. I would throw two hundred balls before school and two hundred when I got back. I would duck walk around the block at least once a day and take batting practice any time Rod could manage it. I also batted rocks for hours on end and worked on my swing. And I would do all this before baseball season. Most of West Texas would still be delirious with football fever but I would be working on throwing behind the runner at first base.

▪ ▪ ▪

The violence of baseball was adult violence, not big children pushing and hitting each other. It was a fastball moving toward your head, and the deep cut of steel into your leg as you blocked home plate, and bad hops off a brown dirt infield that popped you in the face. Even as a child, I never understood how anyone could find that hideously maddening game to be soft or sweet or pastoral. Baseball is about as heartwarming as heart surgery, and to people who don't know the game, just about as much fun to watch.

When I was a teenager, our baseball team, the Jim Ned Indians, won district and finished second in the tournament in Abilene against the largest of the local schools. But the next summer, our best pitcher Ryan Glaze and our shortstop Donny Graham were lost to the age limit of sixteen. Rod was what might be called the "shadow" coach of the team. He couldn't be the official coach because of his constant drunkenness and his temper, so W.B. Maywell took that job.

W.B. showed up at our door and discussed the pitching problem on the first day of spring practice. He was a good baseball man too, and so he understood that pitching was the key to the whole game. He reminded Rod that we would have only nine players with no room for injury and no one at all who could really play shortstop. We needed three recruits who were sixteen or younger and could live in Tuscola during the summer. Finding good players was the kind of thing my old man would normally dismiss out of hand, but he had a strange look in his eyes and he agreed with enthusiasm.

The next day, Rod and I drove twenty miles of dirt road to the little farming town of Winters, Texas. It was even poorer than Tuscola and everyone I saw on the streets was black or brown. We pulled into the one café in town, aptly named Café, and had a fine fatty barbeque beef sandwich and ice cold Cokes. Rod and I were the only white people in the place, and from the looks we got, we may have been the only whites to ever eat there.

My old man began asking around about baseball. Did anybody in town play the game? Did the young guys have a team? At first, no one wanted to talk to us. But Rod ordered another Coke and, without invitation, began to describe the game he saw Satchel Paige pitch in the Negro Leagues. He talked about the fastball that you could barely see and the hesitation pitch and how Satchel could knock a nickel off the top of a balanced broom on home plate without disturbing the broom. They all seemed to know the stories, but Rod had really seen him pitch. He bought a round of Cokes, and after an hour or so, everyone in the café was talking baseball.

The town didn't have a team for teenagers, but most of the older men did play on Saturdays and Sunday afternoons after church. They mentioned a young pitcher named John Lee Townsend. Rod explained that he was fielding a team and asked if he could come back on Saturday and watch.

A discussion about the white man and his son must've taken place, because when we returned to Winters the next weekend, everyone seemed to know us and treated us very nice. This was my first contact with a community of black people and it left a lasting impression. The bleachers were composed of wooden boards laid over a few rows of cinderblocks, and the large black woman sitting next to us offered chicken from a covered basket. Rod sent me to buy Cokes, and I passed drinks around to whoever wanted one, and we ate and drank together, something that was rare in those racially divided times.

The baseball field was carefully chalked, but the infield had almost no grass and the outfield no fence. These were concessions to weather and the cost of watering and maintaining a field. The players varied in age from fourteen to forty. Cheering erupted when John Lee Townsend walked out onto the mound. He looked to be about eighteen or nineteen, but Rod seemed sure he was younger. John Lee began to warm up as if he owned the world, and I still remember the first pitch he threw. It was a fastball the size of an aspirin. He was big and powerful, with a pitching motion that was naturally smooth and graceful. My old man smiled at him like a gold miner smiles at gold. It was the fourth inning before anyone got a hit off him, and that swing was an accident.

Rod didn't talk much at baseball games. He watched and studied and fretted, but that day was different. He joked with everyone around us and praised the young pitcher's stuff. As it turned out, the woman sitting next to us was John Lee's mother and she took an immediate liking to my dad. Rod kept on eating her chicken and biscuits and drinking Lone Star beer wrapped inside a brown paper bag without letting the liquor interfere with his running commentary on the potential of her son.

The hit in the fourth inning had angered the young pitcher, and he struck out the next three hitters on eleven pitches. The first score of the game came in the eighth inning on a home run that might have landed in the next county. It was hit by Rabbit Johnson, the shortstop on John Lee's team. He was the smallest and one of the youngest players on the field. We found out that he was called "Rabbit" because he was also the fastest runner in town. "There's our shortstop," Rod leaned over and said to me.

He asked if Rabbit's mother was at the game, but John Lee's mother told us he had no parents that anyone knew of, and so he lived with different families around the little town when and if they could afford his rather healthy appetite.

The game was fast and beautifully played and John Lee closed it out in the ninth inning with a fastball as quick as the first one he threw. After the game, Rod talked with him and his mom and Rabbit Johnson. He asked the young men if there was another outstanding ball player in Winters as young as they were, and they both said "Toliver" at once and explained that while he was only an average player, he hustled harder than anyone else and he was funny and made a great teammate.

Toliver had played with the losing team that day and he'd had no more success than the older players at hitting John Lee. But Toliver was a good outfielder, and almost before we knew it, his mother had joined our little group. Rod took everyone to the local café, and while we ate, he invited the three young men to come and play with our Tuscola team. He said he would handle driving back and forth to Winters and find some money to make up for lost wages at their odd jobs and he surmised it might do some good in the world for black kids and white kids to play on the same baseball team. The only stipulation was they couldn't be older than sixteen. Before anyone else could speak, I said, "They look sixteen to me" and everyone laughed.

A few weeks later, we had three houseguests with temporary birth certificates and proof of residence. That was how baseball had finally become integrated in Tuscola, Texas, in the summer of 1964.

The first night the three recruits spent at our cinderblock house required a shuffling of cots and pallets, but all went well and we got to sleep after talking baseball late into the night. In the morning, El cooked a breakfast big enough for a road gang and John Lee, Toliver, and Rabbit Johnson dug in. Townsend was quiet and dignified and always seemed calm and deliberate. By contrast, Rabbit did everything fast and nervously. Toliver was funny, as we'd been told, and by the end of our first day together, he'd shown us his "white person" smile and explained how it was designed to comfort simpletons, and he also did an imitation of the way white boys walked that was so dead on that Rod and I couldn't stop laughing. We liked our three guests right away, and I believe it's fair to say they thought we Rodericks were not too bad or too crazy or too dangerous.

When Rod introduced them to the new team, everyone looked stunned. Coach W.B. Maywell asked, "Are these the recruits?" He and Rod walked away from us so we couldn't hear their conversation, but it was certainly animated. It took a while, but they came to some agreement. Maywell walked back to us players and announced that Rod was now responsible for the team, and he illustrated that point by leaving the bag of equipment and driving away.

There were more stunned looks as my old man pulled the big duffel bag full of bats and balls onto his shoulder. "Let's start by playing some catch and getting limber," he said. For a brief time, no one moved. Then Freddy Sims said, "I ain't playing with them niggers."

"That's right, Freddy," Rod said, "because you ain't playing at all. Go home."

And he did.

Mickey stepped forward, grabbed a ball, and tossed it to Toliver and said, "Well, hell, let's play catch, then." Toliver laughed and said, "With those hands, you don't need no glove, man."

Everyone laughed and baseball practice was underway. It didn't seem like much at the time, but on that hot summer day in West Texas, our whole world shifted a little.

▪ ▪ ▪

Two nights before the season opener against the Wylie Bulldogs, while I was sleeping in my usual spot on the couch, I woke to the sound of gunfire. I thought I was shot and I rubbed my hands over my face and they were bloody, but I didn't feel any pain. I pulled on the light cord and the room went bright. I was afraid and confused, and I searched around the couch. My dog Blitz, who'd slept on the floor next to me since he was young, was shot through the chest. He was dead. The impact of the rifle bullet had thrown his blood all over my face. Rod came rushing over and I told him I was okay. He looked at the front door, open to Main Street because of the heat, and he began to curse. El woke up, saw our dead dog, and glanced away. "At least the young men weren't here for this," she said.

John Lee, Rabbit Johnson, and Toliver were back home in Winters that night, as they would be all summer during the middle of the week. But maybe that bullet had been a message to them.

The room smelled like rifle smoke and blood. El brought a wet towel for my face and Rod dragged our dog out onto the sidewalk, cursing as he did.

I couldn't stand to look at Blitz. The rest of the night we drank coffee and cleaned the floor and checked our own weapons. When it was daylight, Rod and I dug a deep hole behind the house and buried our dog.

We didn't tell anyone about the shooting. When Rod returned on Friday with the recruits, it was as if nothing had happened. Mickey came over, too, and we all pulled on our game gear. I put on my catcher's cup and pants and sat down to file my spikes. I liked them sharp to dig in and hold my position at the plate. Mickey sharpened his so he could slide into people. Rod wrapped John Lee's powerful arm in a warm towel. Danny and Randy showed up and asked for a ride to the game because their parents couldn't make it, they said. Between the '57 Chevy and my old man's pickup, we could just about do it. The rest of the team was riding with Billy Mack and his mother in their station wagon.

"We're not going to have a lot of fans in Wylie," I warned our teammates.

"Or in Tuscola either," Mickey replied.

▪ ▪ ▪

Wylie, Texas, was very different from Tuscola. It was a suburb of Abilene and it was almost affluent. The town had several fancy shops and restaurants and the citizens were salesmen and business people, attorneys and accountants, and even a banker or two. They dressed better, ate better, lived much easier, and when we came into contact with them, it was either to work for them or to play sports against their children. Their high school was much bigger, so they tended to dominate us in every sport except baseball, and even that was always close. The kids from the two towns would get in fights for no reason except being caught in the wrong one, and that happened to us far more than it did to them. They basically thought we were country trash and we thought they were bogus urban cowboys with those funny hats and pointy boots you never ever saw on a real farm or ranch, but only on the Porter Wagoner television show or at one of the new Abilene shopping centers. Over the years, true hatred had grown between our towns, and I'm sure my old man knew that bringing three black players to Wylie would just about cause a riot. But he was calm and told us to ignore whatever was said from the stands and play hardball.

Wylie had a great field with tall wooden fences and green grass and an electronic scoreboard. It was a fine Friday night for baseball. When we took the field for warm-ups, we could hear the murmur from the crowd. Our three black players did their best to ignore the catcalls, but it was ugly and we all felt the tension.

Rod was asked for their birth certificates and residency forms right away by the umpire in charge, which was not a good sign for John Lee and me, the pitcher and catcher who would depend on that umpire to call a fair strike zone. Rod handed over the papers and they were in order, so the game could begin. The bleachers were by now overflowing, and the usual jeering that went on at Wylie vs. Tuscola games was twice as loud. Within that noise, we could hear the faint taunts of "coon" and "nigger." I was scared, but some part of me embraced the pressure, too. I wanted to show up those bastards and rub victory in their clean, smug faces. John Lee was unruffled as he threw warm-up pitches. He smiled and looked at the crowd the way Sitting Bull must have looked at Custer.

I walked out to the mound before the first batter to do the standard catcher check-up and ask him how he felt. He was good, he said, and ready. I asked him to throw the first pitch high and very hard into the backstop. He looked at me and laughed for the first time since I'd known him.

The first batter dug in hard, crowding the plate. I adjusted my mask and put down the one finger for fastball and John Lee let it rip. It hit the top of the backstop so hard you could hear it in Abilene. I glanced up at the batter and said, "Sorry, man. I have no idea where he'll throw that damn thing. But I sure as heck wouldn't crowd the plate."

No one else dug in hard for the rest of the game.

▪ ▪ ▪

If life was like the movies or television, I would tell you how well we fought and how we overcame the odds and won as underdogs in the bottom of the ninth on some heroic play. But it didn't happen that way. My old man had picked the right players and the game was as boring as could be, except for making side bets on the inning when the crowd would be numbed into total silence. Rod had designed the team to be unexciting and brutally effective. John Lee allowed one hit, a flare over first base, and I picked that runner off when he tried to steal. We scored three times in our half of the first inning and no one who was watching and had the brains of a rock lizard ever thought we would lose. We played with efficiency and purpose and, finally, with great joy.

We won that day and every game the rest of the summer right up to the end of the season. As we traveled to the small towns of West Texas with our team, we ran into "Whites Only" and "We Reserve the Right to Refuse Service to Anyone" signs everywhere and we ignored them. At some of the cafés, the service was rude, and El had to raise her voice once or twice to scold a waitress or get their attention. John Lee, Toliver, and Rabbit Johnson were patient and courageous in dealing with the occasional name-calling and a few weak threats, but no one was hurt. None of those good old boys actually wanted to tangle with our black players and Mickey Sansom.

▪▪▪

The last game of the summer was for the championship of the West Texas teenage summer leagues. It was against the same team that beat us the year before, the River Oaks Colts from Abilene. I can still remember nearly every pitch from that championship game. And it wasn't boring, not to me. John Lee was throwing very hard that night, on fire, and I called the fastball again and again. They couldn't get around on it. But we were having almost as much trouble hitting Charlie Wilder, their left-hander. So the innings flew by and the game was hanging on whoever made the first mistake.

Rick Roderick, aging softball player, with his sons Marshall (*right*) and Travis in Austin, early 1980s. *Photo courtesy of the Roderick family*

It was a hot night and the sky was clear and shimmering. The crowd was huge and they understood the game and they roared at every long foul ball or potential error. The tension unique to baseball built as the game went on.

In the bottom of the eighth inning, Danny Phariss leaned into a pitch and it barely hit him, but he made a dramatic fall and he was given first base. On the fourth pitch of the inning, he stole second by a few inches. Rod signaled Rabbit Johnson to bunt and he managed to lay one down that sent Danny to third base with one out. When I came to the plate, I knew the game was over. Rod had drilled me at bunting at least ten thousand times, and all I needed to do was get wood on the pitch no matter what and bring Danny home. My old man signaled for a suicide squeeze right away and I glanced toward Danny at third. He'd read the signal, too. As Wilder went into his wind-up, Danny took off running. The high fastball was coming in on me, trying to brush me back, but my hands relaxed and I kissed the pitch with the fat part of the bat. Danny slid across home plate in a cloud of dust with the only run we would need that night. Many years later, Danny Phariss told me that was the happiest moment of his life.

Rod and I took the trophy back to Winters. The little town welcomed John Lee, Rabbit Johnson, and Toliver with a barbeque celebration. Someone laid open a copy of the *Abilene Reporter-News* on a table so everyone could read all about the game in the sports section. The paper even printed a photograph of John Lee on the mound. We partied until it was nighttime and the lightning bugs appeared in the warm air all around us and seemed to blink in time with the last notes of the music, little flickers of light in the vast and empty darkness. Before we left Winters, Rod asked John Lee's mother how old he really was. "Twenty," she said, and everyone laughed wildly. That championship baseball season may have been the biggest scam my old man ever pulled off.

It was the end of the summer of 1964. A year later, our laughter was gone. Private John Lee Townsend lost his life in Vietnam, and the US Army brought him back home to Texas in a wooden box. No one even tried to explain it to his mother.

BASEBALL JONES

IN THE 1950S AND EARLY 1960S, baseball was the one language we Texas boys spoke in common. It transcended all our differences. The ball fields and diamonds may have varied from cow pastures to vacant corner lots, but the rules were universal and the fever was contagious. My younger brother Frank and I always carried a ball, gloves, and bat in the car trunk on family vacations, and we had no trouble finding local kids ready to play the game wherever we went, whether to a fishing cabin near Waxahachie, a dude ranch outside Bandera, or a schoolyard in a Fort Worth suburb. If I had met Rick and Mickey in Tuscola in those days, we would've ended up at their nearest baseball field, shagging down fly balls with sweat pouring from under the billed caps we always wore to ward off the unyielding Texas sun.

Ah, baseball. Ever since the sport's infancy, our nation's best poets have admired the game and praised its appeal in verse—Walt Whitman, Robert Frost, Marianne Moore, William Carlos Williams, the Beats, Donald Hall, and dozens of lesser-known bards. It *is* a pastoral game, almost a family picnic, with long stretches of inaction, and there's a fine line between a boy playing right field and that same boy wandering around in a grassy meadow, picking flowers.

When I was growing up in the 1950s, Texas City was a racially segregated town, like everywhere else in the South and many parts of the country. I don't recall seeing "Whites Only" signs, but there was definitely an unwritten social code: *Don't come to our side of town.* African Americans had their own school and swimming pool in what was shamefully called "n****rtown" by whites. Their neighborhood was shabby and unappealing and too close to the toxic emissions from the refineries and chemical plants, a condition that would later be known as environmental racism. Located in a kind of buffer zone shielding the rest of the town, their homes and housing projects had suffered the greatest damage when two cargo ships blew up at the Texas City docks in 1947.

There was a Mexican American barrio near Monsanto and a wood-frame Catholic church named Our Lady of the Snows for Hispanic worshippers in that neighborhood. But Hispanic kids attended schools with the Anglos, at least by the time I started the first grade at Our Lady of Fatima in 1954. They were also integrated into the public schools and played on all the sports teams, including Little League and the teenage baseball leagues, and many of them were standout athletes.

Rick was introduced to racial integration during Tuscola's championship season when he was a teenaged catcher, and he witnessed firsthand how his black teammates were harassed by bigots in the small towns where they played. Baseball was a good teacher.

One summer at the end of the 1950s in my hometown, a group of older Anglo and Hispanic boys decided to play each other in a series of unofficial, unsanctioned sandlot baseball games. The games were organized by the boys themselves, with no adult supervision, and it promised to be the baseball equivalent of the gang war between the Sharks and the Jets.

The first game took place at Tarpey Park, itself a rule violation because the field was limited to scheduled Little League play. The two teams made it clear they were ready to bolt on foot if the cops showed up to bust everyone. I was too young to play and sat watching the game with a handful of neighborhood boys on top of the home dugout, an old wooden shed-like structure painted the same dark green as our garage doors. The players ranged in age from twelve to fifteen, and my heroes were pacing around in the Anglo dugout, the stars at every sport they played. At school, they were the older boys scuffing along the corridors between classes with their *Rebel Without a Cause* attitudes and Elvis hairstyles and the clickety rhythm of metal taps on their loafer soles. They were the gods of cool.

One of my favorites was a teenager named Sonny Lockwood who was a stellar running back and champion sprinter. I'd seen him carry the football on long breakaway runs at Stingaree stadium. He was tall and muscular, with a blond crewcut and the same All American male face as the future sniper Charles Whitman's yearbook photo. Sonny worked behind the soda fountain at a pharmacy down the street from our house, and Frank and I would sometimes ride our bikes there and occupy stools at the counter, savoring the icy air conditioning and splitting a chocolate milkshake because our mother couldn't afford to buy us two separate drinks. Sonny was friendly and talkative and teased us about our freckles and red hair, wondering if we were twins.

Tom Zigal played on the Hawks in the teenage baseball league in Texas City, Texas, 1963. *Photo courtesy of Thomas Zigal*

That morning at Tarpey Park, with Sonny pitching, I figured the game was in the bag for the Anglos. But Ray Farias was on the mound for the Hispanic team, a breaking-ball specialist with a nasty curve and sinker, and a nightmare for any batter. His team was well ahead in the game when I heard the first catcalls from the Anglo dugout. "Beaner." "Taco vendor." "Chili choker." A couple of the white players were hurling racist slurs at Farias, hoping to rattle him, I suppose. Sonny Lockwood was the ringleader, raking the dugout's chain-link screen with a bat and inciting his teammates: "spic," "wetback," "greaser."

I was shocked and embarrassed to hear those insults and deeply disturbed that my hero was the instigator. Regardless of my allegiance, it was poor sportsmanship, something I'd been conditioned to oppose and avoid. I couldn't believe that Sonny and his friends were behaving that way. Ray Farias glared at them from the mound between pitches but held his tongue, focused on maintaining his concentration. He kept throwing slow-breaking curveballs that the Anglo batters couldn't touch.

In the next inning, angry words were exchanged between the two dugouts when a base runner named Ricky Yanas slid into second base on an attempted steal. He insisted he was safe, and Buddy West insisted he'd tagged him out. There were no umpires, and calls were made on the honor system, as they were at every sandlot game ever played. A loud argument erupted at second base, soon followed by some shoving and the threat of a fistfight. The dugouts emptied quickly, players scrambling onto the diamond. Team leader Ray Farias walked slowly over to confront team leader Sonny Lockwood, a much larger young man. After a short, fairly composed discussion I couldn't hear, the Hispanic team packed up their gloves and equipment and left the field. They were fed up with the racial taunts and bad blood. The white players hooted and derided them for quitting the game, but the Hispanic players carried themselves with poise and dignity as they departed. The truth was, the Anglos were behind by at least four runs, and although they were acting like they'd won the game, they'd been roundly outplayed.

I was disillusioned. I walked home with a burning ache in my gut as if my soul was on fire. It was perhaps the first time in my life that I'd faced a purely moral dilemma. Were Sonny and those older boys my heroes anymore? I was ashamed of their conduct. They were poor losers who'd resorted to name-calling when things weren't going their way. I felt let down and deflated, as if I'd suddenly discovered that my idol Elvis was a meanspirited bully. (Not remotely true about Elvis.)

I told my mother what had happened, and she was appalled. Even though she believed in the superiority of the white race, she was strongly opposed to insulting or mistreating people of color. As a waitress off and on when we four children were growing up, she often worked with African American cooks and busboys, and she always befriended them and fondly introduced them to us when we dropped by to eat at Ellis's restaurant or Bostick's or wherever she was waiting tables.

When I walked home and told her about the game at Tarpey, it wasn't clear which disturbed her more—the poor sportsmanship or the racist name-calling. She rested a fist on her hip and said, "Don't ever be like those boys, Tommy. Don't call people ugly names. When you lose a game, act like a gentleman. It's just a game. Shake their hands and tell them 'good game' and don't be a shitass about it."

Words I have endeavored to live by.

NO ROAD BACK

IN MY JUNIOR YEAR OF HIGH SCHOOL, Rod started a little hamburger stand. Money was very, very tight and he simply had to contribute something to the family pot. I was working after school hauling hay for sixty cents an hour and El was breaking her back in the beauty shop. Somehow, Rod managed to rent a stand with money he borrowed from his cousin Mann, and he dug up a grill, a large refrigerator, and a snow cone machine for next to nothing. The stand sat on a grassy lot on the way to Abilene State Park, on the edge of Buffalo Gap, Texas, about seven miles from our house. It was a good location and I agreed to help him. Rod erected an extendable tent behind it for sleeping over when we worked late, and there were a couple of nice large tables for customers.

Buffalo Gap was halfway between Tuscola and Wylie, and it was by far the prettiest, greenest town in that whole area. It was filled with girls my age who went to Wylie High School, so that was my opportunity to date someone who didn't already know me as "the fat kid with the pimples" or as "one of those thugs." By that time, I was not as fat, the pimples were better, and I wasn't a convicted felon, so I figured I had a chance.

Every day after school I would drive over to the Gap, as we called it, to cook hamburgers and make snow cones and flirt with the new girls. Rod did the side work, cleaning and chopping, and we started to make money. He paid me infrequently but generously. Every Friday night we would play poker on the big table next to what our sign called "Burgers and Cones." My poker skills were growing, and I managed to put away some additional money taken mostly off the local airmen from Dyess Air Force Base who came out to play. I learned the three basic poker laws. First, play with people who are not as good as you. Second, play with bigger cards. And third, push the hand with raises or throw the hand in. In other words, you cannot lose money you do not bet.

Finally having a bit of folding money, I began to date, and the new girls were even more fun.

▪▪▪

The hamburger and snow cones were selling very well and our little joint was becoming a favorite hangout for the kids in Buffalo Gap. After we closed on weekend evenings, I would pick up a car full of the local girls and take them driving in the '57 Chevy. We would explore all the hidden little dirt roads and play the radio very loud and everyone would squeal and laugh. It was around this time that my opinion of the Beatles changed. One night, after dropping everyone off, I heard them come on the radio. This was no love song; it was "Eleanor Rigby" and the compact little story spoke to something deep and sad in me as I heard the refrain "all the lonely people" repeatedly in the hollow of my ear. I felt a tear run down my face as I thought of the secret and divided beings that we all are and how we hide from each other and from our own selves. Could such hidden, damaged beings really love one another? I was not at all sure, but I knew the Beatles would never again be able to sing those simple love songs without irony or self-deception or both. They had grown up and so had I.

▪▪▪

It was a rainy Saturday night and I closed the hamburger stand a few minutes early. Two girls I had never met were visiting Buffalo Gap and they wanted to go on one of the drives they had heard about. Rita and Tate were very attractive and a year or two younger than I was. They were sisters and would be in town for a month while their father looked for work and considered the possibility of moving to Abilene. They knew Cynthia, a Gap girl who nearly always joined the crowd for a late night ride. Along with Danny and Randy, the '57 Chevy was soon full of giggling girls and excited boys. We pulled out into the night and the rain, and I played the radio full blast. No one paired off into couples, but everyone seemed to like everyone else.

The new girls were funny and smart and I especially liked Rita, with her short brown hair and twinkling eyes. I tried to talk to her and drive at the same time, but it caused me to go slower and everyone thought I should go faster. So I did. We passed around some Dr Peppers and Randy called for beer, but we didn't have any. The radio was playing the Rolling Stones and they wanted to "paint it black." It was fine rock 'n' roll and Cynthia moved to it in her seat.

I don't remember when I realized I was lost. I knew almost all the roads around the whole county, but I had never been on this one. I slowed the Chevy down and tried to see through the light fog and rain. Rita and Tate kept sticking their heads out of the car window, yelling and letting the rain fall on them. I saw an ancient railroad underpass up ahead and I slowed down. I would need to turn slightly on the dirt and gravel road to make it through. When I moved the steering wheel, the car drifted. It couldn't have been more than a foot or two. The Chevy didn't hit the underpass, but I knew immediately that something horrible had happened. I could hear everyone screaming in an awful, inhuman way. It felt like it was raining inside the car, a flood of sticky liquid. I turned to look, and Rita's headless body was shaking like a hideous cartoon character. A long and rusty steel bolt jutting out from the railroad trestle had taken her head off as she stuck it out of the car window into the rain. The smell of death was everywhere. It smelled like dirt and vomit and spoiled buttermilk. The amount of blood was unbelievable. I could feel my senses shutting down and the onset of deep shock. I pulled over and stumbled out of the car and pulled Cynthia with me. I tried to turn back for the others, but I simply couldn't. I started walking down the road to get help, although what help could do now, I had no idea. I don't remember how long it took me to find the nearest farm, the Rackow place. They rushed to the telephone as soon as they saw me. The next thing I remembered was waking up in the almost perfect white of a hospital room.

Everything seemed unreal. I couldn't focus my mind and I actually wondered if I was dead. Flashes of the accident would come back to me, but only as gruesome fragments. Finally, a nurse came in to check on me. She took my blood pressure and my temperature and smiled weakly at me. "How long have I been here?" I asked. "Three days," she said. It was hard to believe. I remembered none of it. After she left, El came in. I was glad to see her. She explained to me that I had almost died from shock, that the other kids were still in the hospital, too, and that we would be getting out in the next day or so. I tried to follow what she was saying, but it was very hard. "She's dead," I said. "Yes, son, she is," El replied. I began to cry quietly and for a long time. Finally, I was still. "When is the funeral?" I asked. "Tomorrow morning," El said. She knew I would find a way to go, so she didn't try to argue with me. The doctors may have felt the same way, too, because I was released early enough in the morning to attend the funeral. Rod brought me a black suit borrowed from Tim Kelley and it almost fit. I dressed carefully and then walked out on my own. The early morning air was cold on my face. Had the season changed while I was gone? I looked back at the hospital, speckled with lights in the predawn dark. I felt shaky, so El helped me into Rod's truck. We drove in silence down to the highway and back toward Buffalo Gap.

■ ■ ■

It was a graveside service, and half of Taylor County was there. I stood away from the crowd, but I could feel people looking at me. I didn't see any of the other kids from the accident, but I did see Mickey and our classmate Sharon. They walked up to me and stood on either side like guardians. I wanted to say something very quietly to them, but I couldn't. The Baptist preacher from Abilene offered a prayer and the music began. It was a single bass voice, singing "Amazing grace, how sweet the sound." I could see the lovely young girl's family crying. Her mother was inconsolable. It was cold that morning and all the voices made trails in the air. I shivered deep inside. "That saved a wretch like me . . ." I wanted to hide from myself and from the world. As the song trailed away, the preacher explained how God let things happen for reasons that we didn't understand but that it was all for the best in the overall scheme of things, and how we would learn from it and go to heaven. Everything he said was absolutely crazy. Did anyone actually believe it? Did *he*? The words made me angry and I wanted to tell him how nothing in this world or out of it would ever make up for the horrible death of this young girl. I wanted to say that I would rather be dead myself than carry the guilt of having killed her for the rest of my life. But I didn't say anything. I couldn't even cry. I looked up, but the sky was empty.

▪ ▪ ▪

A week later the police questioned me. They determined that it was a simple accident and I didn't even get a traffic ticket. Rod lost the hamburger stand in the accident settlement, and we had to sell my '57 Chevy. It didn't matter. I never wanted to see that car again. It would be more than a year before I would drive at all.

I stayed inside the house and read. I didn't want to talk to anyone or to see anyone and I finished most of my junior year by doing schoolwork at home. No one treated me the same, and I was always aware of how the accident had made me even stranger to our little town than I was before. Mickey would come over and play chess; otherwise, I cut myself off from the world.

The Abilene Public Library sent a vehicle called the bookmobile to Tuscola once a week with volumes that were specially ordered and a selection of other reading. I used it as my lifeline. They must have brought me two hundred books. I read Dostoyevsky, Tolstoy, Melville, Flaubert, Steinbeck, Hemingway, and the Brontë sisters. I read Copleston's comprehensive *History of Philosophy* straight through. I read many of Plato's *Dialogues* and Aristotle's *Nicomachean Ethics*. I tried modern philosophy and read Descartes, Hume, and Kant with care. I devoured Nietzsche and Kierkegaard. They filled my damaged heart with a dark comfort. I didn't neglect Freud. And I didn't leave poetry entirely alone. I read T.S. Eliot and some small pieces of Ezra Pound and Walt Whitman's *Leaves of Grass*. I pushed my unschooled mind as far and as fast as it could go and still I felt lost. In fact, I was more lost than ever. But it was too late. There was no road back.

RIBBON OF DARKNESS OVER ME

RICK TOLD ME THAT STORY one evening after we'd finished our shift washing dishes at the new Dobie dormitory on the University of Texas campus. He said that the night after the accident, the determined fathers of Tuscola and Buffalo Gap had driven out to the old railroad trestle, which looked like a small square mine entrance carved into a loamy hillock, and with their hacksaws they'd sheared off the bolt that had killed the girl. It was a heroic gesture, truckloads of farmers and oil-field workers with flashlights and hacksaws and their need to make the world safer for their reckless children. Did those men really do that? I don't know, and I don't want to know. As Rick said in his Teaching Company lecture "Heidegger and the Rejection of Humanism" (1993): "About someone's life story, if it's powerful, interesting, and it grabs you and you can find meaning in it, it's not the best question to ask about a narrative, 'Is it true or false?' That's the best question to ask about an argument, but believe me, I am from Texas, and when you hear a good story, you don't go 'Is that true?' because that takes all the fun out of it."[7]

Rick was a gifted storyteller, colorful and witty and melodramatic, and he had a way of transforming a seed of truth into a dense forest with hidden trails and deep rich hues. He always found the nuances where the emotion lay, where it hurt, where it outraged, where it brought tears or laughter.

After years of repeating our shared stories to friends, he and I knew every line by heart, as if they were from well-rehearsed theatrical plays. We would usually complement each other's narratives, adding magic and humor and wildly obvious hyperbole as we went along. We relished the exercise, and the stories improved with each telling. It was more than a game with us, and more than mere entertainment for our listeners. Storytelling was essential to his nature and mine.

The sky was heavy and moonless on the night Rick told me about the girl's death. We had emerged tired and sweat-soaked from the steam heat of the scullery where we washed dishes for pocket change. We needed the night air to cool us down, so he and I ambled past the cascading Littlefield Fountain and up through the lane of oak trees lined with Confederate generals and statesmen. Couples were making out on the grass of the South Mall. Their dogs roamed and frolicked and barked at us. Rick and I were getting to know each other, and he clearly needed to bare his chest. The accident had happened less than four years earlier, and the pain was still raw. I was startled by the story. I couldn't imagine what I would've done if I'd been behind the wheel. I had studied enough Catholic theology to know that his period of guilt and self-doubt and despair was truly what St. John of the Cross meant by "the Dark Night of the Soul." I had never experienced anything like it or known anyone who did.

The death of that young girl colored everything that came afterward. Rick had lost all his mirth, and his entire childhood seemed like a frivolous carnival to him. He wondered if he would ever laugh again. He was only seventeen years old. He never got over it.

Neither did the others in the car on that terrible night. Decades later, when Rick was living with his sons across the street from Ramsey Park in Austin, he found a story on the Internet written by one of the girls who'd been sitting in the backseat. She had won a short-story contest and her work was posted on the web. She identified Rick Roderick by name as the driver of the car.

I sat and read the story in a respectful silence. I was curious to see how an eyewitness—a traumatized participant—would portray the tragedy more than thirty years later. I read her story slowly, carefully, and soon realized she was recounting the incident word for word as Rick had always told it. He had not exaggerated the horror or the suffering.

"Did she get it right?" I asked him after I'd finished reading.

He nodded solemnly. "Except it all happened quicker. And with more blood."

I asked if he was offended that she'd used his real name. He wasn't.

"I'm going to send her an email," he said, "and ask her how she's doing."

He didn't really know her. He hadn't met her before that day, and the last time he'd seen her was at the funeral. But he remembered her name.

I don't know if Rick wrote to her. I hope he did, but he never mentioned it again. If they exchanged emails, I wonder what they said to each other? The tragedy had taken place so long ago, yet they both still carried that one staggering moment locked away in the darkest corner of their hearts.

The car accident was the awakening of Rick's intellectual life, but it also gave him *soul*. The girl's death taught him that everything was temporal and that he should accept his own mortality and the fragile bargain we've all made with the pale horseman. The Rick Roderick I knew at age twenty-one was a tragicomic figure who had *character* as deep as a West Texas rock quarry. But without that horrible tragedy when he was a teenager, I wonder if he and I would have ever met.

GALVESTON, OH GALVESTON

MICKEY PICKED ME UP on the first day of our senior year. After the girl's death and my long hibernation, I was apprehensive about what school would feel like. By noon, I was amazed to find that everyone seemed to have forgotten all about the accident. At least no one mentioned it. The same old routines and schedules were in place, and that made me feel comfortable. It was actually a relief to be back in this little social world and away from the solitude of my books. I felt like a traveler returning from a long journey, deeply changed, but glad to see the familiar outlines of home in the distance.

■ ■ ■

High school ended with the senior trip. As a reward for graduating, the senior class could pick any place in Texas and the school would provide transportation by bus and three days of vacation fun with your classmates. As unbelievable as it may seem, the senior class the year before ours picked a dude ranch only a hundred miles away. I suppose they figured they would be drunk most of the time and less likely to kill themselves or someone else in a familiar environment. And it was true that these trips involved a kind of competition over which class could be the most unforgettably stupefied and depraved.

After twelve years at Jim Ned, we were more than up for the challenge. With lobbying from Mickey, Sharon, and me, we picked the Million Dollar Inn in Galveston, which was built on a pier out over the Gulf of Mexico. Principal Weeks chose not to go, so we ended up with old Mrs. Holliday and the bus driver, Mr. Mackey, to keep an eye on us. I packed my fishing tackle, one good outfit of clothes, extra cutoffs and t-shirts, a pack of Camel cigarettes, some Swisher Sweets cigars, and a fifth of Wild Turkey hidden as well as I could hide it. I had never been to the Gulf Coast, but like many landlocked boys, I had read about it, dreamed of it, and longed to see it firsthand.

It was easy to understand why some parents didn't let their kids go on the trip. However, David Elder's parents put aside their doubts and decided to let him join us. David was what was then called retarded, but he'd always been in our regular classes. To Mickey's credit, he never let anyone pick on David or make fun of him. David's unpredictable behavior was sometimes a source of amusement. Because of his condition, he had the freedom to say anything that passed through his mind. And like the fools in Shakespeare's plays, David would often say something oddly appropriate and even true.

▪▪▪

The bus trip was long and hot, and I don't remember when we started slipping drinks from our bags, but it wasn't very far down the road. Galveston is a long, narrow, barrier island that runs parallel to the Texas Coast, two miles offshore. When we finally made it across the causeway bridge and into the city, half of us were drunk. Galveston was a ruined shell of the days when it was a booming trade center with an opera house and theater to go along with the fabulous old saloons and hotels. The island had been devastated by the 1900 Storm, the worst natural disaster in the history of the country. More than eight thousand men, women, and children died, and the winds and the tidal surge and the flooding flattened almost everything in the city. Afterwards, they built a huge seawall, but in the decades that followed, most of the beach had been blown up against the wall, until all that was left was a small sandy strip.

The Million Dollar Inn was part of yet another attempt to restart the city. It was ten stories tall and built on a pier supported by giant concrete pillars. Its exterior was hot pink, yellow, and hideously garish, and the entrance was designed around a sea chest full of gold doubloons and a dolphin being ridden by a cartoon cowboy jumping over the coins. The staff was dressed as buccaneers, pirate lasses, Hollywood gunslingers, and saloon girls, and they hurried out for our luggage. Mickey and I followed the buccaneer carrying our stuff up to a corner room, which was on the second floor facing the beach on one side and the Gulf out another window. We staggered inside, fairly drunk, and the room was air-conditioned and clean, and I could see all the way to the horizon.

Mickey and I ordered a shrimp salad and coffee from room service. That was my first time, and I thought the very idea of someone bringing food to your room was metaphysically outstanding. The food arrived and I began to sober up as I ate and drank coffee. It wasn't long before I was almost human again.

We left the room and checked out the entire hotel. It was teeming with tourists and local Texas groups like ours. We bought a huge sack of bloodworms for bait at the twenty-four-hour fishing pier built at the very end of the hotel. When we got back to our room, our plan was to fish and drink all night. I loaded my Mitchell 300 spinning rig with a large spool of ten-pound test line and a treble hook with a sliding sinker for end tackle. Mickey dumped out the ice from a plastic hotel container and put our bloodworms in it. We were ready to hit the pier when we heard the knock at our door. It was Sharon. She was wearing a short white sundress that showed off her deeply tanned body. I was amazed at how Sharon always looked like she *belonged*, wherever she happened to be. She wanted to spend the evening with us, but not at the pier. She preferred alcohol, music, and room service. Mickey preferred fishing.

"Why not both?" I suggested.

Mickey ordered Cokes and Seven Ups and shrimp with a huge basket of fries, and I opened the window overlooking the surf. "I think we can do this," I said and cast my rig out the window. I could barely see the line hit the water two stories below. Mickey and Sharon joined me, and soon we were fishing from the comfort of our hotel room with our rods balanced next to one another on the window ledge.

After room service came, Sharon made us drinks, mixing the Cokes with the Bacardi Rum she'd brought from home. She turned on the music box sitting on the hotel television set and then served us little plates of shrimp. We took turns dancing with her, moving free and easy around the room. The station from god-knows-where was playing excellent music by the Stones and the Beatles and Jimi Hendrix and a new group, the Doors. That was the first time I heard Jim Morrison sing "Come on, baby, light my fire." I held the waist of the lovely Sharon, swinging her around like a soft cotton doll. Cool sea air filled the room from the open windows, night was down, and stars were twinkling above the Gulf. We were laughing and getting drunk and the joy of living was as tangible as our young flesh. How could I be so happy, I wondered, remembering that terrible night in the Chevy and knowing all that I already thought I knew? It was in that sweet moment, dancing with Sharon in the tropical moonlight, that I finally understood, to my amazement, that not even despair could last forever.

▪ ▪ ▪

Around ten o'clock, the tide shifted and the clicker went off on my rod. I'd caught something and Mickey laughed, watching me reel the fish very carefully up the side of the hotel. It was a small croaker, and it was making that irritating sound for which it's known. Mickey's rig went off, too, and soon we had another fish flopping on the carpet. Mickey wasn't going to throw back his first ocean catch, so he filled the bathtub with cool water and tossed in the squawking little fish, and I tossed mine in, as well.

For the next couple of hours, we couldn't stop catching croakers, and the bathtub was swimming with them. Other classmates came in and out of our room while we fished, and Sharon played hostess to the ongoing party. Our friends were getting drunk again and much too soon, and room service was very busy and more than a little suspicious about the croaking noises coming from the bathroom. At some point I stripped off my t-shirt, smelly from the fish, and Sharon latched her arms around my neck and we slow danced through the room and around Mickey and past Patty and Randy, who were making out on my bed. Sharon's arms slid down my bare back and I wanted her so badly I ached throughout my entire body. We danced like that until the room cleared out and Mickey was asleep in a chair with his fishing rig in his hands.

It was almost morning when Sharon looked up at me and smiled softly. Did she want me to kiss her? It was unthinkable after all those years of platonic friendship. I lifted her luscious body into my arms, kicked the door open, and carried her down the corridor to her room. Her roommate Carol was long since asleep in one of the beds and I took Sharon to hers. She was barely awake as I settled her in bed and pulled the covers up over her. She dragged off her dress underneath the spread, took my hand and squeezed it gently, and pulled me down close to her. Breathing into the hollow of my ear, she whispered, "Rick, you are my best friend. My very best."

Her face in the moonlight made me want to die. "I know, beautiful," I said, and I turned and walked back to my room.

▪ ▪ ▪

I woke the next morning to the sound of screaming. It was the maid. Prickly bloodworms were stuck to her hand, the croakers were still croaking in the tub, and the entire room looked like a nuclear test site. Randy had passed out in our room and his naked body lay asleep on the floor. Someone had thrown up in the bathroom, and even the sea air didn't improve the smell. The maid's screaming woke Mickey, too. He had a powerful hangover and wasn't in a hospitable mood.

"Shut her up, old son," he said to me, "or I'll throw her out the window."

I pulled on my Levi's, hurried over to the maid, and put my hand over her mouth so I could reason with her. "I know this looks bad. I know," I said. "But we're all good people here. Farm boys. Country folks. Salt of the earth."

She was shaking and trying to free herself. I wasn't getting through. Then Randy woke up and leapt to his feet, naked and confused and afraid. When he saw me holding the maid, he began to make a very loud inhuman moaning sound. I took my hand off her mouth and let the two of them wail. Mickey crawled out of his bed, snarling in an ugly and violent way. The maid and Randy took one look at him and bolted, escaping through the door together, with Mickey scrambling after them on his knees.

"We might be in trouble," I observed.

We washed as best we could and dressed and went to Mrs. Holliday's room on the floor above. I explained to her how a gang of thugs from some big city high school in Dallas had ruined our room and that a few of them, naked and shameless, had stayed around to frighten the maid. Our sweet old English teacher was sympathetic. She called down to the front desk and, to my surprise, smoothed the whole thing without the intervention of hotel security or the local police. We stayed to have coffee with her via the magic of room service, and the added charm of a good strong lie filled me with hope.

Mickey and I went outside and walked along the strand of beach next to the hotel. I sat down in the sand and pulled off my t-shirt, gazing out across the Gulf, breathing the salt air, feeling the warm sun on my face. A fat seagull swooped down, caught a fish, and flew away with it. This was paradise. Nothing could destroy my tranquility.

Mickey looked back at the hotel and the large display sign below the marquee: *Welcome Texas Young Republicans - Annual Banquet.* He read it aloud. "Old son," he said, "we've found our destiny. We gotta party with those fine upstanding citizens."

▪▪▪

We knocked on Sharon and Carol's door. They were awake and in good spirits. "Would you ladies accompany us to a banquet tonight?" Mickey asked. "Everyone is invited."

"Hell yeah," said Carol, a big and strong country girl.

Sharon was delighted by the idea and began phoning our classmates' rooms, arranging the evening. Darrell Graham and Pete Kendall, the only two Republican sympathizers in our class, refused her invitation. "I find that odd," Sharon said in mock surprise.

Shortly before the banquet, I took a shower as hot as I could stand it and donned my one good outfit, khaki pants and a white shirt with a blue blazer. Mickey dressed in his church clothes, a black suit and tie, and we drank Wild Turkey over ice as I sat smoking a cigar and peering out the window at the deep blue of the Gulf. Mickey found the last container of bloodworms in his bag and said, "These will be useful, don't you think?" He wrapped the container in a small plastic ice bag and slipped it into his suit pocket.

We collected Sharon, Carol, and the rest of our party and passed around the Wild Turkey, and someone opened a bottle of Johnny Walker Red Label scotch. When we arrived at the entrance to the hotel's main ballroom, a Young Republican staff member stopped us. "Invitations? Credentials?" he asked.

"We're the Tuscola contingent," I explained. "Our credentials didn't come in time. My father is a close personal friend of Dick Nixon, and Mr. Nixon is looking into the matter. Personally, I don't believe that communist dupes were behind it, but my father isn't so sure."

"Your name?" he asked.

"Darrell Graham," I said.

He smiled broadly. He knew my father, Jimbo Graham, from business dealings between his dad and the Cross-Graham Grain and Cotton Elevator Company. He let us inside.

The banquet room was filled with shining young conservative faces. When everyone settled down, they brought plates of fabulous seafood and huge salads. Before we could eat, everyone fell silent and a short and very fat man wearing an expensive suit said grace. He prayed for God's help in defeating the communists, both inside and outside our country. He asked God to help keep the races from mixing and to ensure prosperity for all right-thinking people. He prayed for America to become a more Godly place, with stronger law and order and better prisons.

The prayer was too long for Mickey. He began to eat rather loudly. Some eyes in the room looked up, and a young woman sitting near Mickey put her finger to her lips to signal quiet. Mickey got up slowly, walked over to her, and whispered something in her ear. I could see the blood drain from her face.

A chorus of *amens* ended the prayer. I leaned over to Mickey. "What the hell did you say to her?"

"I asked her for a date," he said. "She's thinking it over. Look."

The young woman was trembling.

Our little party devoured the food and asked for seconds. Sharon and Danny kept ordering more club soda and mixing in the scotch they'd hidden in her handbag underneath the table. Mickey had concealed a pint of Everclear, 150-proof pure grain alcohol, in his jacket. I took one drink and thought my teeth would explode. By the end of the meal, the Tuscola contingent was very drunk and very loud. Mickey was wandering around the ballroom. Carol was hitting on all the young Republican guys at nearby tables, but her big country shoulders and drunken smile scared them. A Lawrence Welk-style band began playing polkas on the ballroom stage. The music was beyond human endurance, and our table called for someone in charge to throw the rascals out.

One of the older organizers of the banquet marched over and asked us to settle down or leave. That's when we noticed that our special-needs friend David Elder was making a horrible face, as if the whole world stank in some indescribable way. This banquet, in particular, seemed to offend his malfunctioning brain. He squatted in the middle of the ballroom, pulled down his pants, and vacated his bowels. It was unbelievable to see what could come out of such a little guy.

The entire audience was stunned into silence and the band stopped playing. David took his time, as though he were at home in the safety of his own bathroom. When he finished, he used one of the formal white napkins to clean himself, then pulled up his pants, said "thank you," and walked out of the ballroom.

Someone shouted "Good god, call the police," and yet the crowd remained frozen in disbelief until they discovered the first of the bloodworms Mickey had dispensed at all the tables. A blue-haired lady jumped to her feet and almost yanked her dress off grabbing at her neckline. Others turned surly when they found bloodworms in their drinks and on their chairs. A squad of well-scrubbed young men stormed our table, chairs were overturned, a few punches were thrown, and my classmates and I made the wise decision to scramble for the exits.

Stumbling through the ballroom doors, I saw Mickey standing in the lobby, laughing like a drunken fiend. "We have to get out of here!" I yelled.

As drunk as I was, fear had set in. He saw the terror in my eyes—it grabbed his attention—and we both raced out of the hotel and down to the beach.

▪ ▪ ▪

It was dark and windy and cool on the sand, and we ran for almost a mile before stopping. I stripped off my clothes down to my underwear and rushed into the surf. The gray tide washed over me and I felt sick to my stomach, but I didn't throw up. Mickey soon joined me and we dog-paddled around, letting the tide carry us up the shoreline. A couple of hours later, Danny and Mr. Mackey, the bus driver, appeared on the beach with flashlights. We trudged out of the water and put on our clothes. Mr. Mackey was, well, angry. The deal was simple. The only way we could stay out of jail was by paying for the damages and leaving the hotel that night. We would never be allowed to return to the Million Dollar Inn, not as a school and not as individuals.

Mr. Mackey said, "It's a good thing a nice kid like Darrell Graham got everyone into that damn banquet. If y'all had crashed the banquet without Darrell, things'd be even worse."

Rick fishing on the Texas Gulf Coast, early 1980s. *Photo courtesy of the Roderick family*

Back at the hotel, Mr. Mackey confiscated our remaining money and our booze and gave us fifteen minutes to pack. By midnight, we were all on the bus going home. In the years ahead, our senior trip became legendary. The Class of 1967 was used as the perfect example of what *not* to do as representatives of Jim Ned High.

BIBLE COLLEGE

THE SUMMER AFTER my high school graduation was the Summer of Love elsewhere in the world, but I worked twelve and thirteen hours a day in the West Texas oilfields and read myself to sleep every night. I had worked hard since I was eleven or so, but this was different. It was longer and hotter, regular and deadening, the adult world of work. But I lost my potbelly, and my body turned hard. Mickey worked with me and we did our best to find amusement in the jobs. We didn't have much luck. Real work just wasn't that funny. It was horrifying to think that many of the people we knew, like Mickey's father, had spent most of their lives doing this kind of labor. Along with the military draft, that troubling thought inspired me to apply to college. I sent applications to the three in Abilene: McMurry College (a Methodist school), Abilene Christian College (a Church of Christ school), and Hardin-Simmons University (a Baptist school). They were roughly equivalent, and I decided to choose the one that offered me the most financial aid and the best work-study job.

Before being driven out of college by the Great Depression, my mother had attended Abilene Christian College and was only a year away from graduating at the age of seventeen. But she had no loyalty to the college and hoped I would go to one of the others. With two weeks left in summer, I received my best offer from Hardin-Simmons and I accepted.

▪▪▪

On my first night in the dorm at Hardin-Simmons, a bat attacked me. I was lying there feeling out of place and listening to other students move in and actually missing Tuscola and afraid that I wouldn't make it at college with all the middle-class kids and wondering if I should spend some extra money and finally get another car. Suddenly, a bat swooped down from a crack in the dark ceiling and went for my face. I rolled aside and the hideous flying rat missed me. I jumped out of bed, grabbed my baseball bat, and began swinging at the damn thing, but it fluttered out an open window. I could hear it flapping away in search of some other dark place to hide. I don't know how many of those ancient gothic buildings were infested with bats, but I can assure you this one was. I had one of the few single rooms in the dorm, so there was no one to take turns staying up and waiting for another attack. My first night in college was a sleepless bat patrol.

Hardin-Simmons was what used to be called a Bible college and very conservative even by the standards of Southern Baptists. Chapel attendance was required on Sunday mornings (regular church services) and Wednesday evenings (vespers). A year of Bible study was required—a semester of Old Testament and a semester of New Testament—and a biblical perspective was expected in all courses. Female students were required to follow a strict curfew of eight o'clock on weeknights and ten o'clock on weekends. They weren't allowed to smoke or wear patent leather or brightly shined shoes, or to sit in a seat just vacated by a man, or to wear shorts in public, or to curse or even laugh too loudly. Whatever bizarre and twisted sexuality lay behind these rules, not even Nietzsche or Freud could have unraveled. One thing was for sure: far from having the intended effect, the rules kept sex on everyone's mind most of the time. As I had always believed, if a young man wasn't thinking about sex, his mind was wandering.

Hardin-Simmons enrolled about four thousand students divided equally between men and women. There were only four black students, however, and each one was a basketball player. The two other Abilene colleges were not very different in this demographic, or in any other regard.

During the first week of classes, I tried out for the baseball team and made it. The players weren't very good and I was a bit rusty myself. With too much time on my hands, I walked around the small campus and checked out the college women. I listened to music in my room, primarily Jefferson Airplane, Johnny Cash, Janis Joplin, and Jimi Hendrix. I skipped Wednesday night vespers. I finished reading *A Portrait of the Artist as a Young Man* by James Joyce. Toward the end of the week, I found a cheap used Volkswagen Beetle, faded yellow and funky, and bought it with some of my hard-earned oilfield money. The slow and sputtering little toy car filled me with comfort. I was relieved to be mobile again.

My dorm room was connected to another room by a shared bathroom, and I introduced myself to my suitemates, Hunter and Garland. They were both from Wisconsin and had been sent to Hardin-Simmons to improve their moral and religious faculties. They weren't too bad for Yankees, and they were relieved to find someone else who listened to the same music.

By Saturday night, except for my lingering fear of bats, I felt that college just might be tolerable. I took Hunter and Garland out for a quick tour of Abilene. It wasn't difficult to do. If you've seen one cluster of gas stations and churches, you've seen them all. Abilene was so boring that a somewhat famous basketball coach, Abe Lemons, once threatened his players that if they lost to an Abilene team, they would have to spend a night on the town. After nine p.m., everything shut down. Driving through those empty streets late at night gave you the feeling of a *Twilight Zone* episode. You could sense that the alien mothership must be parked around the corner. No Bergman movie I ever saw exuded the kind of bedrock despair that was as common to Abilene as mesquite trees and bad drunks. So the culture shock suffered by my two new Yankee friends was very real, and I could see them almost tear up as I drove around town and they witnessed the horror of where they were.

We returned to the dorm about midnight and went up to my room. As soon as I opened the door, a bat flew straight at me. I ducked and crawled in far enough to grab my baseball bat. A second bat was circling near the ceiling. The two Yankees were frozen in the hall in abject fear. I rose up swinging and hit the winged rat solid and splattered him against the window. When I retreated into the hall, the other bat followed me. I was swinging and yelling, and the Yankees came to their senses and helped me chase that little monster down the stairway, waking up everyone in the building as we clamored after it.

On the bottom floor, we woke up Mr. Dowd, the dorm master. "You boys sound like stampeding horses," he barked from his opened door.

The bat curled back toward us at the dorm's front entrance, and I swung and smacked it against the wall. It was still alive enough to make a hideous squeaking sound, so I stomped it with my boot. Mr. Dowd stormed over to me and said, "Hand me the bat."

I reached down and picked up what was left of the creature by the tip of one wing and handed it to him. His face turned pale and he looked as though he would be sick. "No, no. Your *bat*," he said through clenched teeth.

I flipped the baseball bat end to end and handed it to him grip first. "What is your name, son?" he asked me. I looked at his livid face and knew I was off to a ripping good start at Bible college.

▪▪▪

The bat story circulated quickly around campus. It produced my first disciplinary citation from the Dean's office for disturbing other students. The college sent a handyman to repair the bat hole in my ceiling. These incidents made me one of the better-known freshmen.

▪▪▪

When I returned to my dorm one night, President Johnson was on the recreation room television announcing another escalation of the war in Vietnam. I went up to my room, sat down, and began writing what would become the first article in Abilene's first underground college newspaper, *The Bat Report*.

The first issue was a single sheet of badly written and horribly self-righteous screed denouncing the war, the politicians, big business, racism, and the university. The antiwar movement I had belonged to in spirit, I now belonged to in fact. In my case against Hardin-Simmons, I pointed out obvious and egregious examples of the unequal treatment of women and minorities. I think this is what came to bother them most, aside from the mere existence of the damned subversive rag.

I could only afford to have a hundred copies printed for a student body of four thousand. I showed the paper to Hunter and Garland first. To my surprise, they agreed to help me distribute copies all over campus. Garland even wanted to do a cartoon for the next issue. The newly formed staff of *The Bat Report* spent the rest of that evening slipping the issue under dorm room doors at the rate of about two or three per floor. This included exciting ventures into the forbidden women's dorms, where we were spotted several times by the lovely inhabitants without being turned in.

I made it a point to slide a copy under the doors leading into the suite where the black basketball players lived. We tacked the remaining copies on bulletin boards and trees and we even taped one to the chapel door.

By noon the next day, everyone was talking about *The Bat Report*. A majority of students thought it went much too far or that it was just plain crazy. I was amazed and pleased, especially when I heard that copies of copies were being distributed by parties unknown at Abilene Christian College and McMurry College. I had, of course, overlooked the possibility that anything like that would happen. Which was why I was stupid enough to call it *The Bat Report*, a name that just might help the administrators identify the author.

At two o'clock that afternoon, I was summoned to Dean Cunningham's office. As I sat in silence and looked at this very ugly little man behind his huge desk, I realized for the first time that I might be kicked out of school. And that meant I would be drafted. Dean Cunningham held the sheet aloft by a thumb and forefinger as though it were fecal matter.

"Did you write this?" he asked.

"No, sir," I replied.

He expected Baptist honesty from his students.

"Let me share your record with you, Freshman Roderick," he said. "You've been issued a disciplinary citation for an incident involving bats. Don't you find that odd?"

"It's quite a coincidence, sir. But then I did tell a lot of people about the bats. Maybe someone is out to get me. Or perhaps to bamboozle you, sir."

"I was going to issue a second disciplinary citation to you today even before this business with the scandal sheet came up." Dean Cunningham was almost stammering. "Are you aware that your attendance at chapel services and vespers is required here?" he asked.

"I am, sir."

"My records show that you have attended only one service all semester. Just one." He paused significantly. "Why?"

"Because I didn't have anything better to do that day," I replied.

I could tell he wanted to paddle me. I wasn't worried, because I'd been paddled before and by much bigger people.

"We will kick you out of here, I promise. Just one more citation." He lifted the single sheet again. "One witness will do it. All I need is one!"

▪▪▪

The Yankees were waiting for me when I returned to the dorm. "How did it go?" they asked, showing grave concern.

"I'm fairly certain Dean Cunningham intends to pack my bags for the rice paddies."

That night, as I was bidding goodbye to my fledgling newspaper career, the telephone rang. It was Jimmy Estes, son of one of the richest families in Abilene and a senior at Abilene Christian College. He asked to meet me at the Saddle and Sirloin restaurant at midnight.

I walked into the brightly lit and very busy truck stop on time, and he had no trouble finding me. We sat down and ordered coffee, and he got to the point quickly. As incongruous as it seemed, he loved *The Bat Report* and wanted to pay for the typing and printing and to handle distribution on all three campuses in Abilene. All I had to do was bring him copy. We agreed that it could be no more than a weekly edition and no more than a few pages each. We decided that we would meet the next week at the same time in the Saddle and Sirloin to transfer the draft and talk. As soon as we shook hands to seal the deal, he was gone. I got a refill on coffee and sat there thinking that Jimmy must be a government agent or some other pervert. But I didn't see why that should stop us. So *The Bat Report* was not only back in business, we now had a publisher.

Jimmy Estes was as good as his word. For the rest of that semester, the little paper was distributed all over town once a week. Each issue featured more contributors, and the quality improved. Oddly enough, after months of investigation, Dean Cunningham couldn't find a single witness who knew anything about *The Bat Report*.

PERSONA NON GRATA

I COULD RELATE TO THE STORY about the Bible college dean trying to pack Rick's bags for the rice paddies of Southeast Asia. Before transferring to the University of Texas, I spent my sophomore year studying at a university in the quaint postcard town of Fribourg, Switzerland, and I'd been threatened with expulsion—which meant I would've lost my student draft deferment—because I'd organized a boycott of the university *mensa*, its cafeteria.

The trouble began when I took a job as a dishwasher, my go-to choice of employment whenever I was broke. The silver-haired *patron* who ran the *mensa* treated his student workers like crap, I soon discovered, shortchanging our pay every week. He clearly disliked Americans—or at least American longhairs—assigning us to the sweatiest, most menial tasks. His foreman was a buffed-up, clean-cut law student who had the ambition to work as a diplomat for the UN. His name was Jacques and he spoke several languages, but he was one of this planet's least likely candidates for service in the diplomatic corps. When he lost his temper at his employees, which was far too often, he would bite off a chunk of a water glass and chew it slowly, then swallow the shards, demonstrating how tough and intimidating he was. This was hardly a leadership skill you'd want to list on your résumé applying for an embassy position. We were certain he was clinically psychotic.

Neither Jacques nor *le patron* could be reasoned with. A couple of us tried to speak with them about their accounting system and bookkeeping, but they dismissed us with the usual French scoffs and continued to shortchange our paychecks. After one contentious meeting, the *patron* sicced his German shepherd on my friend and coworker Greg as he was leaving the building, and Greg was forced to jump on the roof of the *patron*'s parked Mercedes to save himself from a vicious bite. That led the old silver-haired tyrant to withhold even more money from Greg's paycheck as reimbursement for the car's tiny scratches.

Furious about all that nonsense, I organized a boycott of the *mensa* and convinced a group of bright, earnest American students to translate our demands into French, German, and English, and we posted the leaflets all over campus. On the day and time announced, I brought my Martin guitar to the *mensa*, and forty or fifty of us blocked the front entrance of the building, sitting on the floor and singing protest songs and chanting for justice. We wouldn't let anyone in to eat.

About twenty minutes later, the police arrived and arrested my friend Brian and me as the two ringleaders. They escorted us into the Fribourg business district on foot, ushering us along a winding cobblestone street to a small Italian restaurant called Frascatti's, where five somber gentlemen in gray suits were waiting for us in dour silence at a corner table: the mayor of Fribourg, the chief of police, a deputy ambassador from the American consulate, the director of the American university exchange program, and *le patron*, who'd thrown a respectable trench coat over his chef's white shirt and white pants. They were all holding cigarettes like Nazi officers in a 1940s black-and-white war movie. That so many local heavyweights had assembled so quickly was a measure of both Swiss efficiency and how boring and uneventful the duties of municipal authorities were in the daily grind of sleepy Fribourg, 1968.

This august meeting of the *Schutzstaffel* was where I first became acquainted with the phrase *persona non grata*. Brian and I were told that if we didn't call off the boycott immediately, we would be expelled from the university, jailed for civil disorder, and then deported back to the United States. The deputy ambassador assured us we would lose our draft deferments and be sent to the US Army's basic training on our way to Vietnam.

"We are not Berkeley or the Sorbonne," the courtly old mayor informed us in French. "We do not have these kinds of demonstrations in Switzerland, and we do not wish to start."

The Swiss, it turned out, admired the idea of democracy but not its practice.

Faced with the prospect of slogging through neck-deep elephant grass in the mangrove swamps of Vietnam, Brian and I skulked back to the *mensa*, tails between our legs, and called off the sit-in. We were both fired from our dishwashing jobs, and Jacques ate another water glass in a victory celebration. I fought the law and the law won.

The night Rick and I swapped tales about our clashes with furrow-browed bureaucrats in gray flannel suits, there was a familiar ring to the threats we'd encountered: expulsion, jail, Vietnam. I admitted that my rebellion had suffered an inauspicious début. But he and I were young and inexperienced and just getting started. A time was coming when that would change.

THE DAY OF THE LOCUST

EVERY GREAT STORY is a love story. Or so I've read. Rick and Elaine's love story began at the University of Texas on May 5, 1970, the day after four students were shot dead by National Guardsmen at Kent State University during what would become the most turbulent period of protest against the Vietnam War. It was ironic that Rick would meet his future wife and the mother of their four sons on that day. Four bodies sprawled on the hard ground in Ohio, four sons who might face military induction someday.

On Monday, May 4, the Ohio National Guardsmen fired sixty-odd rounds of lead bullets into a crowd of students who were protesting the US invasion of Cambodia, which had expanded and escalated the war. Thirteen seconds after the guardsmen opened fire, four students lay dead, and nine others were wounded. Who can forget that photograph of a teenaged girl named Mary Ann Vecchio kneeling over a lifeless body, her arms spread in disbelief as she cried and asked *why?* It became one of the most disturbing and iconic images of our time.

In Austin, the tensions began two weeks before the Kent State debacle, when University of Texas students requested a permit to march down Congress Avenue to protest Nixon's air and troop movements on the Vietnam border with Cambodia. Everyone suspected that Nixon was preparing to invade that country. When the conservative Austin City Council rejected the request for a parade permit, they forced the antiwar march to take place on the Congress Avenue sidewalks instead of in the street. Policemen were stationed along the curbs, and motorcycle cops buzzed up and down, preventing anyone from venturing out to obstruct the nonexistent downtown traffic.

Rick, my brother Frank, my childhood schoolmate Joe Duoto, and I decided to hassle the cops by playing the schoolyard game of Red Rover. We called out to one another from opposite sides of the street—"Red Rover, Red Rover, let your side come over!"—and we took turns dashing across those empty lanes and eluding the Austin police officers who tried to chase us down. At some point a studious *Texas Observer* reporter caught up with Joe and me and, pen and notepad in hand, asked if we were an organized political movement. Were we Weathermen? Yippies? White Panthers? French Situationists? "We're the Red Rovers," we told him, and in the next issue he wrote about the Red Rovers as if we were an underground cell.

On Friday, May 1, 1970, the United States did indeed invade Cambodia in an attempt to hunt down and destroy North Vietnamese regulars and Viet Cong who were hiding across the border. In response to the invasion, spontaneous rallies erupted on college campuses in Berkeley, Ann Arbor, Madison, and all across the country over the weekend, including on UT's Main Mall. The militant clashes with police were gathering strength nationwide and promised to spill over into the next week.

The Kent State students were killed around noon on Monday, May 4, and over the next twelve hours, in those less-media-saturated days when most of us college students had no quick access to television, the news spread across the land. I was incredulous at first, then furious. Maggie and I had already worked ourselves into a fever pitch over Cambodia, and the deaths gave us even more resolve. When we saw the images of four bodies sprawled on the ground and young students who looked very much like us crying over them, our reaction bordered on hysteria.

On Tuesday morning, our Eastwoods Park neighbor Ed Stein raced over to tell us about a rally on campus, and the three of us practically sprinted to the university, stopping by Brackenridge dorm to rouse the troops. It was only three months after the gay dormmates had faced down the Longhorn football champions in the stairwell, and Rick and those surly Brack Boys were ready to hit the streets. Our band hurried toward the South Mall and joined hundreds of kindred spirits pouring out of dorms and cafeterias, chanting and pumping fists and venting our rage over the events in Ohio.

At the ornate Littlefield Fountain, an Italian neoclassical tribute to the casualties of the Great War to End All Wars, more than three thousand students had already massed with hastily fashioned signs and banners. The crowd was dense and restless, and it was difficult to keep our group together. Within minutes, a march had formed without clear purpose or destination, and we surged with an explosive frenzy toward the mammoth football stadium that was being expanded to add a large upper deck for thousands of rabid boosters to cheer from. The expansion had caused a student firestorm the previous semester when graceful old trees were cut down along Waller Creek to accommodate construction. One afternoon, I took my beloved Martin D-18 guitar to the creek and sang protest songs while the cops were dragging hippie protesters out of the trees.

During the Kent State march, our chanting echoed off the high concrete walls of the stadium, and the hard-hat construction workers behind the safety fence stopped work to yell "Fuck you, peace pukes" and wave their American flag. "I wish they'd killed more of you," they shouted, a sentiment fully embraced by the country's "silent majority."

Ed Stein was an Air Force veteran who'd been stationed in Germany for two years but now resembled the Furry Freak Brother named Phineas Phreak, the one with the shaggy black beard and Jewish 'fro. The hard hats infuriated him and he pounced against the chain-link fence, screaming at them and calling them out to fight. Maggie and I pulled him away and told him we needed to keep marching. We circled the campus and stormed onto the Drag, pouring past its bookstores and University Co-op and burger joints, by now four thousand strong, and the students behind the bullhorns were instructing everyone to march all the way to the state capitol and Congress Avenue and to occupy the business district downtown.

As we approached 19th Street (later renamed Martin Luther King Boulevard) at the south end of campus, police cars were screeching to a halt, and a dozen cops hustled out to form a human wall, intent on preventing our mob from leaving the university area and invading the city. Maggie and Rick and I were near the front of the march and we realized, in chorus with a hundred others, that there was no need to continue on another block and confront the police. A side street near the old Nighthawk restaurant provided a convenient detour, and we turned there and began running, and the entire march swerved off the Drag, following the alternate route and effectively sidestepping the police barricade. The cops weren't deft enough to move laterally two blocks and intercept us, so protestors spilled quickly across 19th and into the ghostly netherworld of tall granite fortresses that housed state government offices. Zigzagging along those empty streets, our chants reverberating through the sound tunnel of stately walls, we marchers soon entered the grounds behind the shellfish-pink dome of the Texas State Capitol. There was no sign of police. We had escaped them, and in our giddy delirium we forged ahead, focused on shutting down state government and all city functions and stopping the world itself because the war was wrong and killing students was wrong and somebody had to atone for those transgressions.

Clapping and chanting, thousands swarmed around the east side of the capitol building, but ever the iconoclast and rabble-rouser, Maggie shouted, "Don't go around it, people! *Go through it!*" And soon she was leading a large contingent through the back entrance of the venerable old building itself.

There we were, Rick and Ed and I and a dozen others following this madwoman into the bowels of the beast. The smoked glass panel in one of the elegant doors was shattered by a crazed protestor, and that's when I knew we'd crossed the line of respectable nonviolent resistance and were in for big trouble ahead. As we scrambled across the polished marble floor of the rotunda, secretaries screamed and clattered away on high heels, and a lone security guard held out his arms to stop us but was knocked aside. We darted past Elisabet Ney's statue of Stephen F. Austin and the small brass cannons from the Texas Revolution and burst into daylight through the main entrance of the capitol to discover what we knew in our hearts would be waiting for us. A wide phalanx of state troopers in riot gear was positioned shoulder to shoulder at 11th Street, which separated the capitol grounds from the commercial district of downtown Austin. There were two hundred of them wearing helmets and gas masks and bulletproof vests, and they looked ominous and fearsome with their shields and long black nightsticks, like unearthly dark warriors from a science fiction movie.

"We're screwed," Rick declared as we all stopped to stare at their fierce line of defense.

Sunlight glinted off their face shields, and we could see their sidearms and tear gas launchers, and nobody doubted that these well-trained Texas troopers were more vicious than any weekend guardsmen in Ohio. If given the order, they would've gunned down every one of us like feral dogs. The *Austin-Statesman* had reported that during the sidewalk march two weeks earlier, Texas Ranger snipers were perched on the rooftops of Congress Avenue, ready to shoot anyone who broke storefront windows and looted. We believed the story because we'd grown up in Texas and knew what sinister deeds the Rangers were capable of, especially our Chicano classmates from South Texas and the Rio Grande Valley.

"*Let's all sit down!*" the bullhorns shouted, and we slowed our momentum and proceeded cautiously down the long grassy slope of the capitol grounds to sit like Sunday picnickers at the feet of the silent, menacing troopers blocking 11th Street and Congress Avenue.

It's possible that there was a police spokesman who instructed us by loudspeaker to leave the grounds and return to campus, but I don't remember the police offering any communication whatsoever.

The crowd ranged across those hallowed acres of well-maintained lawn and hunkered down beside the many stone memorials to Texas heroes glorified under the shady oak trees. It was my first confrontation with cops in riot gear, but I felt emboldened, I suppose, by the courage and sheer numbers all around me. Marchers continued to clap and chant antiwar slogans, but we were sitting as compliantly as schoolchildren, and I thought that maybe things would calm down and we'd end this standoff unscathed.

We weren't seated for very long.

A tall, gaunt, stoop-shouldered freak with long hair and a scruffy beard stood up near the front of the gathering, pulled a paperback book from his backpack, shouted something obscene, then hurled the book as hard as he could at one of the helmeted troopers. The pages fluttered like a gamecock and hit the trooper squarely in the chest, and in that instant a barrage of tear gas canisters exploded into the crowd, skipping along the grass like runaway fireworks. The assault was on. Noxious white clouds engulfed us, and our small cadre of friends leapt to our feet and started sprinting back toward the capitol building. My eyes were burning as a canister whistled past my boots and lodged under the tire of a parked government vehicle. The rubber began melting like candle wax. That's when I realized how *hot* those damned things were. I couldn't understand how Parisian students had picked them up and hurled them back at the gendarmes. My eyes afire, I made a quick mental note: Go buy some asbestos gloves.

In the fog and pandemonium of our retreat, I lost sight of Maggie. She was confronting the troopers face to face, trying to talk them out of shooting those gas canisters, but they were stolid and unflinching behind their armor. She jogged side by side with one trooper carrying a rifle with bayonet attached. "We're human beings like you! Stop shooting tear gas at us!" she shouted. He bellowed through his mask, "If you people throw a rock, I'll shoot. If you come at me, I'll shoot."

He could stride through the tear gas but Maggie couldn't, so she ran back into the capitol, where she noticed a silent band of tourists circling the balconies above, watching the students race through the marble rotunda ringed with dark portraits of past governors glowering at all that civil disobedience. As she was escaping toward the north entrance and the shattered door, a state legislator appeared out of the shadows and spat on her. She considered punching him in the face but kept moving.

The disciplined line of troopers slowly advanced on our withdrawing stampede, but in their own haste and panic, they inadvertently fired canisters into the rotunda, causing the immediate evacuation of the tourists and every aide, clerk, and custodian who worked there. The gas drifted high into the vaulted air of the round upper stories and hung suspended and trapped for the next two days, doing something we protesters could not have accomplished: It shut down Texas state government.

In our hectic flight back to campus, I found Maggie but had lost track of Ed and Rick and Joe Duoto, whose cheap rag-cloth sandals had fallen apart in the madness, forcing him to toss them aside and flee like a barefoot country boy on a hot dirt road. Not far from the capitol, Maggie and I stumbled across a Nightingale hippie girl who'd wet her bandana at an outdoor faucet. She offered us the cool wet cloth, and we wiped our faces and burning eyes. It was the first time we'd tasted tear gas.

When we reached campus, the riot squad was only a block behind us, advancing patiently but persistently, still holding formation with shields raised, a taut line of head-busters whose faces were concealed behind gas masks. Two dozen of us were foolishly willing to take them on and had rallied at the corner of Speedway and 19th Street on the perimeter of campus. I picked up a rock from the gravel parking lot, then another, nervously squeezing the rough edges into my palms. I'd thrown a lot of rocks as a kid growing up in Texas City. And a lot of baseballs. My eyes were still stinging, and I was dehydrated and half-delirious and still upset about those students at Kent State who'd been milling about in a parking lot when they were struck dead by guardsmen bullets. And here I stood in a parking lot, rocks in hand, asking for trouble. I knew these troopers would fire on us if provoked, but I didn't care anymore.

"Don't let 'em come on campus!" I shouted.

The squadron had reached 19th Street, the border of campus, two hundred professionally trained troops at a military trot. We were claiming that street as our line in the sand.

Rick appeared suddenly out of nowhere and picked up a rock. I saw others hunting for the best ones they could find. "Hey, Zigal!" he yelled. "Do you think they'll shoot us if we throw?"

"Probably."

"Then throw hard!" he said.

We stood our ground. If they'd marched onto campus, I would've thrown rocks until they shot me dead or there were no more rocks to throw. Fortunately for all of us, their commander halted his troops at 19th and they remained there in formation, stretched horizontally for several blocks, their tear gas and firearms at the ready, no doubt as hot and tired and angry as we were. They held that position for several hours but didn't venture onto campus. It was the wisest decision anyone made that day.

After the confrontation, we demonstrators quickly regrouped on the Main Mall, in the shadow of the looming Tower, to recuperate and recount what had happened to us and to listen to the speakers at the microphone set up in the open plaza. It was a clear day near summertime temperatures, the cicadas were screaming in the live oak trees, and the collective mood was raw and uncompromising. I remember feeling that blood-drained, whole-body trembling sensation I'd always felt after a childhood fistfight.

Joe Duoto had soaked his aching feet in the East Mall fountain, then walked home and put on a more sensible pair of shoes. He and I were standing in the rear of the crowd on the Main Mall, listening to speakers and collecting our wits, when we noticed an older man wearing a suit and tie who was wandering through the crush of students, taking photographs of certain individuals. I pointed him out to Joe. "Is that guy a Fed or something?" We'd heard about undercover cops snapping photos at antiwar rallies to identify potential "troublemakers."

Joe went after him. "Hey, man, who *are* you?" he demanded, moving quickly toward the photographer. I was a step or two behind him. "Who're you working for and why're you taking pictures?"

Joe was tall and rawboned, an athletic six-feet-four with a mop of dark hair and a chiseled scowl when he was annoyed. We'd grown up together, playing football and baseball on the same teams, and I'd never seen Joe back down from anyone. *"This dude is taking pictures of everybody!"* he yelled into the crowd, and when some of the protesters began to question the photographer, he grew alarmed and hurried away in his polished wingtips toward the Supreme Court-like steps of the Main Building, retreating to the safety of the administration offices.

Over the next few hours, Joe and I tried to persuade a group of students gathered under the trees of the West Mall to call for the immediate closure of the university and the cancellation of commencement ceremonies. We argued passionately for the dismissal

Protesters on the University of Texas campus in response to the Kent State University shootings by the Ohio National Guard, May 1970. *Photo by Alan Pogue*

of final exams. "Shut It Down Now!" was our mantra, and we convinced the architecture majors to make signs that delivered this message in bold yet tastefully stenciled lettering.

A short walk away, hundreds of exhausted marchers were resting on the grass of the South Mall in the bright sunshine while guitars banged madly around them and dogs roamed free. Rick and his Brackenridge dormmates were tossing a Frisbee, and it landed next to an art student named Elaine, who was sitting on the grass with her friends from Jester dormitory. The young women were smoking dope and sharing jug wine and nodding "Right On!" to the speakers at the microphone, and the Frisbee brought the two groups together. That's how Rick met Elaine, his future wife.

Her friend Gail took an immediate dislike to the Fat Man from Tuscola and his cowboy twang, and the two of them argued politics for several minutes. Somehow the quieter Elaine mentioned that she'd painted a picture she'd titled "The Burning of Los Angeles," which was hanging temporarily in Parlin Hall, the English Department building facing the oak-shrouded mall.

Rick beamed. "That's the painting in Nathanael West's *The Day of the Locust.*"

Elaine was impressed that he knew the book. She explained that she'd read the novel in her literature class and wanted to render her version of what the painting must have looked like. Rick was intrigued by this cool dope-smoking artist with an enigmatic smile and the unfashionably short hair of Jane Fonda. He found her smart and deep and quietly sexy, and he was elated to be having an intellectual conversation about art, literature, and politics with an attractive college woman. Wasn't that what we were all looking for—a companion and lover who was interested in the same things we were? Wasn't that what was so appealing about my girlfriend, Maggie?

It was certainly portentous that Rick and Elaine's love story began on that afternoon in May 1970 after days of combative protests on campuses all over America. It was almost too Hollywood-perfect. I wonder how many other romances were ignited on that same day, how many chance encounters led to a decades-long bond between couples?

The university was under siege until dark, but no one had been seriously injured, and Austin's commercial district was spared our wrath. A march through downtown Austin was planned for Friday, three days after the tear gas, but the city council once again declined to issue a parade permit. On Friday morning, May 8, hundreds of law enforcement officers were stationed between campus and downtown, prepared to stop any mass movement that constituted a "parade."

By late morning, an enormous crowd of twenty thousand protesters had gathered on campus and intended to march, parade permit or not. I had gone to a messy shack called Academy Surplus (the original of what would become a national franchise) and bought asbestos gloves, ready to hurl hot smoking tear gas canisters back at the police. The gloves were sticking out of my back pocket as I stood in the restless crowd with Rick and the Red Rovers, psyching ourselves up for civil disobedience. But a group of UT law students prevailed, convincing Federal Judge Jack Roberts to overrule the city council at the last moment and allow the march. When the decision was announced, twenty thousand voices roared with gratitude and relief.

It was the largest march in the city's history. Hundreds of frat boys and sorority girls joined an antiwar march for the first time in their lives. The rooftop snipers were in place again downtown, or so we read later, but we marchers gave them no reason to act. I will leave it to the historians to decide if the landmark nationwide marches of May 1970 had a meaningful impact on the course of the war. All I know is that it was important for me as an individual to take a stand, and I'm certain that Rick and our friends felt the same way. But the two sides of the Vietnam War remained divided for several years more, hawks and doves, until the last helicopter lifted off the roof of the US embassy in Saigon and the people of Vietnam took back their country.

In the chaos and charred nerves of the Kent State protest, Rick didn't get Elaine's last name and had no way of contacting that young attractive artist with the enigmatic smile. But he remembered her painting was in Parlin Hall, and he went there the next day and read her name on the wall beside "The Burning of Los Angeles." He looked her up in the student directory and called her dorm room for two weeks, leaving messages with the unfriendly roommate he'd argued with on the South Mall. Elaine found notes on her bed scrawled with Rick's phone number and the comment, "He called again." But she didn't return his calls because she was going to Bogotá, Colombia, for the summer with her family, and she didn't think she would ever see him again.

FROM BLOOD TO BONE

WOMEN PUZZLED RICK. They were mysteries to him. He didn't have sisters, who would've demonstrated what it was like to share a bathroom with makeup and cosmetics and a fine layer of powder sprinkled everywhere, a cabinet full of bobby pins and lotions and boxes of sanitary napkins, a multitude of bewildering straps and cups strewn across bedroom floors. As an only child who ended up living alone with a crank father in that cinderblock shanty, Rick didn't experience everyday interactions with the female gender—mother, sisters, aunts, cousins. And so he romanticized women, put them on a pedestal, admired them from afar.

As he revealed in *Bury Me Not,* he had an inferiority complex about being short, overweight, and scarred by acne, and he couldn't imagine that attractive young women might be drawn to him. He didn't deserve them, he insisted, and he distrusted their motives. *Why would that beautiful girl want to get involved with someone like me?* He was also unconvinced that women could truly devote themselves deliriously and unconditionally in relationships and relinquish complete control during sex. I thought his expectations were unrealistic and possibly skewed by reading too much D. H. Lawrence. Rick was looking for a woman's total surrender—that fabled, starry-eyed, mystical state called for in a dozen popular songs. "My darling, please surrender," Elvis crooned. For Rick, surrender was far more than "please agree to have sex with me." He believed that true love demanded a deeper, more idealistic, almost obsessive commitment. He wanted a lover who would surrender to him body and soul, as if they were taking a deep dive together into a bottomless chasm. As he wrote in his autobiography, "without some transcendent connection, sex was merely a pleasant bodily function like a high-fiber bowel movement. No, I'd waited a long time to have a meaningful relationship, and I wanted it to be all-consuming, from blood to bone. I wanted *Wuthering Heights*, not *Goodbye, Columbus*. And the whole idea scared me a little."

In his early college years, Rick was intimidated by the bold new breed of feminists, and he found it confusing and difficult to simply befriend a woman without sexual intent. My relationship with Maggie became the model for what he was seeking—a real flesh-and-blood bond with a young woman who was his intellectual equal and who loved sex, drugs, rock'n'roll, and radical politics. He wasn't aware that my relationship with her was far from ideal. From the very beginning, Maggie and I argued, disagreed, and competed, sometimes over how many days in a row one should wear the same pair of jeans. All of us in that countercultural world were making our way into new territory without roadmaps. We'd abandoned the certainties of religion and blind patriotism, and within that vacuum, we struggled to define our own values and beliefs.

Rick asked me what it was like to live with a woman. I told him that Maggie was a free spirit and confrontational by nature and that we squabbled a great deal. It was our way of working things out. But we were in love. Our living arrangement was very comfortable. We read the same books, went to films (not movies) three nights a week, discussed the serious issues of the day. Ours was a typical college live-in relationship of that era.

"You're one lucky bastard," he said. "I don't know if I'll ever find someone like Maggie."

Rick admired her politics and passion, her striking blue eyes and the soft, seductive Mississippi accent she used when speaking over the phone. He would call us just to listen to Maggie's voice, quite possibly an early version of phone sex. But Rick was upfront about it, more humorous than coarse, and Maggie always laughed and hammed it up when he called.

One of her most brazen anti-establishment moves was to feed scads of the longhaired freaks of Brackenridge and Jester dorms for free. Her work-study job called for her to wear an official white frock and sit behind a tall podium-like desk at the entrance to Jester cafeteria, where residents showed her their red ID tags to gain entrance to the abundant buffet. Her task was to cross off their ID numbers on a large printout sheet. This prevented subversives from eating and then loaning their tags to friends who didn't have a valid food contract. Maggie, of course, didn't care who ate there. In fact, she believed that the food should've been free to everyone on campus, and she told her dormmates and classmates to come whenever they desired. Rick, Frank, and others made fake red IDs with fake numbers. This went on for most of the academic year 1969–70. I don't know how many people she fed, week after week, three meals a day.

With Maggie in mind, I told Rick, "There are thousands of girls on this campus, amigo. You'll find the one for you. At this very moment, she's studying in one of the libraries. Or having a cup of coffee at the Chuck Wagon. Or maybe she's wandering around campus, looking for *you*. What was that girl's name? The artist you met after the march."

"Elaine," he said. "She blew me off."

Ironically, a few days after the Kent State march, Maggie declared that she felt smothered by our relationship—we'd lived together for all of five months—and she wanted to move out of our cozy little place across the street from Eastwoods Park. It was the beginning of an erratic off-again, on-again relationship that played out over the next three years.

That summer of 1970, she shared a crumbling stucco roach-haven near the state capitol with a melancholy female roommate, and they drove each other crazy. In the fall, our last semester in college, Maggie moved into a one-room garret in that same ramshackle complex and invited me to live with her again. By then, Bill Gallagher had returned from Europe and reclaimed his Eastwoods garage apartment and that sleek sports car under a tarp, so I was grateful to have a place to stay.

Maggie's new garret was so small that I had to sit on the edge of the bed to use the roll-top desk when I worked on a story for my short fiction class. It was the most claustrophobic place I've ever lived, and I knew we would kill each other if we stayed there too long. In October we rented the upstairs half of a shabby old white house, with its own private entrance, on East 45th Street near the leafy Hyde Park neighborhood. Our landlord was a slightly eccentric middle-aged beatnik named Loudon who lived downstairs with his bedraggled wife and a fragile little daughter who looked too young to be theirs. Loudon made it clear from the beginning that he didn't care what we did upstairs as long as the rent was paid on time.

In Austin in those days, there were eccentrics everywhere. Next door to us, an old lady lived in a car parked in the driveway of her home. She preferred the car to her quaint two-bedroom house. The car's back seat was filled to the windows with tissues and napkins and various paper products. On a couple of mornings, I tapped on her driver window and talked to her to make sure she was okay. Her daughter came by every few days to check on her well-being.

Maggie and I occupied the long main room, which had a double bed at one end and a comfortable living area at the other, with a built-in bookcase, a black-and-white TV on a wire stand, and an ancient sofa and overstuffed chair. There was an old spinster aunt of a kitchen with spongy linoleum and a rattling Frigidaire, and a smaller bedroom we decided to rent out. We advertised in *The Rag*, Austin's underground newspaper, and on bulletin boards in the university's student union. Somehow, we settled on a scrawny UT upperclassman from San Antonio who asked us to call him Grover, although we found out later that wasn't his real name. He wore wire-rimmed glasses, and his long, strange, brownish hair was thinning prematurely. He was trying to lose weight because his draft lottery number was thirty-seven and he would soon be called up for military induction. When he finally underwent his official physical, Grover was five foot nine and weighed one hundred and twenty-five pounds, and he looked emaciated and convincingly deranged. He flunked, as planned, and we celebrated in appropriate drunken fashion. A few weeks later, he read that Native Americans had used yucca roots to cleanse their hair, so he packed up his gear and headed out alone into the Chihuahua desert southwest of El Paso to make his fortune as a supplier of yucca roots for his new business enterprise. We didn't hear from him for weeks, and we presumed he'd been killed by a mountain lion or shot and left for dead by Federales.

When French-major Maggie and I graduated together from the University of Texas in December 1970, she decided to take a job as an *au pair* with a family in Bordeaux. This came as quite a surprise. As usual, her decision had been impulsive and she hadn't discussed it with me. She basically said, "So long, I'll see you in about eight months. *Maybe*. Don't forget to write and tell me where you are."

A few days before New Year's Eve, I took her to the Austin airport and kissed her goodbye. She was excited about her new life, and I was depressed beyond words. I wondered if I would ever see her again. I returned to the cold and solitary apartment, sat on the sofa in the chill room that had once been our cozy love nest, and pondered my future. I'd graduated from college with a degree in English, and I had no job and no prospects for one. Even worse, I didn't know what I wanted to do, beyond becoming the next William Faulkner or John Steinbeck. How would I make a living in the meantime? I hadn't given it enough thought.

As I began to reminisce about Maggie, I realized how deeply I cared about her and how lost I would be without her and our comfortable routines. Something gave way inside me and suddenly, unexpectedly, I began to cry. I was twenty-two years old, and it was the first time I'd ever cried over a woman. This disturbed me because I'd worked so hard to perfect my persona as one of those tough, cool antiheroes who avoided sentimentality and emotion, like the knowing, cocky presence behind every tough-love Bob Dylan song. My grief seemed to last an eternity in that desolate room. I eventually got up off the sofa, dried my eyes, went to the phone, and called the one person I trusted to understand my pain.

Rick.

"Maggie's gone and Grover is probably dead by now in Mexico," I told him. "I need a roommate. How would you like to move in over here?"

Rick was sharing an apartment with a guy who'd digested too much LSD and now believed he'd been a dromedary camel in a former life. We called him Camel Man. He drank almost no liquids and could go for days without sleep. The last time I saw Camel Man, he dropped in on me in San Francisco a few years later, on his way to a high-security government job tracking satellites at an isolated outpost in American Samoa. He slept on the floor of my apartment that night but required no water.

"It'll take me about ten minutes to pack all my shit in a shoebox," Rick said. "Is that too soon?"

You don't really know someone until you live with them. And that's when I truly began to know Rick Roderick. We lived together for the next six months on East 45th Street, and our place became Freak Central and one of the craziest transient crash pads in the entire crazy hippie city of Austin, Texas, in the spring of 1971.

THE CIRCUS IS IN TOWN

FROM THE EARLIEST DAYS of our friendship, it was clear that Rick Roderick was a master of performance art. At times he was a boisterous exhibitionist who captured everyone's attention through humor and the force of his personality. He would do outrageous things, like drop his pants and moon the dorm card-players after he'd finessed a hand of bridge. Or he'd stick a lit cigarette in one nostril, fold his arms, and talk poker-faced to someone whose views he found reprehensible. Now and then he would make loud, provocative statements in public, speaking in full voice to random passersby. The night we watched the movie *Carrie* together at the Americana theater, we were surrounded by the entire University of Arkansas Razorback football team in Austin for a game. During the famous opening scene of high school girls in a steamy gym shower room, Rick loudly declared, "This is the best movie I've ever seen!" only seconds into the film, and the Razorbacks exploded in laughter.

Many people, including some in my close circle, thought he was overbearing. I'm not sure how or why I saw through that large Falstaffian façade. Probably because he allowed me to.

Rick was not a man given to subtlety, but he had refined dimensions that weren't obvious. He was tidy, orderly, a frequent shower-taker. He relished silence and would spend hours reading lofty tomes while curled up on the couch in the apartment's big room, smoking nonstop in those more tolerant days of personal excess. He was studious and competitive in academics, making top grades in his classes and maintaining a high GPA throughout college and later in his graduate studies.

One day, I asked him if he'd read Karl Marx and he said that Marx was the one German he hadn't yet absorbed. I loaned him my volumes on Marx, Lenin, and Sovietology, relics from my sophomore year abroad at the University of Fribourg, where I'd studied Marxism taught by a couple of Dominican priests who were remarkably objective about a philosopher who would've hated them. After Rick had finished reading the *Communist Manifesto* that same afternoon, he looked across the room at me through a drifting cloud of cigarette smoke and said, "This makes perfect sense." It was the beginning of his lifelong fascination with Marx and socialism, the subject that would shape his worldview and occupy his scholarly endeavors for the next three decades. It was his Marxist boots-on-the-ground activism that eventually led to difficulties in his academic career.

As an added bonus, it turned out that Rick was a terrific cook of the downhome country style. His dishes were highly seasoned with salt and pepper and soaked in butter or grease and often batter-fried, a cuisine reminiscent of my mother's meals and every café and roadhouse in Texas when Rick and I grew up. He and his dad had been fry cooks at a restaurant called Saddle and Sirloin in Abilene, and Rick showed a zen-like patience with food preparation—as he did with fishing and chess—a slow, monkish, perfected ritual that went on for hours. He measured every ingredient like an alchemist and tasted his work frequently between his readings on the couch. Never did food taste so wonderful: stews and meat loaf and fried chicken and amazing pots of beans and garden greens. You could hear your arteries harden with every bite. But Rick was also allergic to many foods, notably oranges. When he was a child, his windpipe had closed on several occasions after eating something with oranges buried in the recipe, and he'd needed a shot of adrenaline to save his life. He asked me to be aware of that condition and rush him to the ER if it happened.

Penniless and desperate, Rick and I soon realized we needed financial help with the rent, and we put the word out that we were looking for *paying* roommates. No one in our collection of sketchy friends had any money either, but there was no shortage of rascals and rogues longing for a cheap roof over their heads. Sometimes they promised to pay us with what might be called "in-kind gifts" instead of cash. And that's when our apartment devolved into the Big Top with its tent flaps thrown open to the four strong winds.

Every morning when I woke up, there was someone new crashing on the premises, very often just stopping by for a day or two, road-dusty pilgrims on their way to a shinier shrine. We threatened to put a coffee can on the kitchen table for food and rent donations, but we knew the money would be stolen before we could get to it. With all the commotion and chaos and the stream of transients coming and going, Rick and I would occasionally close off the big room for peace and quiet. He was a year behind me in school and still finishing his undergraduate degree, and he needed undisturbed moments to write papers and work on class assignments. So he and I became the house marshals and occasionally booted people out.

My brother, Frank, was always welcome. He and Rick got along famously. Frank admired Rick's intellect and humor, his politics and warped worldview, and Rick was a great fan of Frank's music. When my brother was a teenager, his rock band had recorded four songs at the famous Gold Star Studios in Houston, the same studio that produced Lightnin' Hopkins, George Jones, Roy Head, Freddy Fender, the Sir Douglas Quintet, and the 13th Floor Elevators. When Frank lived with Maggie and me at our Eastwoods Park roach haven in the spring of 1970, he turned away from electric rock music and focused his attention on perfecting a folk-blues fingerpicking style on his acoustic guitar. Eventually he would master the country blues played by Texans Mance Lipscomb, Lightnin' Hopkins, Leadbelly, and a handful of bluesmen from the Mississippi Delta. Over the next few years, Rick showed up at every gig Frank played in the Austin bars, coffeehouses, and cafés where he was a mainstay. Someone once asked Frank about his playlist, and he said, "Rick Roderick is my playlist," because no matter where Frank was booked, The Fat Man would wander in and sit at a table near the stage, drinking Wild Turkey and shouting which songs he wanted to hear.

It's impossible to name everyone who slept or simply hung out or was banished from that upstairs apartment on East 45th, but some were more notable than others.

Frank's future brother-in-law, Stan, a tall rangy ex-surfer zen hippie, arrived one day with a cardboard box filled with government food subsidies. "I don't have any rent money," he announced, "but I've got cheddar." Everyone loved mellow Stan. How could we turn down a guy who offered large blocks of government cheese?

I don't know what brought Mike the Poet to our doorstep. We couldn't figure out who knew him. He was a strange, skinny, long-haired fellow with few worldly possessions, and he wore the same natty black sport coat every day like a stoop-shouldered Jeremiah. There was something heartbreaking about Mike. He was a lost soul, and we all sympathized with him. He would wander through the rooms reciting his poems to whomever was hanging around, and more than once Rick and I had to ask him to leave us alone.

Mike the Poet claimed to be rewriting the Bible and needed a place to stay while he worked on the text. He offered to pay for his lodging by painting apocalyptic murals, in the fashion of William Blake, on every wall in the apartment. He begged us for permission to live on the small square landing where the stairs turned at a ninety-degree angle, but we got tired of stepping over his comatose body every time we went downstairs, so we invited him to find other accommodations. He moved into a tool shed behind the house, where he professed to be in spiritual harmony with a large scary spider building a massive silver web up in a high corner.

One night he came home with a bloody face and told us he'd been walking downtown and was picked up by a car full of men, a father and his three grown sons, and they'd driven him down to the trees along the dark river and had beaten him up and urinated on him. Rick and I offered to call the police and help Mike file a report, but he didn't want to involve the authorities. I didn't know if Mike was gay and this was a "queer roll" or what, but he certainly had the cuts and bruises to back up his story. It took him a long time to recuperate, and then one day he disappeared. Rick and I checked the tool shed and found it empty of Mike's paint tubes and brushes and the writing tablet he carried everywhere like a sacred scroll. The spider was still there in the corner, spinning its malevolent web, but we never saw Mike the Poet again.

Like San Francisco and most college towns in those days, Austin was rife with stoners wandering the streets and babbling out of their heads. One day, in a Mother Mary act of kindness, Frank's girlfriend and future wife, Beverly (Stan's sister), picked up a young blonde hippie girl stumbling around disoriented on a public sidewalk, obviously zonked on acid or some other hallucinogen, and brought her to our place, hoping that Rick and I would know how to calm a lunatic acidhead on a bad trip. We did not. I tried to talk to the girl, but she became hostile and violent, grabbing a vinegar bottle off a shelf in the kitchen and hurling it through a glass window. As Charles Manson and his "family" had proved, acid and weed didn't mellow everyone out. As we hippies used to say, "Drugs make you even more like you already are."

"Let's pack her up and deposit her somewhere," Rick proposed, and the three of us wrestled the fighting girl into Bev's VW Beetle. (Did everyone own one of those tin cans back in the day?) I tried to hold the girl's flailing arms and legs while Bev drove to Brackenridge hospital, where we dropped her off at the ER, trusting that the medical staff would know what to do with her.

Around the same time, Gypsy Dave—a Harley-riding biker I'd met at a Fasching celebration in Munich two years earlier—had somehow tracked me down in Austin (damned phone books and directory assistance) and asked if he could crash on our floor for a few weeks. Every square inch of bedroom space was already occupied, including a corner where some idiot had scratched a mark on the wall every time he had sex with a girl in his sleeping bag. But Rick and I agreed to give Gypsy Dave three days on the kitchen floor, between the old Frigidaire and the broken window (vinegar bottle) we'd patched up with cardboard. He arrived wearing a Lincolnesque stovetop hat and said he was no longer Gypsy Dave; his new moniker was "Hat." He was a Long Tall Texan with flowing black hair, a devil's goatee, and a mad glint behind wire-rimmed glasses. He said he'd spent the past two years as a roadie for a band and then was involuntarily committed to a mental institution in Arkansas for drug addiction and paranoid schizophrenia. He implied that he'd escaped a few days earlier and he needed a place to hide out.

Rick avoided the guy. "Heavy vibe" was his conclusion. I did my best to carry on conversations with Hat late into the night. There was a gentleness about him, but also a deep well of racist resentment toward "spades" and others he thought were stalking him in the dark shadows of the daytime world. He was certain there was hidden meaning behind every human word and deed, and like Manson with the Beatles' *White Album*, Hat was beginning to decipher all the cryptic messages.

One morning, he left with his backpack strapped over his hunched shoulders and never returned. I ran across him every few years after that, usually at music venues. The last time I saw him, more than thirty years after he'd crashed on our kitchen floor, he was gaunt and in poor health, panhandling on the Drag next to the university. Even though I was wearing a suit and tie, with reasonably short hair and bifocals, he recognized me right away and hobbled over to say hello. He was living in low-income Section Eight housing, receiving disability payments from Social Security, and suffering from a number of serious medical conditions. I was surprised that he was still alive. Because of my fond memories of hanging out with him in Munich decades earlier, I was feeling both sadness and guilt. I gave him all the cash in my wallet and wished him well. He told me where his apartment was located and invited me to visit him, but I never did. I sincerely hope that Gypsy Dave was able to pull his life together and live comfortably and well-cared-for by those who loved him.

■ ■ ■

My old high school buddy Armand Doucet, a Cajun boy from James Lee Burke's small bayou town in southwest Louisiana, phoned me one night to say that he and his younger brother, Blaise, were in trouble for suspicion of drug use and needed to get out of New Iberia fast. The sheriff had informed their father, a prominent businessman in town, that the Doucet boys were about to get busted for possession of weed. After backhanding Armand across the face, their father drove them to the bus station and insisted on buying them tickets to anywhere in the Lower Forty-Eight, as long as it wasn't in Louisiana.

"What's Austin like?" Armand asked over the phone. "Can we come crash with you till things mellow out here?"

Things never mellowed out in his hometown. More than fifty years later, Armand still lives in Austin.

The Doucet brothers were handsome, dark-eyed young Cajuns fond of the outdoors and burnished by the sun. Once in Austin, they wasted no time finding work, first as street-corner flower vendors (a popular job in those days) selling carnations and roses to drivers daring enough to pull over in heavy traffic. They eventually graduated to selling ice cream from what looked like canopied golf carts, until Armand was held up three times by robbers demanding his money bag. Three different heists with three different weapons—a metal bar, a knife, a gun. After one of their fellow ice cream truck drivers was shot to death in his cart at a rock concert on the outskirts of town, our boys turned in their keys and called it quits.

Armand and Blaise (he soon changed the spelling to "Blaze") had no trouble attracting young women of the counterculture, those delightfully unfettered and hirsute female baby-boomers who populated Austin in those days, happily liberated by the sexual revolution and occasionally infected with the clap. (Some of our male friends discovered that the hard way.) Armand had let his hair grow natural in a thick mess of small tight curls, and Blaze had long, straight, mane-like brown hair and an angelic face that made him appear younger than his twenty years. He was short and compact, a former jockey for the ponies at Evangeline Downs, a racetrack north of Lafayette. More than anyone else in the house, Blaze was a magnet for hippie chicks, consorting with them on the roof of the church across the street if the spare bedroom was occupied. Rick and I were concerned that our reckless new housemate was going to get busted. The last thing we wanted was cops showing up and searching the premises. We lectured Blaze, to no avail.

The Doucets didn't own a car, and late one night, Blaze asked me to drive his date home. I was reluctant to get involved in his folly, but Blaze was Blaise, charming and likable and my adopted little brother. The girl lived in the suburbs in a cookie-cutter ranchstyle home, and Blaze was gallant enough to walk her to her front porch, where a floodlight was beaming like a lighthouse beacon. Within seconds, I heard a grown man bellowing, and I glanced out the passenger window to see Blaze bolting toward the car. *"Go, go, go!"* he was shouting as he yanked open the door. The girl's father was chasing him across their manicured lawn.

▪ ▪ ▪

Sometime that spring, Grover returned with his arm in a plaster cast and many heavy-duty black lawn bags stuffed with dry, dirt-encrusted yucca roots. He'd sliced his arm with a machete while chopping cacti in Mexico and had nearly bled to death. But he'd dragged himself out of the desert and into a clinic in Ojinaga and then back to East 45th Street, where he set about packaging the roots in baggies to sell as shampoo to a natural foods store near campus.

I tried the concoction myself, following his crude instructions scribbled on the package, and my hair began to fall out. After numerous customer complaints, the store returned his product and demanded their money back.

Poor Grover was ahead of his time. A few years later, a large corporate manufacturer began marketing yucca root shampoo and made a quick killing. Today, if you search the Internet for yucca root products, you'll find more than three million hits, all New Age products with reputable trademarks and spiritual endorsements. Grover isn't the CEO of any of those companies.

■ ■ ■

The most mysterious figure who lingered around our doorstep in those days was a drug dealer we called "The Dude from Cal." Nobody knew exactly what he looked like. Longhaired, possibly bearded, tall and malnourished and perpetually high. We heard he'd drifted into Austin on the lam, a fugitive from a minimum-security jailbreak out west. Always hipper than you because he was from California, and not unlike the Dude in *The Big Lebowski* nearly thirty years later, our man was the answer to every stoner question. "Who can we score weed from?" The Dude from Cal. "Who knows where Shiva's Headband is playing tonight?" The Dude from Cal. "Who can tell us which pasture has magic mushrooms growing in cow patties?" The Dude from Cal. "Who stole my friggin' Moody Blues album?" The Dude from Cal.

The truth is, Rick, Frank, and I created that mythic nobody ourselves, based on the brain-baked rumors that floated around the Austin counterculture like Day-Glo tracers in a room full of acid-heads. We referenced The Dude from Cal often and with tongue firmly in cheek. Like Beckett's Godot, the Dude was always out there somewhere, on his way to meet you in a back alley with a brown paper bag full of mushrooms, but he never actually arrived in the flesh. He was ethereal, clandestine, a shadowy glimpse in the imagination. We embellished his legend among our friends, a joke we all shared. Everyone knew he didn't exist. But if the cops ever busted us for drugs and tortured us with thumbscrews to disclose our dealer, we all agreed that we'd rat him out in a heartbeat. No, we had no clue what his real name was. We knew him as The Dude from Cal.

THE ABILENE BOYS

IN THE SUMMER OF 1968, Turner Williamson was a lifeguard at Abilene State Park, a rare patch of green in the midst of scrubland and flat dirt fields sixteen miles southwest of the city. Turner was an Abilene city slicker who'd just finished his freshman year at Texas A&M University. The park's swimming pool was a popular spot in the scorching dog days of June through August, and he did his best to supervise the horseplay of the "inbred psychotics," as he called them, the rednecks from little towns like Tuscola and Lawn and Buffalo Gap who were prone to chugging beer in their pickups, stumbling into the pool area, and cannonballing into the water. Their behavior was often dangerous to themselves and others. On one occasion, Lifeguard Turner got into a heated argument with a local tough and made the mistake of saying, "Let's take this outside," meaning beyond the fenced pool area. Turner was tall and in good shape, with a medium build and thick glasses, but oddly enough for a Texas boy, he'd never been in a fistfight. When he regained consciousness on a bench in the park ranger's office, having been knocked out cold, the ranger said, "Son, you're a lifeguard. It's not your job to fight these people. Just save them from drowning."

One blazing hot afternoon, when Turner blew his whistle at a boneheaded incident in the pool, he heard another whistle echoing his own. Every time he blew his whistle that day, another whistle would follow in mockery. It was Rick, messing with the authority figure in charge. Turner climbed down from his stand and walked to the shallow end to confront the culprit, and that's when he first encountered a rotund nineteen-year-old Hardin-Simmons student saddled with a barrel gut and pockmarks all over his back and chest from bouts of body acne. Turner informed Rick that he had to stop blowing the whistle, and strangely enough, Rick complied without a hassle. Inexplicably, he took a liking to Turner and soon discovered that the lifeguard was very well-read and something of an intellectual. Turner and his younger brother, Holt, were the sons of a junior high history teacher and a former semi-pro baseball player who'd tried his luck in the oil business but eventually built a career with the US Postal Service in Abilene.

Over the next few weeks, while Turner was making his periodic rounds of the pool, Rick patrolled with him and they discussed the books they'd been reading. Before long, Rick and Turner became good friends, and Rick invited him to Tuscola to play cards and hang out in the Roderick cinderblock bunker. As Turner put it, "Rick and I joined forces. The two of us brokered deals with wayward adolescents for guns and whiskey, listened to Steppenwolf, talked

Turner Williamson (*left*) and Rick, mid-1980s. *Photo courtesy of Thomas Zigal*

of Camus and Dostoevsky. We played a lot of poker in his mom's beauty parlor in Tuscola, taking money from oafs with beetling brows. It was the Season of Rick."

They began to introduce their friends to one another, the city boys from Cooper High School in Abilene and the country boys from Jim Ned High School in Tuscola. A few years later, after I'd met several of them in Austin, I affectionately dubbed their entire gang the Abilene Boys. Because of their geographical spread, it would've been more accurate to call them the Taylor County Boys, but that wouldn't have carried the same western movie mystique.

Not everyone in Turner's circle liked Rick. He'd already earned a reputation as a "loud mouth." A few of them had played against the Tuscola baseball team and knew Rick as a trash-talking catcher. The conservative, gung-ho "America, love it or leave it" types disdained his outspoken liberal views on civil rights and the Vietnam War. Others blamed him for the death of that teenaged girl.

Even at age nineteen, Rick gave no quarter to the dullards and the wishy-washy, nor to the kneejerk patriots and social climbers. He challenged people, pushed their buttons. You either "got" Rick or you didn't. Turner got him, and over that summer they enjoyed each other's company, playing cards and chess together, shooting pool and driving the endless hours to a Mexican border town for paid sex, all the things that West Texas boys did for pleasure and amusement in those simpler days. Rick thought Turner was an absolute genius, the brain equivalent to his friend Mickey's brawn.

Holt Williamson was taller and thinner than his older brother, Turner, with thick wavy blond hair and a starter mustache like a wispy caterpillar. He reacted to things with a mischievous smile that narrowed his eyes into a whimsical, half-crazed gleam. Turner was intense and deadpan ironic, Holt was satirical and entertaining. The two brothers eventually earned a bushel basket full of degrees from the University of Texas at Austin and Texas A&M—Turner in English, library science, and geology, and Holt in classics and marine biology.

Holt Williamson (*left*) **and Tom, 1980s.** *Photo courtesy of Thomas Zigal*

One afternoon in Holt's sophomore year at UT Austin, he saw Rick walking on the university Drag and recognized him instantly. He'd met him through Turner and had heard his brother sing Rick's praises. "I was diddly-bopping down the Drag when I saw him, and it was too late to dodge," Holt once told me. "He'd already spotted me in the throng and made a beeline over to me as if I was a long-lost friend."

Holt wasn't as enamored of Rick Roderick as Turner was. "Friends of mine who knew Rick warned me to beware and to steer clear. He was a bad boy, a bad influence. As they saw it, Rick was a troublemaker, an agitator, clearly operating outside the bounds of acceptable society. Rick was not fit to be among decent people. One thing really stuck in their craw. He thought he was smarter than everyone else."

On the Drag that day, Rick greeted him with such genuine amity that Holt softened immediately. Rick explained that he'd transferred from Hardin-Simmons, and he was happy that he and Holt were both UT students and suggested they get together. "So we did," Holt said. "I think Rick's instant and insistent attachment to me was in large measure because of his adoration for my brother. With Turner, Rick had finally met his intellectual match, and that meant to Rick that I was also as good as gold. Unlike them, I was not an intellectual, far from it. But from that point on, I tried to be. Rick was my teacher."

Holt fully accepted the challenge. "Rick opened my mind and heart. Conversations with him were like Socratic journeys or explorations. His book-reading and hunger for knowledge were infectious. To meet Rick on level ground, I had to read. And his thirst for social justice opened my eyes to the trials of the poor and dispossessed. Our mutual anger and protests against the Vietnam War bound us even closer."

Holt told him that Turner often made the two-hour drive from College Station to Austin on the weekends to visit him and other Abilene friends. Turner had come to terms with the fact that Texas A&M was a cesspool of conservatism, with a military culture for buzzcut cadets yearning to die in foreign fields of glory. He escaped to the People's Republic of Austin as often as he could.

I saw immediately why Rick liked the Williamson brothers so much. Their intelligence, their humor, their leftist political convictions. They came to our East 45th Street apartment for long days and nights of music and Rick's cooking and endless bull sessions fueled by liquor and illegal substances. Turner and Holt also started showing up to hear Frank perform his solo acoustic guitar act at Hansel and Gretel's beer garden and other venues. It was the beginning of my lifelong friendship with a couple of brilliant and hilarious Abilene Boys who have remained among my very best friends for five decades and counting.

THE DANISH SURFER

NOT LONG AFTER RICK moved into the East 45th pad, where we were both ingloriously broke, I snagged a job as a dishwasher at the brand-new Dobie residence hall on campus, and I brought Rick onboard when there was an opening. The twenty-seven-story residence was the most expensive on campus, run like an exclusive hotel, and the students eating in the dining hall appeared to be privileged white kids from wealthy Texas families. That year's Miss Texas beauty queen was a UT student and held court among them. After eating meals, they were tasked with placing their messy food trays on a conveyor belt that disappeared into the bowels of the scullery, where we troglodytes stood waiting to dump their leavings into garbage bins and to load their gooey plates, glasses, and silverware into various baskets and racks for cleaning in a roaring, water-blasting Hobart dishwashing machine. The trays were often smeared with what looked like the handiwork of angry toddlers and sometimes carried love notes to us peasants scribbled on paper napkins: "Lick my plate, hippie scum!" It was hot, brutal, gritty labor, and we sometimes sang work songs ("Eww, ahh. Eww, ahh. That's the sound of the men . . . working on the chain . . . ga-ah-ang."), until our supervisor received too many complaints from the offended students and ordered us to stop all the noise.

One day Rick was handling the trays by himself because a fellow worker didn't show up. As that endless line of trays was rolling into the scullery along the little railroad tracks and clacking against one another, edge to edge, he struggled to keep up with the sorting. I couldn't help him because I was assigned to "pre-wash" the silverware, an onerous task that involved sponging off a ton of sharp metal utensils soaking at the bottom of an industrial sink full of greasy suds. I was examining my raw red hands, wrinkled like an old man's face, when Rick began to yell that the trays were in danger of slipping off the end of the conveyor belt.

The supervisor of the food services was a thickset, rugby-loving white South African named Sebastian, a few years older than us, the son-in-law of the business manager of the entire Dobie megaplex. It was clear how he'd gotten his job. Sebastian spoke with a proper British accent, not a hint of Afrikaans, and he was a humorless autocratic bully lacking the slightest social skills or leadership qualities. He reminded me of that glass-eater Jacques at the Fribourg *mensa*. Sebastian regarded us dishwashers as *kaffirs* to serve at his pleasure, and he routinely meandered into the steamy scullery to bark orders and complain about our slowness and inefficiency.

On the day in question, he heard Rick yelling and rushed out of his air-conditioned office and into the steam, demanding that Rick stop complaining and work faster, harder. Rick stared daggers at him and said, "Listen up, Johannesburg. Reassign some of these guys to help me unload this shit or the trays and glasses are gonna end up on the tile floor."

There was a tense standoff. Sebastian began to issue more orders to Rick, who continued to stare at him in silent defiance. I watched Rick retrieve a cigarette from the pack in his hip pocket, stick it unlit into one of his nostrils, and fold his arms. His signature play. He didn't move an inch or even glance at the trays as they began to slide off the end of the conveyor belt and crash onto the floor in an echoing clatter of plastic dishes and broken glass. Sebastian pulled at his thick dark hair like a distressed child, then began commanding other crewmen to rescue the trays and restore order to the belt system. In a furious spew of spittle, he fired Rick on the spot. And that's when I noticed Jim Bogard standing in the doorway, calmly observing the chaos. We called him the Head Dish because he was our floor manager, and he'd been taking his fifteen-minute break somewhere in the storerooms, cooling down and probably toking on a joint.

Bogard was a huge, fair-skinned guy with a grand Norseman's head and long stringy blond hair, and it was easy to see why he'd played lineman on a Houston private school football team and had given thought to "walking on" the Texas Longhorns junior varsity squad. He was only twenty years old but looked thirty-five, and he was incredibly well read, outgoing and quick to laugh, with a magnetic aura and a mind full of zany ideas, and already a fully formed radical leftist by the time we met him. His daily uniform was a puffy white peasant shirt halfway bare at the chest, with sandals and blue jean cutoffs no matter the season or temperature. (Wearing shorts year-round wouldn't become a high school and college fad for another thirty years.) He wore a small glinting gem in one earlobe, giving him a piratical air, and he often tied his hair in a ponytail. Nobody gave Jim Bogard any grief over his appearance. Even in Texas, he was too large to mess with.

Although Sebastian was Bogard's boss, our towering friend took the older man by the arm and walked him back to his office. I don't know what they said to each other, but the conversation was very loud and animated. We could hear them shouting even above the Hobart machine, which roared nonstop like an airplane engine. Bogard returned a few minutes later to tell Rick he wasn't fired and that changes would be made to manage those trays better. We never saw Sebastian again. He hid in his office until a couple of weeks later, when his father-in-law replaced him with a kinder, gentler MBA grad student who treated us with respect.

Bogard was a radio-TV-film (RTF) major at UT, and he aspired to write and direct feature films. Although two years younger than I, he knew more about "cinema" and introduced Rick and me to the term *auteur* and a handful of European filmmakers he admired—Truffaut, Godard, Fellini, Antonioni, Bergman. In those days, films flickered every night in a half-dozen theaters and venues on campus, including an outdoor screen under a stand of oak trees behind the art building, and there were three busy movie theaters on the Drag and two more downtown. Without televisions and long before the Internet, we students packed into those campus theaters to watch the new auteurs and the latest experimental films (*Bambi vs. Godzilla*) and to catch up on the classics, like Chaplin and the Marx Brothers.

We referred to Bogard as our "activity director" because he would often arrive at East 45th with the evening's entertainment, usually a new record by the Stones or the Grateful Dead or a bootleg copy of Dylan's *Basement Tapes*. He introduced us to the madcap hilarity of Firesign Theatre, and we would sit around the big room smoking dope and listening to their skits and laughing out of control.

Sometimes we tuned into the ludicrous rantings and con pitches on late-night AM radio, preachers like the Reverend Ike and his "prosperity theology" ("Forget about the pie-in-the-sky; get yours here and now") and the Reverend Don Stewart in Miracle Valley, Arizona, selling "compassion explosion kits." The world out there in the cosmic ether of radioland was as bizarre as any magic mushroom high.

Bob Dylan's long-awaited book *Tarantula* was finally published that spring, and one night a group of us dropped acid and went to the spare bedroom to lounge on the Doucets' waterbed and take turns reading the entire book aloud. Bogard and Rick were especially good readers, and in our psychedelic mind-warp we chortled and snorted at Dylan's surreal, whimsical writing. Halfway through the night, we dubbed Jim Bogard as "Bodeguard the Danish Surfer" after a character referenced in the book ("Bodeguard, half danish & half surfer"). Under the influence, this coincidence seemed positively mystical and meaningful, although we couldn't figure out what it really signified.

Bogard had learned a great deal about camera technique while earning an RTF degree at UT, and he became a skilled cameraman, which he considered essential to understanding how movies were made. In the late 1970s, he and his wife, Debbie, moved to Los Angeles to pursue his career in the movie business. They started a family there, and he knew he would have to earn a living as a cameraman until he could break into the fiercely competitive world of screenwriting and directing. He found ample work behind the camera during the day, and at night he wrote screenplays and tried to network them to the right people. As Jim eventually discovered, writing for money and recognition leads to a long and frustrating life.

Jim Bogard died when his large heart ruptured while he was lugging camera equipment through LAX. Rick phoned to tell me the sad news. I hadn't seen Bogard in several years, but he was a soul friend for life, and I'd always intended to get back in touch with him. Losing him brought me to tears.

The Danish Surfer didn't fulfill his dream of becoming an auteur. He didn't write a lucrative screenplay or direct a feature film. But he got halfway there. He made a living as a cameraman in Hollywood and in the bewildering world of television, and maybe that's the important lesson to consider. It sounds like a line from his beloved Firesign Theatre: Halfway there is better than nowhere at all.

LOVE AND FEAR

THAT CLASSY ART STUDENT named Elaine had made a lasting impression on Rick. Despite her discouraging silence, he was dogged in his pursuit. She finally agreed on a first date, nine months after they'd met during the Kent State turmoil, and they went to an Austin folk club called the Chequered Flag to see the singer-songwriter Jerry Jeff Walker, famous for his song "Mr. Bojangles" (Richard Nixon's favorite song). The club was overcrowded and too noisy for conversation, so they ended up sitting on a pool table in the back of the place and talking. Years later, Elaine told me she thought Rick was cool and mysterious that first night, and she liked his "rap," as we used to call it—his facility with words and stories, his humor and hip style, his radical worldview.

But what happened next left Rick perplexed and devastated. Elaine stood him up on their second date. He couldn't understand what he'd done wrong. He thought they'd connected, that there was a strong attraction and a prospect for romance and a deep and abiding friendship.

Elaine's life had become very complicated over those nine months since Kent State. She'd dated other guys and had received a marriage proposal from one of them, and she was overwhelmed by the abundance of attention. Did she need another young man in her life? Dropping Rick would have slowed things down and simplified her choices.

Elaine's father was a university professor, and two weeks after the Kent State marches, he took his family to Bogotá, Colombia, where he'd lined up a summer teaching position at the Universidad de los Andes. They lived in a modern high-rise apartment, and Elaine spent the summer typing her father's notes and frequenting the chic clubs that were open all night. But the summer of 1970 was an unstable period in Colombia. There were military tanks in the streets of Bogotá during an ongoing state of siege. The presidential election in April had been declared fraudulent by the supporters of the defeated former president (and one-time dictator) Gustavo Rojas, and riots continued to erupt throughout the city. In the midst of the chaos, Elaine became romantically involved with a young Colombian, and on one occasion their car was stopped and searched by government soldiers. First, tear gas at the Texas State Capitol, then tanks and soldiers in a foreign city. Within that brief historical moment, the professor's daughter from a comfortable college-town upbringing had experienced love and fear in a time of revolution.

Because Elaine's life had become more serious and consequential, more burdened by the drama she'd lived through in less than a year, there was a new intensity about her. She wasn't the same young woman Rick had met sitting on the grass of the South Mall, smoking dope and drinking jug wine and dodging Frisbees. She stood him up on their second date to warn him that she was different now and that he should proceed at his own risk.

It didn't scare Rick off. He'd found the woman of his dreams.

One night at our upper floor on East 45th, Blaze brought home two young women. One was a cute blonde named Emily with intelligent eyes behind her rimless granny glasses. After speaking with her for five minutes, it was clear to me that she was brighter and more sensible than his usual "dates." For one thing, she could carry on a coherent conversation. I was sitting on my bed, reading, and Blaze, Emily, and her girlfriend were sharing a joint at the other end of the big room, listening to records when I heard footsteps coming up the stairs. Rick walked in with Elaine. His perseverance had been rewarded. Even after being stood up, he'd finally persuaded her to go on a second date. I smiled and said hello to her, introducing myself to the woman Rick had been obsessing about for months, but she turned immediately toward the girls with Blaze and said with suspicion and surprise, "Emily, what are you doing here?"

Emily was Elaine's younger sister. What were the odds of two sisters meeting like that at the same house, on the same night, in a city of two hundred thousand people?

The situation was indeed tense. The calm, protective Elaine was mortified to see her sister smoking a joint in a crash pad with a degenerate like Blaze. But strangely enough, it didn't ruin her evening with Rick. In fact, the two of them had scored a lid of grass and began to roll a few joints of their own. I was impressed with Elaine. She was measured and cool and sophisticated, and I was happy to see Rick so courtly and attentive to her, another side of him I hadn't seen before. It was clear to me that The Fat Man was in love.

ROD

IN THAT WILD MERRY-GO-ROUND of friends, crashers, and hangers-on at our place in the spring of 1971, no visitor was more colorful and entertaining than Rick's dad. His name was Marshall Roderick, but everyone called him Rod. In Rick's pantheon of vivid boyhood gods and titans, Rod loomed as large as Cronus. When I finally met him, he was already a firmly established legend in my mind—and if Rick was to be believed, a crackpot legend in all the beer joints and baseball fields within fifty miles of Abilene.

Rod drove down to Austin unannounced one day in a trashy, beat-up gray Plymouth that died with a rattle and backfire next to the house. He'd stopped every half hour during the three-hour trip from Tuscola to check his oil gauge and pour in more oil. Everything Rod owned was held together by rusty wire and duct tape, or else caulked, spliced, jerry-rigged, re-routed, stitched together, or ignored entirely. Except for a very short career as a baseball pitcher in the Texas League and then a West Texas scout for the St. Louis Cardinals, he'd been unemployed and poor for most of his life. Down-and-out, pinching pennies, Depression-era broke, he'd often resorted to flimflammery and con games to make ends meet. On one occasion, in a bold swindle to convince an oil executive to invest in an imaginary oil patch, he'd filled a Mason jar with Pennzoil, brought it to a meeting at the corporate headquarters in Abilene, and set it before the executive, saying, "Here's a sample of the refined crude from one of my rigs. Test it in your lab. It's damned near as good as Pennzoil."

Over the years, Rod had launched several chain-letter scams

and Ponzi schemes, and most of them had paid for groceries, but he wasn't always successful. His wealthy cousin lived a country-club life as a local banker, with a large ranchstyle home and swimming pool, and Rod allegedly colluded with him as a silent partner in what amounted to financial fraud. Rick told me that the only thing that kept the cousin out of prison was Rod's perjured testimony in court, which somehow got them off with probation and a huge fine paid by the cousin. In gratitude for that testimony, Rod received periodic cash "gratuities" from his cousin for the rest of his life.

Like a latter-day Fagin in *Oliver Twist*, Rod taught his son all the tricks of the con underworld. In time, Rick became a seasoned thief, using his skills on large corporate supermarkets and big box stores, often finding a cheaper price tag for something he wanted to purchase—a baseball glove, a rod and reel, a book or record—and simply switching the tags. Years later, after reading Marx and Engels, he justified his misdeeds as class warfare, and he was certainly correct about that. Growing up in poverty had led him to separate the rich from their money whenever and however he could.

When Rod came to visit us, he ingratiated himself to everyone in the house by cooking tasty meals, usually in large pots that would simmer on the stove all day and could be eaten at any hour, which suited the stoners passing themselves off as our roommates. One of Rod's best meals was chicken cacciatore (or at least that's what he called it), a simmering stew of chicken parts, tomatoes, bell peppers, onions, and government cheese. He also specialized in large greasy breakfasts and hashes of every kind.

When I first met him, Rod was in his mid-fifties but he looked twenty years older. Living in a small cinderblock shanty for decades without proper health care, sensible nutrition, and physical exercise had taken a toll on his body. He was a big man, tall and overweight, with a swollen belly underneath the same khaki shirt he wore every day. The shirt was stained with tobacco juice, his sunken mouth and chin were stained with tobacco juice, and he was virtually toothless, which made his speech sound like gummy old Gabby Hayes.

Having played and coached the game, he loved baseball more than any other sport, and he rarely removed the ancient sweat-stained baseball cap he donned day and night, outdoors and indoors, no matter the season.

Every evening after we'd eaten our fill of Rod's cooking, he would sit in a straight-back chair in the big room, nursing a forty-ounce bottle of Old Milwaukee beer, watery and weak but hobo cheap, and discourse on whatever crossed his mind. We gathered around him like Athenian students gathered around Socrates, anticipating wisdom and profundity. Rod's soliloquies lasted for hours, a stream of entertaining biographical anecdotes, West Texas yarns, and comical one-liners, plus the occasional political critique (he was a Democrat) and harangues about middle class mores and the evils of religion. He would punctuate his remarks with an incongruously high giggle and occasionally pick on someone in the room—Armand or Holt or whomever—for no apparent reason. "Are you paying attention, dummy?" he'd ask. Few of us dared to interrupt him while he was performing, because that could bring his ire, usually an edgy put-down leavened with humor and a wink.

It was clear where Rick had learned most of his chops. The equation was something like this:

> Rod's shaggy, irreverent, verbose style + an encyclopedic knowledge of philosophy and literature = Rick Roderick

Turner Williamson had known Rod longer than any of us, and he described him with affection as "loud, fat, dirty, profane, and totally hilarious. Listening to his commentary would put you on the floor, exhausted from laughing. He was a backwoods Hunter S. Thompson."

Beverly observed, "I had never met anyone like Rod before. I realized pretty quick that he probably skirted the law a bit, and you certainly didn't want to buy any swamp land from him. He was long of tooth, and all of us listened to him expound on a wide range of topics (although he had his favorites) for as long as we could before we had to ease ourselves out of the room."

I remember a few of Rod's one-liners:

"It's hotter than a preacher in a border town."

"Tight as a bug's boot."

"*Spit* in one hand and *pray* in the other, and see which one gets wet."

"It's better to be a lawn than an old person in this country. Lawns get better care."

"I can sit on a stump and wipe duck butter off my shoes and make more money than that." (I still have no idea what that means, but it's pure poetry. His use of "duck butter" meant something different than the current urban slang, but I'm not sure what it was.)

One of Rod's most memorable lectures was directed at the young male knuckleheads in the room. "If a woman says stop—*stop*!" he insisted, long before the popular aphorism "No means no." "If you stop when she says to stop," Rod said, "she'll start trusting you and you'll get a lot fu'ther the next time around." It was more battlefield strategy than feminist ideology, of course, but sage advice to all the cock hounds sitting around on the floor.

Rod loved big band music and classic country, with a special fondness for torch songs and ballads, and to illustrate a point, he would sometimes sing a few lines of a song we'd never heard before. He was a great admirer of my brother Frank's singing and guitar playing, and he was always offering to book him in *this* charity benefit and *that* fundraiser, usually in Abilene or Dallas. But Frank had zero interest in charities sponsored by lounge singer has-beens (think cheesy Jerry Lewis telethons) and was too savvy to consider Rod a legit booking agent.

During those long evenings, as soon as Rod began to tire from his nonstop monologues, we would invite him to go drinking with us in the Austin bar scene and listen to live music. But his response was always the same: "I've been to bars," implying that he'd been there, done that, way too often. Besides, drinking in bars was much too expensive. He'd just as soon sit on a stump, wipe duck butter off his shoes, and sip forty ounces of Old Milwaukee until bedtime.

Rod was an acquired taste, like mescal with a worm disintegrating at the bottom of the bottle, and not everyone partook. Holt Williamson was wary of him. "I was always uncomfortable around Rod," he recalled. "To me he seemed bitter, resentful, judgmental. I can't say he felt at all deprived or unlucky. He seemed in charge of himself and he lived the life he chose. He just seemed to be misanthropic. He was always hospitable and had a good greeting for me, but I felt like it was mostly because I was a friend of Rick's."

Elaine would eventually dislike Rod on a deeper level, not only for his demeaning treatment of her, but also because of the festering and largely unacknowledged animosity between father and son, a resentment Rick felt toward Rod but never discussed with his friends. She was aware that Rod had criticized and belittled Rick when he was growing up. Rod's expectations were too high, too demanding, and his biting sarcasm was confusing to a child. And yet in spite of poor treatment, Rick mythologized his father as an antihero who not only tilted at windmills but had actually knocked a few down in that vast prairie of windmills in Taylor County, Texas.

TUSCOLA

THAT SPRING, Rick and I drove up to visit his parents in Tuscola, a two-hundred-mile trip northwest of Austin through post oak woodlands and cedar thickets and the grazing pastures of family farms. The land was beautifully verdant in that rainy season, but as we journeyed farther into the rural countryside, passing through the quaint towns of Lampasas and Brownwood and the nearly shuttered Coleman—once a cattle-drive supply center that Rod insisted was the meanest town in Texas—the green foliage began to wither and turn arid brown, and the fields were dried up as we reached the rocky, mesquite-choked sparseness of West Texas.

Rick had told me many stories about Tuscola, but it was smaller and even more black-and-white than Larry McMurtry's Archer City. When we pulled up in front of the Roderick cinderblock in the "business district," Rod was stirring a pot of beans on the stove and baking cornbread. The scene was exactly as Rick has depicted it in his manuscript:

> The sidewalk was our front yard and the backyard was old cars, various broken fans, stoves, blown-out tires, and an assortment of stray dogs and cats. Across [the street] was the old Fiesta Theater, which opened only on weekends and sometimes showed the same picture for six months.

I tried to imagine what it was like growing up as Rick did, sleeping on a couch only a few feet from the front door and "downtown" sidewalk. There was a small narrow room just off the entrance, empty when I visited, that had been his mother's beauty parlor when he was a kid and then a walk-up hamburger stand for awhile. Rod grilled burgers on the kitchen stove and served them out the front window to schoolchildren, store clerks, bank tellers, any hungry souls with a buck in their pockets.

Rick was raised without the latest modern conveniences of 1950s America, but Rod and Elwynn certainly weren't destitute or helpless. Rod had a strong, willful aversion to the middle-class values of hard work, ambition, and financial achievement. He was who he was, blustery and obvious, a peevish malcontent whose schemes and dreams hadn't worked out to his liking. But to me, Elwynn was the most puzzling parent of the two, because she'd grown up in a stable family environment in a stately old home only a few blocks away, and that cozy life was an available fallback whenever she tired of the privation and unhappiness in Rod's cinderblock. She could always go home to mom, and at some point, she did go home and never returned. As Holt Williamson put it, "Rod and Elwynn liked each other well enough but couldn't live together. Their stars were misaligned."

Elwynn wasn't cut out for the traditional domestic duties of hearth and home. She'd shown great academic promise early, precocious enough to attend college in her mid-teens, but that ended when her family's finances evaporated in the Great Depression. She was as unconventional in her way as Rod was in his, and their lifestyle choices were no doubt compromised by a shared addiction to alcohol. It liberated them and wrecked them, and it left their only child wondering why he wasn't better loved. Rick felt more like a companion than their child, and their lack of physical affection toward him caused him to doubt if unconditional love was possible at all.

Knowing there wasn't enough room in the cinderblock manse for both of us to stay overnight, Rick drove me over to Elwynn's family residence, where she'd grown up and which she now shared with her aging mother, Viola Reddell. It was an old-fashioned white wooden home built in the 1910s, like the one-story house with high ceilings and long front porch that my grandparents had moved to

Elwynn Roderick's beauty shop in Tuscola is still intact but vacant. *Photo courtesy of Brenda Saling*

after they'd sold their farm in Fayette County. Elwynn's new beauty shop had once been a stand-alone garage built for the family's Model T, but her renovation created a modern, clean, well-lighted place with a salon chair, utility room, bathroom, and much-needed air conditioning in that hot dry climate. The shop was so comfortable that Rick often slept there on a cot.

Seeing Elwynn for the first time, it was apparent that Rick was more of a short, squat Reddell than a stringy, long-legged Roderick. Like Rod, she was in her mid-fifties but looked older. She was nearly as wide as she was tall, slow-moving, with thick glasses, graying Mamie Eisenhower hair, and a West Texas accent like a croaking frog from decades of cigarettes and vodka. But she was friendly and sincerely happy to meet me and see her son. They said hello with genuine enthusiasm and embraced in a quick, perfunctory way, and I thought of how I greeted my mother on my infrequent visits home. I would sometimes lift her off her feet in a bear hug and swing her around, beaming and happy to see her, and she'd laugh and say, "Put me down, Tom, before you drop me on my head!"

Compared to Rod's financial circumstances as a pauper and his broke-ass living quarters, Elwynn's home was a palace, and I wondered why she hadn't fought for custody of her son. Perhaps Rick had chosen to live with his dad, and the three of them had reached a mutual agreement. Rod and Elwynn never divorced but remained separated in a fluid, quasi-friendly arrangement in which she visited the cinderblock freely to see her son, and Rod visited the Reddell home whenever he wanted the companionship of the smartest woman he'd ever met. No one else in town would speak to him.

Years later, when I asked Elaine about Rick's parents, she felt strongly that a duplicitous Rod had manipulated the family dynamics, driving a wedge between Rick and his mother at every opportunity. That doesn't surprise me. But Rick loved and admired Elwynn. In one of our late-night conversations, he and I discussed our mothers' reading habits and discovered they shared the same approach to literature. They read trash and they read the classics, usually if their sons recommended something of a more challenging nature. Books were books, both *Lady in Lust Land* and *The Razor's Edge*, all equally worthy of their attention, no matter how the snooty librarians categorized those titles.

In my case, a bookmobile from the Rosenberg Library in Galveston came once a month to the parking lot of Our Lady of Fatima Catholic School in Texas City, and I stocked up on books I thought my mother would like to read as well. I remember when we read *Ivanhoe*, *Rob Roy*, and *Lorna Doone* together—she would read when I was at school—and we binged on Edgar Allan Poe, Robert Louis Stevenson, Charles Dickens, and many others.

One summer when I was in high school, I decided to read a few Shakespeare plays on my own because my English teacher, Brother André Pierre Lacoste, had inspired me to love the Bard. On nights when my dad was working the evening shift at the refinery, I would lie on a bed in my parents' bedroom with the AC window unit cranking icy temperatures, and my mother would lie on the other bed, reading quietly as well. Every now and then I would recite a beautiful passage aloud to her and explain it or give its context, and Mom was always enthralled by the majesty and wisdom of Shakespeare's language. We enjoyed those leisure hours very much. It connected us and gave me a great sense of peace and contentment, raising a smile even now when I remember those summer evenings. Rick had experienced the same thing. As he wrote in *Bury Me Not*, his mother had begun reading the classics to him when he was a small child.

Elwynn had been cutting hair professionally since 1937, and her renovated shop had become a gathering place for the blue-haired ladies of Tuscola. She shampooed, cut hair, permed, and styled, but her appointments were also occasions to visit with old friends. When I stayed overnight in a small but comfortable bedroom in what was referred to as "Granny's house," my hair was shoulder length and Elwynn insisted on cutting it. "Let me take a little off the back and sides," she said, and I thought, "Okay, fine, how bad can it be?" She seemed to approach her work as a social service, a mission to keep America well-trimmed, if not clean-cut. She was openminded and certainly not anti-hippie, but my unruly long hair brought out the missionary zeal in her, and she offered her hairstylist skills as a generous gift. It would've been rude to reject her offer—a decision I would soon regret.

Working a comb and scissors through my hair, she was heavy-handed and graceless, smoking Pall Malls and sipping vodka on ice the entire time and chatting about the books she was reading. When I returned to Austin, I tried to trim and even-out the mess she'd made, but it took another month before I looked normal again. I pitied the poor women of Tuscola and wondered how Elwynn had stayed in business for so long. A few years later, my future sister-in-law, Beverly, had a similar experience:

Rick and I drove my car (pulling a trailer) to Tuscola to pick up some of his furniture and belongings. I met Elwynn on that trip and stayed overnight in Granny's house. El was great to talk to when sober, earlier in the day. Very Tennessee Williams / Faulkner. But later on, she insisted that I let her shampoo my hair in her little beauty parlor, and she was quite inebriated by that time of the day and wouldn't take no for an answer. After all, I was doing this nice thing for Rick by using my vehicle. Well, I wasn't sure if she was going to scrub all the hair off my head or drown me. It was the only life-or-death experience I've ever had in a beauty parlor.

On our way back to Austin after our trip, Rick and I compared notes about our upbringings. I had now seen firsthand where he'd grown up in Tuscola, and he would soon see where I'd grown up in Texas City. Our respect for each other was already mutual and unassailable, but it solidified even more after those visits. We were two working class Texas boys, Rick's parents closer to the poverty line than mine, and we were determined to rise above it all and distinguish ourselves in some pursuit we hadn't yet discovered. There was no going home again to small-town Texas, no turning back. Not after Austin and our intellectual interests and the delicious ways of the flesh in that time and place. Our minds had expanded and our hearts had been opened to love and other mysteries, and we were feeling arrogant and invincible at twenty-two years of age. Like that long, blistering Texas highway we were traveling on, the world unfurled before us, promising a thousand glorious adventures.

For three or four years I'd been thinking of myself as a writer, but recently I'd given up composing poetry and songs because I realized how terrible I was at those crafts. I'd started writing short stories instead, and I'd received compliments from my classmates in the only creative writing class I'd taken as an undergraduate.

"I dig your stories," Rick said. We were on the road somewhere between the dry open prairies of West Texas and the mineral springs of Lampasas. The highway smelled like the rubber sole of a melting tennis shoe. "They're really good, Tom. Whatever you do, keep writing. The only thing that'll stop you from becoming a success is if you get discouraged and give up. Don't ever give up, man."

He knew I'd applied to three graduate programs in creative writing but hadn't heard from any of them yet. I'd learned about those master's degree programs from a classmate in one of my English courses, and I was surprised that such programs existed. Your thesis could be a novel or a collection of short stories. I went to the library and found a catalog that listed the few universities that offered those graduate degree programs. Stanford and Iowa were ranked as the top two.

Rick was scheduled to graduate from UT in the next few months, and I asked him what he intended to do with a bachelor's degree in speech.

"I have absolutely no idea," he said with a raspy laugh. "Keep speechifying, I guess."

"You're good at that."

He was considering graduate school as well.

"In speech?" I asked.

"In philosophy."

His minor. He explained that he'd have to take a few more undergraduate courses in philosophy to earn a second bachelor's degree, and then apply to grad school.

It was philosophy that had engaged his prodigious intellect. In an interview with an Irish professor named Anne Buttimer more than a decade later, Rick explained that his orientation toward philosophy was influenced by the real-life struggles he'd witnessed in that era of the Civil Rights Movement, political assassinations, and the Vietnam War. His interest was driven

> by passion and by horror of the conditions around me, to try to understand them and make some kind of sense out of them, and that's what initially led me to philosophy—as well as the way I personally reacted to [those events] with such utter outrage.

> And that outrage was mixed—well, to be honest—with a kind of joy . . . As I began to see the structures around me falling apart, I began to see the hidden past of America—the past that was there in the 1930s, that was there when I listened to Woody Guthrie—which I came to after [listening to] Bob Dylan . . . and I began to see a hidden past of America. A past full of promise that had basically been taken over by a bunch of shoddy insurance salesmen and techno war bureaucrats. And I began to see and feel part of an America that's been hidden and is still hidden and it's certainly systematically hidden at the university.[8]

I'd observed his infatuation with philosophy in the two courses we'd taken together at UT, metaphysics and symbolic logic. Rick had shown remarkable perseverance and a whimsical curiosity about the metaphysical noodlings of Professor Richard Zaner while I eventually dropped the course because every discussion seemed self-evident and I was bored. (We learned later that Zaner's course was being monitored by an ultraconservative mole, posing as a student, who'd been assigned by some reactionary academic outfit to keep tabs on liberal professors.) Rick also had a mathematician's flair for the algebraic codes and propositions of symbolic logic, and he'd helped me on several nights, patiently showing me how to decipher and solve logic equations. Those two courses convinced me I was not philosopher material.

As I steered the Dodge Dart through the highway's spring glare, Rick was twisting the radio dial, searching for a rock music station in the middle of nowhere. "Amigo," I said with a smile, "philosophy may be the only degree less employable than speech and creative writing."

He flicked cigarette ash out the window. We glanced at each other and exploded with laughter. Apart or together, living in the same household or growing up four hundred miles away, when had either one of us ever done the sensible thing?

THE ISLE OF MISFORTUNE

A FEW WEEKS LATER, Rick drove with me to the Texas Gulf Coast to visit my family, eat Mom's homecooked meals, and stroll along the beach in Galveston for only the second time in his life. I showed him the Bay Street seawall in Texas City where sometimes as a child on an autumn night, I would sit and watch a huge orange harvest moon dip slowly off the dark end of the earth. Unfortunately, that view was forever obstructed by the high earthen levee built after Hurricane Carla had flooded the city a decade earlier. The levee ran parallel to the town's shoreline, and the only way to see the open bay now was to drive up onto the road atop the levee's grassy slopes.

I parked my Dodge Dart at a lookout point and we sat on the hood, watching mullets leap in the dull gray water. It was a warm spring day, and a few miles across the bay, the bank towers and insurance buildings were gleaming in the sun on Galveston Island. Rick lit a cigarette and told me about his only visit to "The Queen City of the Gulf" on a senior trip in high school. His story brought back memories of that enchanting isle, a paradise of sandy beaches and towering palm trees and oleanders blooming pink and white year-round, its tropical gardens a hundred shades of deep rich green. Galveston was infinitely more exotic than our small refinery town on the mainland fourteen miles away by car.

I was born in Galveston's old St. Mary's Infirmary, built in 1867 as the first private (and Catholic) hospital in the state of Texas and only partially destroyed by the infamous 1900 Storm. At the time of my birth in 1948, my parents were living in Texas City, whose long steel tangle of oil refineries, tin smelter, and chemical plants is visible to drivers on I-45 when approaching the island city, especially at night when the glowing towers create a mirage of urban skyscrapers. My mother had given birth to my older sister at St. Mary's, and she probably felt more comfortable delivering another child with the Sisters of Charity of the Incarnate Word rather than at the newly opened and understaffed little hospital in Texas City.

"So I am B.O.I. Born on the Island," I told Rick that day. It was a playfully elitist appellation claimed by those who were delivered in Galveston, as if we were royal-born under the stately pleasure dome of Xanadu instead of on a narrow sandbar once inhabited by Karankawa Indians living in portable animal-skin dwellings. In 1528, the Spanish explorer Álvar Núñez Cabeza de Vaca and forty crewmen washed ashore on the island after their makeshift raft, assembled in Florida from the mangled wood of their shipwreck, broke up in a storm. "We named this place *Malhado*—the Isle of Misfortune," he wrote in his recollection of the ordeal. He feared being killed and eaten by the Kronks.

"This sure beats the hell out of staring at cactus and rocks out in Tuscola," Rick said, squinting toward the Bolivar peninsula barely visible on the horizon. "Is it too late for your family to adopt me?"

Our home in Texas City was eight houses from Bay Street and the low seawall. I grew up gazing out at the murky, gray-brown waters of Galveston Bay and watching fat white gulls hover in the air currents, screeching and searching for food. On clear days, we could see the tall buildings of Galveston shimmering in the sunlight like an exotic Oz, an apparition spectral and mystifying. There was always a smell of salt and sea-life decay wafting in those Gulf breezes, and often a petrochemical stink from the mess of industries nearby. In decent weather, my neighborhood pals and I bounded down the wood steps braced against the seawall at 18th Avenue, our street, and followed the worn trail through a strip of scrubby saltgrass to the shore. It wasn't a sandy tourist beach like the one in Galveston, only a crusty rim of coastline littered with driftwood and dead jellyfish and rotting crab shells and every manner of strange debris washed up from a bay whose waters were nearly as dead as the Dead Sea. Galveston Bay had been polluted for decades by city sewage and pesticide runoff and fuel leaks from the towboats and giant oil tankers making their way to Texas City's docks a couple of miles from where we lived.

When Rick and I were parked on the levee that day, I told him what had happened to our family when Hurricane Carla battered the Texas Gulf Coast in September 1961. I slid off the car's hood and pointed back toward town and that old seawall that was supposed to protect our neighborhoods from tidal waves.

"Carla overtopped the wall and gushed three feet of salt water and mud into our house and a thousand homes all over the city." I located the exact spot where our street ended at the seawall.

Like all of our neighbors, we spent months replacing our belongings, tearing out carpet and soaked sheetrock, floating and taping and repainting everything, and hauling away mounds of snake-infested driftwood that had settled in our yard after the flood. Dad used a shovel to chop off the heads of water moccasins slithering around in the debris.

We did most of the work ourselves. My sister was fifteen, I was turning thirteen, and Frank was turning eleven, and we became our father's bumbling helpers. From time to time, my uncles and aunts drove down from Houston to assist with the rebuilding. An insurance adjuster dropped by to tell us we didn't have a policy that covered "rising water"—flood insurance—so all he could offer us was two hundred dollars to repair the small patch of roof that had been damaged. Dad grew angry because he'd been paying home insurance to the man's company for fourteen years and had never used it. He told the adjuster to get the hell out of our house.

A few days later, when Dad, Frank, and I were on the roof with a bucket of boiling hot tar and a bag of gravel, fixing that hole and covering areas blown bare by the hurricane winds, my mother yelled, "Emil, the insurance man is here again!"

The three of us wandered over to the edge of the roof and peered down into the front yard. The bespectacled insurance adjuster was standing next to Mom in his suit and tie and polished wingtips, a hard-shell briefcase at his side. "Our company's final offer is three hundred dollars, Mr. Zigal," he said to my father. "I can cut you a check right now."

Dad grabbed a claw hammer and flew down the ladder, cussing at the man, and the adjuster took off running down the sidewalk with the briefcase knocking against his leg. My mother shouted up to me, "Go stop him, Tommy! Do not let him hurt that man!"

I was too young to stop my dad from doing anything. But at my mother's frantic insistence, I slid down the ladder and raced after them. Dad was an incredibly fast runner, but the insurance adjuster had a head start and was sprinting away with Olympic-caliber speed in those Mercury-like wingtips. I kept yelling, "Don't clobber him, Daddy! Don't clobber him!" My father finally slowed down and grabbed his knees, huffing and out of breath. I was surprised to see that he didn't have his usual herculean stamina. When I reached him, he was staring off down the sidewalk to where the adjuster was only a speck in the distance. "Jesus, that son of a bitch can run!" he said.

"Give me the hammer, Daddy." He grinned and handed it to me.

"I wasn't gonna hit him," he said, still breathing hard. "I just wanted to scare the bastard."

The rest of that fall and well into winter, the entire city was still renovating, remodeling, recuperating. In the midst of the wreckage and hard labor, Dad suffered a heart attack at age thirty-nine. But that World War Two veteran, who'd earned a Bronze Star for the liberation of Dachau and for serving as a Czech interpreter at the all-female work camp at Unterschleissheim, was too tough to lie around in a hospital bed. Within a few days he was back repairing the house and working his daily shifts at the oil refinery.

"That hurricane," Rick said, toking his cigarette thoughtfully. "Did you guys lose it all? I mean, clothes and furniture and beds and everything?"

“We lost it all,” I said. “We had to start over.”

Rick and I watched the choppy waters of the bay in silence for a long time, cooled by the pleasant breeze gusting across the levee. The ever-present seagulls were squawking overhead, buoyed in the wind.

“Come on, let’s drive over to Galveston and check out the bikini scene,” I said finally, opening the car door. “I know the beach pretty well.”

▪ ▪ ▪

Galveston’s Seawall Boulevard got its name from being constructed above the massive seawall built after the 1900 Storm, and when I turned the Dodge Dart onto the wide boulevard, Rick roared with delight at seeing the open Gulf and the beach, thirty miles of glaring sand from one end of the narrow island to the other. It was a spring break weekend for college students, and bumper-to-bumper traffic was cruising the street elevated above the half-naked sunbathers down at the water’s edge. This celebration had been called Splash Days in the 1950s, when thousands of college kids swarmed onto the Galveston beaches as they did at Ft. Lauderdale every year. But after too many fights and a riot in the early 1960s, the Galveston city council eventually shut down Splash Days and their official festivities. By the time Rick and I were of age, the city elders and the Galveston police were discouraging young people from visiting the beach at spring break. Their pleas went unheeded, of course. The crowds were spontaneous and undeterred.

Beautiful surfer girls and young hippie chicks strolled along the seawall sidewalk wearing skimpy bikinis and dark sunglasses, many of them on roller skates, and carloads of college boys were slowing down to admire their tanned bodies and long flowing hair. Frank had once rear-ended the car in front of him because he was ogling the girls on the promenade.

“I’m in love!” Rick declared, resting his forearm on the open window and flicking ashes into the sea breeze.

“Which one?” I asked, glancing toward the stream of beachgoers.

“All of them.”

Glen Campbell's hit song "Galveston" was blaring from a loudspeaker. Its lyrics described a soldier in Vietnam pining for his dark-eyed girlfriend back in Galveston. The soldier envisioned her staring out to sea and waiting for him on the beach where they used to run barefoot in the sand. The song's over-orchestrated background music and country-cracking warbles sounded schlocky and sentimental to Rick and me, and we sang along with cruel exaggeration: "Galveston, ohh Gal-ves-tununuh!"

I told Rick about Frank and me dashing into those pathetic Gulf waves when we were kids, the whitecaps a staggering six feet tall on the rougher, windy days at high tide. Underwhelming by Maui standards, but strong enough to knock over a nine-year-old forging out into the breakers. As we grew older, my brother and I became more fearless, paddling our inflated innertubes (which my father stored in the garage) out to where the water rose to our necks. My mother was always screaming, "Come back in, boys, you're out there too far!" and Frank and I would catch those monstrous six-foot waves and ride them in on their crests, laughing like wild jackals and pitched high into the air more often than not, losing our tubes and tumbling head over heels into the surf, salt water burning our nostrils and eyes.

"Ahh, the scene of the crime," Rick said as we approached the Flagship Hotel perched at the seaward end of a long pier. It was the hotel where Rick and his classmates had fished from an upper window on their senior trip. "I am officially banned for life from entering that illustrious establishment."

The boardwalk structure had once been the mighty Pleasure Pier before it was destroyed by Hurricane Carla. Back then, it was like a gaudy amusement park on stilts, and in my earliest childhood memories, that weathered mélange seemed ancient and preserved in the aspic of time. It was a denser version of the Santa Monica Pier, with a jumble of food stands, an open-air movie theater, a ballroom, an aquarium, and a carnival midway at the tip of the pier. The hurricane's damage was so extensive that the city didn't bother to restore the amusements. Now only the Flagship Hotel occupied the pier, corporate and starkly alone where so much innocent joy had once flourished.

When Frank and I and our buddy Doug Kirby went cruising down Seawall Boulevard on those dark hopeful nights in our teen years, the humid Gulf air pressing a low cloud cover over the island in a sticky fog, our destination was usually the east end near Stewart Beach, where the two most popular live-music clubs, the Bamboo Hut and the Grass Menagerie, were plunked down next to each other like Caribbean juke joints, with hot rods and convertibles and pickup trucks parked all around them in the sand.

The beach scene had its own clans and cliques: surfers tanned by a concoction of iodine and baby oil, redneck wannabe cowboys we called goat ropers, a small scattering of hippies. The hippies hated the surfers for being shallow muscle-heads, the surfers hated the goat ropers for being clueless country bumpkins, the goat ropers hated everybody except their Skoal-dipping buddies who waved Old Glory down at the courthouse but wouldn't volunteer to fight in the Vietnam War they blindly supported. Music was the only thing that brokered a truce between warring tribes, if only for a few hours on a summer night. At those two clubs, everyone dropped their bigotries and grooved on the sounds of the Boogie Kings, the Countdown Five, Neal Ford and the Fanatics, Gee Gee Shinn and the Roller Coasters, and the great Roy Head.

There was a shared sentiment on the mainland. Our parents felt that Galveston was a wicked, heedless, heavy place, where only the wicked survived—*Malhado*, the Isle of Misfortune. It was a tough town, and violence festered in the outer darkness on those balmy nights. The late 1960s were a volatile time everywhere in America, especially in the inner cities with their rampant poverty and explosive racial tensions, and even a beach resort like Galveston could be a dangerous place if you found yourself in the wrong neighborhood after dark.

"Let's park and go down to the beach and wade around," I suggested to Rick.

We hadn't brought bathing suits, so we rolled up our jeans and splashed along in the shallow surf with our manly footwear in hand, laughing and talking to the children digging in the sand with their plastic shovels and toy buckets. "Holler if you find Jean Lafitte's treasure," I told them.

Rick tried to bum a cigarette from a camp of bronzed sorority girls sunbathing on large beach towels. One of them lifted her chin a few inches off the towel and appraised us through rose-colored sunglasses. "Where are you *from* with that accent?"

"France," Rick said.

We sat cross-legged in the sand next to their camp and did our best to engage in conversation, but they weren't interested in a couple of longhaired freaks who showed no potential for financial stability and suitable attire. They didn't even offer us a beer from their ice chest.

The next day, after we'd packed up and hugged my parents good-bye, I crawled behind the wheel of my faithful Dodge Dart and the damned thing wouldn't start. My dad, the supreme master of all things mechanical, tinkered under the hood for half an hour with Rick and me looking on, but he couldn't figure out what was wrong. He suspected it was the carburetor. It was always the damned carburetor.

Rick had classes the next day, and I was writing for a small newspaper in South Austin that expected me to show up on Monday morning. I said, "Let's hitchhike, Rick. I'll take a bus next weekend and come pick up the Dart after Dad fixes it."

At that point in my life, I'd hitched all over Europe, the UK, and parts of Scandinavia. It seemed like a free and easy way to travel back to Austin, which was only two hundred miles away. Rick was from a small town, with a car of his own, and he hadn't done much hitchhiking, but he was game.

It was another clear warm day, and we were standing illegally on the shoulder of I-45 on the outskirts of Texas City with our thumbs out, when a vehicle full of partying frat boys driving northbound from spring break in Galveston slowed down and hurled cups of ice and beer on us as they whizzed by, laughing and screaming and calling us "hippie faggots." Traffic was slow and heavy on the freeway, the well-baked throngs returning wasted to Houston, and within minutes a car pulled over to pick us up—a Plymouth Belvedere muscle car.

"What happened to you boys?" asked the older guy riding shotgun. He'd noticed our wet clothing.

We told him about the frat boys, and he turned to the quiet driver with a menacing grin. "Let's go catch those fuckers," he said.

The older guy was what we used to call a "hood" or a "greaser," a white man in his thirties, smoking a cigarette, slicked-back hair and long hillbilly sideburns and a hardened face you'd expect to see on a Post Office Wanted poster. The driver was much younger, maybe in his late teens, with glasses and long brown hair tucked behind his ears. Although grateful for the ride, I was leery of them. They'd clearly been drinking at the beach. There were two empty whiskey bottles and a dusting of sand on the floorboards in the back seat, and one glance at Rick told me he was as nervous as I was. We could hear something rattling around in the trunk, a shovel or some other yard tool.

"Is that the car up there?" asked the older guy, the gangster.

I craned my head out the window, my long hair streaming in the wind. "That's them," I said.

Weaving through traffic, the driver eventually pulled alongside their vehicle. We were in the middle lane, they were on our right. The frat boys noticed the older guy smiling and smooching his lips at them, our car pacing them side by side, and they made the mistake of sneering and screaming and giving him the finger.

"Yeah, they're assholes," he said, flipping his cigarette out the window at them.

He laughed a giggling demented laugh like James Dean in *Rebel Without a Cause*, then opened the glove compartment and withdrew a handgun, what looked like a blue-steel .22 revolver. With

Rick on a fishing trip to the Texas Gulf Coast. *Photo courtesy of the Roderick family*

his arm fully extended out the window, he pointed the pistol at their driver. To this day, I can still picture the sudden panic in their faces. When the driver saw the gun, he hit his brake and their car skidded and faded behind us. Rick and I looked back and saw them swerve over to the shoulder.

"I hate rude college boys," the older guy said as he slipped the gun back into the glove compartment. He and the driver were laughing wickedly as if they'd done that sort of thing before. "Didn't their mommas ever teach them respect?"

He asked us if we had any weed, and we didn't. When we reached the Houston city limits, he invited us to smoke dope with them at their crib in the Heights neighborhood. Rick and I glanced at each other again and declined, making excuses about getting back to Austin as soon as possible. The older guy said, "Suit yourself. But you're gonna miss a fucking killer party."

A couple of years later, Rick phoned me in Palo Alto, where I was a graduate student in the Stanford Writing Program, to tell me about a story breaking in the local news. A Houston mass murderer named Dean Corll, an older man with a teenaged accomplice, had drugged, tortured, raped, and murdered at least twenty-eight young males who'd partied at Corll's house in a Houston suburb. Some were strangled, others were shot to death with a .22 pistol the police had recovered. Corll and the teenager had buried several bodies on a Galveston-area beach.

"They showed a photo of the older guy. I'm pretty sure it was them," Rick said. "Didn't you hear that shovel banging around in the trunk?"

Maybe I had. Maybe it *was* them.

Over the next three decades, unrelated to Dean Corll's atrocities, the bodies of thirty missing young women would be discovered near I-45 between Galveston and Houston, the heinous acts of at least three different serial killers who worked alone. The area became known as the Texas Killing Fields. Was there some inexplicable psychotic sickness imbedded in the character of the place where I'd been born and raised? So much violence so close to *Malhado*.

While everything was unfolding in what felt like protracted slow motion that afternoon in the muggy, springtime heat on I-45—the ice and beer splattering us, the .22 revolver in the glove compartment, the car swerving away—that old transistor radio in my head kept playing and replaying Glen Campbell's song about the young soldier longing to run with his sweetheart on the sandy beaches of his island home. Because like me, he was B.O.I.

INK-STAINED WRETCH

EARLIER THAT SPRING, I'd become so desperate for income that I drove to Houston to answer a newspaper ad about selling the Great Books door to door. It sounded like the perfect job for someone with a degree in liberal arts. But I was unhappy as a trainee living with my parents again in Texas City and driving nearly an hour each way, back and forth to Houston every day. I arrived at the office one morning and turned in my training kit, confessing to the regional manager that I missed my friends and my brother and I didn't want to relocate to Houston. I had never liked that sprawling, soulless, traffic-clogged city. I longed for the onions and fleshpots of Austin.

"Why didn't you say so?" he beamed. "You can go to work for the Great Books in Austin tomorrow if you want. I'll give their manager a call."

I bid goodbye to my parents and moved back in with Rick and pals at my old crib on East 45th, euphoric to be home in that hippie sanctuary again. But I wasn't cut out to be a salesman, and I ended up losing more money than I gained. So I began to look for another job, and I told Rick I would find one where we could work together again. He was burned out from the hellish nightmare of washing dishes at the Dobie dining hall.

As a foolhardy English graduate, I felt destined to be a journalist or editor, and I scoured the newspaper job listings and even the yellow pages of the Austin phone book for potential employment related to the scribbler's craft. I discovered a small newspaper consortium that published community tabloids aimed at two underrepresented neighborhoods in East Austin and Montopolis, where the African American and Mexican American populations of the city had resided for a century during the long and abhorrent era of racial segregation. When I phoned the company to ask if I could send them a resume, I was surprised that my call was taken by the publisher himself. Rudy Martinez explained that they published "positive, inspirational stories" about and for those two communities, promoting black and brown capitalism and the American dream.

"That sounds right up my alley, Mr. Martinez," I said, a closet socialist desperate for income. He invited me to their office on South First Street to meet him in person and to determine if my writing skills and personality were a good fit for their organization.

I wasn't expecting a small older house on a quiet street corner. It was once a family residence whose living room had been converted into a reporter pool of desks and whose dining room was now dominated by a copy machine, a water cooler, and a light table that looked as if schoolchildren had used it for an art class and left their gluey mess everywhere. Rudy's private office was located in a back bedroom next to the rear door and loading dock where they parked the pickup truck that delivered the newspapers.

When I arrived, Rudy was in the midst of a heated argument with his only reporter, Domingo Hernandez, a scruffy, bushy-haired La Raza Chicano wearing sunshades indoors. His thick, unkempt Zapata mustache disguised his mouth and most of his chin. The Anglo editor-in-chief was sitting on a nearby desk with his arms folded, silently tracking the confrontation as the two men went at it, flinging insults in a seamless fusion of English and Spanish.

The editor's name was Sherwood Carlisle, a lanky UT journalism graduate in his early thirties who sported a well-trimmed mustache, quite distinct from Domingo's, and more bare scalp than hair. He and Rudy were wearing ties, and I was happy I'd decided to clip on my only tie for the interview. In those days, long hair was a strike against you in any professional setting, so I did my best to spruce up in what might've passed for business attire back then—creased slacks, a blond corduroy sport coat for all seasons, leather shoes with a smear of polish. I'd given careful consideration to a recent comment from one of my female friends: "I knew I wasn't going to wear a bra to the interview, but I couldn't decide if I should wear shoes." Austin, 1971.

Rudy was refusing to print an article Domingo had written about the police shooting of a Hispanic teenager for stealing a package of bologna at a Safeway in East Austin. Domingo was passionate and loud, insisting that the story couldn't be ignored, and Rudy was standing firm that they only published upbeat news about community role models, blood drives, bake sales, Lion's Club awards, and minority-owned businesses that were contented and thriving.

"Let the *Statesman* and the news stations cover the shootings," Rudy argued. "We tell our readers what they should be proud of."

"This *pinche* so-called newspaper is total bullshit!" Domingo barked as he grabbed his notepad and brushed past me on his way out the front door.

Rudy smiled wanly at me. "He'll be back. Nobody else will hire him."

Rudy was a short, stocky man with a head full of dark hair, a soft voice, and an even softer handshake. He'd grown up in a border town on the Texas side of the Rio Grande River forty years earlier, and he'd put himself through UT by hustling frat boys at pool, much like Rick had hustled poker games in the dorm. I soon learned that Rudy also ran a side business buying and selling what he called "Aztec pottery," which was essentially a black-market enterprise conducted from the trunk of his car. But his most surprising talent was as an opera singer. He'd starred in several opera productions while at UT, and he would occasionally burst into an obscure Italian aria at the top of his lungs, usually when tensions were high and the situation called for comic relief. He sounded like Caruso to my untrained ear, and after I got to know him, I requested performances at least once a day.

“Here’s what you need to understand about us,” he said, showing me the gallery of framed black-and-white photographs of himself with Lyndon Johnson spaced along the walls. “LBJ is a good friend of mine, and he funds a big chunk of this company. He said to me, ‘Rudy, we need brown voices and black voices to speak up about the great opportunities this country has provided to minorities. Nowadays, too many Negroes and Mexicans are complaining about every little piss-ant thing.’”

He maintained that his good friend, the former president, had worked his butt off to make America a better place for everyone, and yet the whining continued.

“He wants me to print stories that inspire people to enjoy the American miracle. To make everyone realize that with hard work and ambition, they can succeed.” He was totally sincere when he said to me, “My people gotta learn to pull themselves up by their own huarache straps, my friend.”

The photographs were fascinating. LBJ eating chili with Rudy. LBJ driving in a top-down convertible with Rudy. LBJ handing Rudy a fountain pen after signing a bill. LBJ wrapping a long arm around the shoulders of the much shorter Rudy. There was even a framed certificate, signed by LBJ, officially proclaiming Rudy Martinez as a hardworking, ambitious, non-whining, pulled-up-by-his-huarache-straps success story. I don’t recall the *why* or *what* of that certificate, but it validated Rudy as a man of respectable achievement.

“I like Domingo, but he’s pretty damned radical,” Rudy said. “He refuses to accept where I’m coming from. Or this company’s mission. He just doesn’t get it.” He took the folder with my resume and writing samples from my hands and transferred it to Sherwood’s hands without a word between them. “But if *you* get where we’re coming from, my friend, you’re hired.”

Sherwood shook my hand and asked, “Can you start right now?” He gestured toward a desk with a telephone, an old Smith Corona typewriter, and a scattering of gnawed pencils. “We’re way behind schedule this week, and we need to fill column space in a real hurry.”

And that's how I was hired as a cub reporter for the River City News Consortium. We didn't discuss salary, and I was at Rudy's mercy for the next five months.

I sat down at the desk, and Sherwood consulted his notes and reeled off several assignments while I scribbled at warp speed. "You're gonna have to get on the horn and interview people," he said. "There's no time to drive over and visit them in person."

Interview people? I'd taken only one journalism course in four years of undergraduate studies, and my sole experience was interviewing the leader of a hippie commune in the hills outside Taos, New Mexico.

Sherwood hit me with a daunting list:

Feature stories on two religious pillars of Austin's minority communities—a legendary black Civil Rights minister and a Catholic pastor who'd built a gym and community center in the city's poorest Hispanic neighborhood.

A new data-processing training center in East Austin, a subject that intimidated me because I had no idea what data processing was. (And probably still don't.)

A mom-and-pop bicycle shop that showcased new and used bikes and repaired bikes. "The old gal that runs the place is a little batty," Sherwood said, "but go ahead and listen to her. She's pushing for bike lanes on city streets, mixed in with cars. Dream on, lady. In Texas? That'll be the day."

The oldest Hispanic family-operated brake service in town. "The owner has a chip on his shoulder about mechanics getting a bad rap for ripping people off. Let him vent."

A new café with a choo-choo-train motif that specialized in fondue and folk singing. Sherwood shrugged and couldn't stop laughing. "Normally I would tell you to grab some free meal coupons, but nah, I'll pass."

A feature story on a black Kiwanis Club leader who chaired the Crippled Children's Camp of Hutto, Texas. "Do *not* write a single cynical sentence about this guy and his cause. He's an ex-Green

Beret and he'll bayonet us both and burn this place to the ground."

I liked Sherwood from the start. He was a kind soul, thoughtful and well-read, with a wicked sense of humor. As an editor and ink slinger, he was cut from the same leather breechcloth as the rare moderates working at small-town newspapers throughout the Dixie South at that time, levelheaded and cautiously pushing boundaries, a steadfast believer in the cleansing ablution of objective journalism. We didn't become close friends, but we enjoyed each other's company, and during those long listless moments of downtime in the office, often waiting for Rudy to show up and approve copy, Sherwood and I would shoot the breeze about books, movies, politics, and Longhorn sports. He was also a fount of sleazy gossip, the first wag to tell me he'd heard from reliable sources that Rock Hudson had married Jim Nabors and that Marlon Brando and Wally Cox were weightlifting buddies and gay lovers.

I got busy and phoned clergymen and mechanics and the bicycle shop owner and interviewed everyone at least once. I kept phoning and fielding return calls, and I finally hammered out those articles over the next thirty hours. Both Sherwood and Rudy were delighted, and the boss took me under his wing and gave me spare keys to the company's pickup truck and the office doors, front and back.

"I'm gonna teach you the business," Rudy said, "in case Woody here gets hired away by the *Wall Street Journal*."

He called Sherwood "Woody," but Sherwood asked me not to call him that.

The next day, I met the two most important people in Rudy's life: his wife and daughter. Paulette was a second wife, mid-thirties, scion of an old and wealthy South Texas family agri-business that harvested vast acres of corn, grains, and citrus fruit. Rudy may have thought he was scoring a blonde trophy wife with this former UT Tri Delt who favored expensive dresses and jewelry, even around the office or when out grocery shopping. But Paulette was a savvy businesswoman, remarkably unspoiled, with a genuine smile and easygoing personality. She kept the volatile Rudy in line when he erupted over some inconsequential issue, usually involving bills and expenditures. And she seemed to be the brains behind their "Aztec pottery" side hustle, whatever that was about.

Rudy's daughter, Teresa, was a pretty sixteen-year-old girl from his first marriage, a Hispanic beauty with long raven hair to mid-back and the voluptuous figure of a grown woman. "Don't hit on her," Rudy warned me. "She's in charge of newspaper distribution, and you'll have to work with her."

After my articles were completed and red-penciled by Sherwood, he photo-typeset them on what looked like a bulky electric typewriter that produced strips of text, and then that copy was waxed and mocked-up on the light table by an X-Acto-wielding committee of Rudy, Paulette, Teresa, and her teenaged boyfriend, Spud, a skinny blond white kid with impeccable manners. When the layout was finished, Rudy asked me to drive with him to a small print shop in the quaint country town of Seguin, fifty miles south of Austin, where the newspapers were printed on-the-cheap by an old buddy from Rudy's hometown. In Seguin, the printers fed our pages through a chemical process and burned them onto film, which Rudy and I examined for errors, using a little brush to paint over pinholes and cut-lines with what looked like red nail polish.

Rudy's River City consortium printed three different weekly newspapers at the same time—*La Gente* for Hispanics, *The Heritage* for African Americans, and the *South Austin Gazette* for Anglos in the funky white working-class and hippie neighborhoods south of Town Lake. The front pages were the only differences in the three publications, each with its own masthead and lead stories focused on issues relevant to the target audiences. The guts of the newspapers were exactly the same, mostly community and church events and copious ads listing grocery store discounts, tire sales, air conditioner and TV repairs, bakeries, dry cleaners, restaurants, used car dealerships, and beauty shops that specialized in "ethnic hair." There were photos and captions about active military servicemen from the Austin area, paid promos for candidates running for local political offices, an entire page of squeaky-clean classified ads (no "personals"), and a respectable number of short filler articles about upcoming plays, new books, and cultural programs aired on the university's KUT radio station.

I had to give credit to Rudy Martinez. He'd found a niche that nobody else had explored: buoyant, feel-good stories emanating from Austin's minority neighborhoods. His weekly tabloids portrayed those communities as large, vibrant, self-contained, economically viable, roll-up-your-sleeves-and-do-it-yourself populations that LBJ had always supported and encouraged. Although I was an edgy young blade, questioning everything at that time in my life, I had no desire to denigrate Rudy and his admirable (if misty-eyed) raison d'être. I was very happy to have left sales behind, and I was eager to learn about newspaper journalism and the alchemy of offset printing.

Advertising was essential to keeping the doors open and the lights on, and Rudy spent most of his time on the phone, hustling ads in his somnolent voice. I sometimes eavesdropped on his passive-aggressive pitches, listening to him mollify the business owners who suspected they were throwing away money in those tabloid pages. "Just give it a little more time," he always insisted, "and it'll pay off." He promised new customers they'd be overwhelmed with business even if they took out a modest ad the size of a calling card. Occasionally Paulette joined him, working a phone at an empty desk in the pool. She was articulate and persuasive, with a winning persona, but it was a tough job selling advertising in obscure tabloids catering to black and brown populations. "Do your people have money to *buy* anything?" was usually the first question business owners asked.

Late one morning during my second week, Rudy emerged from phone-calling in his office and stood staring at Paulette, Sherwood, and me working at our desks. Clearly something was on his mind. He waited melodramatically in a long pregnant moment of silence, studying us with deadpan intensity, and then he launched into a beautiful Italian aria from god-knows-what opera. It was a stirring, glass-shattering performance, and the three of us gave him a standing ovation. Afterwards, Rudy slumped over as if punched in the solar plexus, straightened again, and declared that selling ads would lead to his imminent death by heart failure if he had to make another *pinche* phone call begging for money. There were better things a publisher should be doing, he said, like schmoozing at lunches with politicians and fat cats.

"Tom," he pleaded, "do you know anybody who'd be good at selling ads over the phone? Somebody who can sling *mierda* around real smooth to a bunch of mom-and-pop *gringo* business types, speak their redneck lingo, and convince them that a display ad in our papers will make them rich overnight?"

My smile was so large it brightened the room. "Yes, I do, Rudy. I know exactly who we need."

Rick came with me to work the next morning. He assured Rudy that he could sell ice to the Eskimos, or something like that, and the boss listened to Rick's West Texas drawl for about three minutes and hired him on the spot. He understood that Rick was finishing his last semester at UT and could work only part time, but he offered Rick a small guaranteed salary plus generous commissions for every ad he sold.

I was ecstatic that Rick was gainfully employed and sitting at the desk next to mine. He was very grateful to have escaped the steamy scullery. Between his phone calls and my pounding on the typewriter keys, we fell into our comfortable comedy patterns, wisecracks and whoops and off-the-cuff banter, trotting out our tried-and-true routines, and Sherwood and Paulette were greatly entertained and couldn't stop laughing. Our friendship was contagious.

The impromptu repartee didn't slow Rick or me down; in fact, it energized our work. After school, Teresa and Spud would drop by the office to sit quietly and listen to our verbal jams. We had an audience. Even Rudy was amused, and his opera performances increased in joy and exuberance. And every time he sang, his booming baritone rattling the frames of the LBJ photos on the walls, Rick would flick on his cigarette lighter and hold the flame high in the air until Rudy concluded the aria, often on his knees with his arms outstretched.

While banging out my articles about a new blood bank in East Austin and low-cost housing units being built in Montopolis, I listened to Rick talking on the phone to dozens of potential advertisers—funeral homes, gas stations, lumber companies, pharmacies, and even the mother superior at a convent for cloistered nuns. He was a natural at it, as folksy and down-to-earth as he needed to be, occasionally showing off his intelligence with a knowing quip to someone he sensed would appreciate a more worldly, well-educated presence behind the cold call. What Rick didn't anticipate was that Rudy would send him out to collect on delinquent accounts—businesses that had run ads but failed to pay for them—and sometimes I would ride along as company and potential muscle, in case things didn't go well with, say, that mother superior. I recall driving to a tortilla factory only a few blocks away, a sweat shop swarming with cute young women who giggled and flirted with us until the *patrón* appeared with his check book and paid the bill.

The River City News Consortium was clearly a shoestring operation, and Rudy asked Rick and me to perform "other tasks as needed and previously undiscussed" in our verbal contracts. We didn't mind. Those tasks took us out of our cramped desk pool and let Rick smoke in the fresh air. We routinely picked up copy written by two shut-ins who had no means of transportation or easy access to a post office. One was a retired military officer who lived in a nursing home, and I was assigned to make sense of his rambling op-eds on patriotism and the absence of decency and proper hygiene from the hippie generation. The other was a weekly crossword puzzle written by an elderly cat lady who always offered us home-baked cookies and lemonade when we showed up at her door. Rick was assigned to fix the puzzle, because it never worked. Some words needed more squares, some less, and some didn't connect to their crosswords in the grid. Rick would laugh his wheezing belly laugh as he sat at his desk and struggled to reconstruct the damned thing. Sometimes he was forced to change a clue-word to something entirely different, and that would give him the darkest pleasure. "I think I'm going to use *Wittgenstein* as the answer to fourteen down," he once declared.

When it was time to deliver the newspapers, I usually drove the pickup truck and Rick rode shotgun, smoking and trading stories while the two lovebirds, Teresa and Spud, hunched together in the truck's bed and hurled rubber-banded papers onto the random lawns we slowly rolled by. There were no subscriptions—the tabloids were free—and we would leave small stacks at grocery stores and laundromats in targeted neighborhoods.

We carried bundles of the three different editions—*La Gente*, *The Heritage*, and the *South Austin Gazette*—and the throwers' primary job was to identify which communities we were cruising through and therefore which papers to toss from the truck. Unfortunately, the teenagers were madly in love, flirting nonstop and distracted beyond reason, and they sometimes threw the African American edition into Hispanic yards and vice versa. Rick and I didn't care. We were too busy discussing Dostoyevsky's *The Possessed* and the films of Ken Russell and laughing about our favorite French philosopher, Nicolas Malebranche, and his Theory of Occasionalism. It addressed the classic theological question, "If all ideas come from God as divine illumination, how often does God illuminate us?" Malebranche's airtight theory: "Occasionally."

Rick was very proud of me for being accepted into the Stanford Writing Program. But because I hadn't notified Rudy yet and I needed the income for the next couple of months, we agreed not to talk about it in the newspaper office and around our fellow employees. One day when we were coasting through an East Austin neighborhood and the two lovebirds in the truck bed were throwing newspapers like German stick-handled grenades onto the lawns, Rick lit a cigarette and said quietly, with devilish mischief in his eyes, "You realize, of course, that you'll never be able to reach California."

I laughed, knowing where Philosopher Rick was going with this. Zeno's Paradox of Motion was part of our comedy routine. The gist of the paradox: Before I could reach California, I had to get halfway there, say, to Arizona. But I couldn't reach Arizona until I got halfway there, say, to El Paso. And I couldn't reach El Paso until I got halfway there, etc. In short, no one could ever reach their destination.

He and I had become best friends, but in that fitful age of serendipitous connections and sudden disruptions, the easy come-and-go of flash acquaintances, I didn't know if my friendship with him would bear the test of time. Distances seemed farther in those days, without the instant contact of emails and cell phones and Google maps and Zoom. The San Francisco Bay Area, eighteen hundred miles away, may as well have been on the dark side of the moon.

I was nervous about leaving Austin and all my friends. I had no idea if I would succeed at earning a master's degree at Stanford or what I was going to do after my studies were completed. I didn't know if I was ever coming back to Texas.

PYRAMID POWER

AT OUR DESKS EVERY DAY in the pool, we sat under the vigilant gaze of LBJ peering down at us from that row of photographs. I had mixed feelings about the former president. While I respected him for passing praiseworthy Civil Rights legislation, instituting Medicare, and lifting up the poor and elderly with his Great Society programs, it was the Vietnam War that had turned our generation against him. When he announced that the dedication ceremony for his new presidential library would take place in May 1971, he'd been out of office for three years but his war was still killing thousands of young American soldiers and the Vietnamese population under his successor's sweaty-lipped watch.

Rudy was a loyal Democrat and despised the Richard Nixon regime almost as much as Rick and I did. Rudy's wealthy wife, Paulette, was privy to LBJ circles and had seen the list of VIPs who'd accepted invitations to the library dedication: Nixon, Spiro Agnew, Vietnam commander General William Westmoreland, Henry Kissinger, Dean Rusk, and future convicted Watergate felons Bob Haldeman and John Ehrlichman, among others. It was a rogue's gallery of war criminals and yes-men enablers, and Rick and I decided we would join the demonstrations that were being planned to disrupt the dedication ceremony.

After LBJ's $18.6 million presidential library was completed that spring, the Texas journalist Gary Cartwright wrote in a *New York Times* article, "Situated on the East Mall of the University of Texas campus, the LBJ Library rises, like the Great Pyramids of Egypt, above all things."[9] He noted that the library was the largest and most expensive presidential library ever built and the first one constructed on a university campus.

In the *Texas Observer*, legendary Molly Ivins called the massive library a crypt, a mausoleum, a tomb: "Lyndon Johnson in cement."

"The tomb effect stems largely from the lack of windows—those great slabs of walls," she wrote, "plus the oppressive roof, set like a heavy, over-large potlid atop the windowless walls. The redeeming feature of the exterior is the tapering curve of the walls: were it not for the potlid, the thing might almost have a galleonesque grace."

She concluded, "my conviction grows that Lyndon Johnson's most enduring monument will be the war in Vietnam."[10] She was expressing how we all felt at street level—tired of the war and the unconscionable napalm bombings and the corrupt South Vietnamese puppet government and the secrets and deceptions of the last three presidents.

Neal Spelce—a well-known local television newsman from the 1950s and 1960s who many viewers thought of as "the most trusted man in Austin"—was hired by his old boss, Lyndon Johnson, to manage the library's dedication ceremony. In his memoir *With the Bark Off*, Neal humorously describes the trials and tribulations of planning that historical event. He was on the receiving end of the infamous Johnson Treatment a time or two. "If there's any way to fuck it up, Spelce, you will," LBJ told him on one occasion.

Neal points out that the dedication planners knew that demonstrators intended to spoil the party, so they set the date for after UT's spring semester had ended and most of the students had gone home for the summer. The planners also created a security team "that involved local, university, state, and federal law enforcement agencies, the fire department and EMS, and the Secret Service. We had meetings on a regular basis to coordinate their roles. Fortunately, they were all very professional and experienced, and they knew what to do in any given scenario."[11]

A preemptive blow was struck by the State of Texas itself with an injunction described by journalists Kaye Northcott and Jay Brakefield in the *Texas Observer*:

> The injunction, requested by [Texas] Attorney General Crawford Martin, named twenty-seven individuals [several staff members of the underground newspaper *The Rag*] . . . and fourteen organizations, including such diverse groups as the Armadillo Mayday Tribe, Children of God, Community United Front, Peoples Party II, the American Friends Service Committee, and the John Brown Revolutionary League. They were enjoined from doing practically anything within a proscribed area around the LBJ Library. For example, "conducting or participating in, or encouraging, aiding or urging any other person to conduct or participate in a mass demonstration on May 22."[12]

The message: Don't rain on LBJ's parade. But someone had neglected to remind those geniuses that there's a First Amendment right to demonstrate in our country. And that includes the right to encourage, aid, and urge our friends to join us.

The people's response to the injunction? Nobody's listening, you gutless functionaries, and you should've realized you were totally hosed when a brood of self-proclaimed witches showed up at the library a few days before the dedication and began circling the fountain, singing and beating drums and chanting "the blood of the Vietnamese people will haunt you forever," putting a hex on the building. Not certified witches but badass female radicals in witch costumes. Seven of them were arrested for trespassing and hauled downtown. (My future friend Alice Embree was one of them.) That hex was probably why the university had to sue the contractors two years later, when those heavy travertine slabs began to erode and buckle and fall off the building in the relentless Texas heat. Somebody should've told them this ain't Italy.

Neal and his team were prepared for us. As he wrote in his memoir, "On the day of the dedication ceremony, National Guard troops were stationed under the stadium, at the ready, in case things got out of hand. Secret Service and agents from the Bureau of Alcohol,

Tobacco, and Firearms (ATF) were sequestered in the law building. The public didn't see these backup forces. Austin police officers, Department of Public Safety [DPS] troopers, and Texas Rangers were assigned to the barricades, prepared to stop protestors from breaching the perimeter."[13]

May 22 was a windy day and the flags were snapping in the stiff breeze, ruffling the Sunday-best clothing of three thousand invited guests milling about the immense travertine plaza, all of them decked out in formal suits and dresses and hairstyles at least a dozen years out of fashion. Rudy and Paulette were among those invited to the party by the great man whose long arms had affectionately meat-hooked Rudy in those framed photographs on his office walls.

The guests took their seats in the roped-off area on the grassy knoll just below the plaza and the eight-story, cube-like repository of all things Johnsonian. The Reverend Billy Graham delivered the invocation, the much-hated chairman of UT's Board of Regents, Frank Erwin, welcomed guests, and Tricky Dick paid generous tribute to the former president. We protesters hated Nixon even more than we hated Lyndon Johnson, and it was Nixon's presence, more than anything else, that incited us to make our voices heard.

After the speeches and formal ceremony, Nixon and LBJ stood shoulder to shoulder, waving from the plaza as the new fountain gushed upward in public for the first time. Those shifting wind gusts blew the giant plume of water over the entire audience, showering VIPs in all their finery. Many of them quickly retreated to the library tour, others to the long tables arranged beneath striped tent-like awnings to feast on Texas barbeque.

Earlier that morning, protesters had assembled at what the hippies called Peace Fountain at the end of UT's East Mall, the water flowing down a hillside above a traffic circle in front of the theater building. Rick and Frank were among the thousand protesters who left the fountain and approached the police barricades at San Jacinto Boulevard, the street running alongside the football stadium and the art building. The barricades were blocking a direct route up the hill to the new presidential library and its dedication ceremony.

A band of Vietnam veterans were the first to confront the phalanx of DPS troopers standing in formation behind the sawhorses. The vets declared that they wanted to return their medals to LBJ and Richard Nixon in protest against the war. When they were informed they wouldn't be allowed to cross the barricades, they threw their ribbons and medals at the troopers in an aggressive act of defiance.

A motley crew called Direct Action released eight hundred black balloons that drifted in those strong wind currents toward the ceremony and were visible to the speakers at the podium and the audience listening reverently on the grassy knoll. Militant chanting erupted at the barricades, and a DPS squadron in riot gear moved into place, prepared for a confrontation.

Searching for a way to breach the restricted area, Rick and Frank decided to outflank the riot squad and started running north on San Jacinto, leading protesters up a hill in front of the Texas Memorial Museum. They'd found a chink in the armor. The troopers gave chase, but Rick, Frank, and a hundred others outraced them over the hill and past the law school, where another unit of troopers was in hiding but chose not to leave the building.

I was stationed with friends and fellow troublemakers behind barricades at the broad intersection at 26th and Red River (now Dean Keeton Street and Robert Dedman Drive), about two hundred yards from the speakers and the closest access point to the library. We were shouting at a double column of cops, DPS troopers, and Texas Rangers preventing us from getting closer. Frank and Rick arrived like the Seventh Cavalry with their large, ragtag cohort of yipping disruptors and joined us in chanting the usual repertoire of "Hey, hey, LBJ, how many kids did you kill today?" and "One, two, three, four, we don't want your fucking war!" Several protesters were banging trashcan lids in a crazy raucous rhythm. But despite our best efforts, our incantations weren't loud enough to interrupt the program going on at the dais up the hill.

Demonstrators began to gather at the barricades below "Peace Fountain" (the East Mall fountain) to protest the dedication ceremony for the LBJ Presidential Library, May 1971. *Photo by Texas Student Media, UT Texas Student Publications photographs, camh-dob-037945, the Dolph Briscoe Center for American History, The University of Texas at Austin*

Turner Williamson was at the barricades with me and our friend Alan Feld, who was wearing his motorcycle helmet for protection against nightsticks. Beverly rode up on her bicycle and found us. The *Austin Statesman* published a provocative photograph of Frank leaning against a sawhorse and taunting the defending officers on the other side. He was angry and hurling insults, daring them to come fight him man to man, and I was worried he was going to get his skull busted. But before long, we heard the Longhorn Band playing "The Eyes of Texas" in the grand finale. The ceremony was over, and the invitees were herding toward the long tables for lunch.

Nixon hurried off to his helicopter, and the remaining dignitaries fed their faces before returning to the Hardin House residence in West Campus, where many of them were staying. Protesters followed them and clashed with the Tact Squad in the street out front. Thirty were arrested, the only arrests of the day.

After the city cops and DPS troopers retreated to their vehicles and departed—leaving the barricades in place but unguarded—Frank, Rick, and Alan Feld marched up the hill to the striped awnings to eat leftover barbeque. I'm not sure why I didn't join them. Fear of arrest? In those days, my view was I couldn't afford to waste money on bail, and I certainly didn't want my parents or friends to dig into their pockets and rescue me at a downtown lockup. So I always pushed it to the limit and then hauled ass when the tear gas and nightsticks were close enough to cause pain.

Rick, Frank, and Alan were prepared to clash with a security force at the barbeque tables, but everyone had disappeared except the cleanup detail, which was mostly African Americans wearing white aprons. "Hey, y'all take as much of this food as you want. There's too much left over," said the boss of the outfit, inviting the three intruders to help themselves at the serving pans. Bartenders brought tumblers of vodka tonics to the trio while they filled Alan's motorcycle helmet to the brim with a mush of chicken, brisket, sausage, and potato salad.

Later that afternoon, we all ate well at our place on East 45th Street and regaled one another with tales of our brave failure to shut down the dedication ceremony of the Lyndon Baines Johnson Presidential Library. But amid the boisterous laughter and our dramatic reenactments, we were collectively relieved that no one was hurt or in jail and we would live to fight another day.

CALIFORNIA DREAMIN'

BEING ACCEPTED to the Stanford Writing Program began to scare me. I'd written only four or five shorts stories in my life, spurred on by my UT creative writing class, and I'd sent two of those stories to Stanford in my application packet. I realized I needed to write more fiction in preparation for a highly competitive program, but finding a quiet space to write in the maelstrom of East 45th Street was proving impossible, given the round-the-clock partying. So a few days after the LBJ Presidential Library protest, I decided to move out. Rick understood why and said that he and Elaine needed more privacy as well, and they might be looking for a place together by the end of summer.

The owner of the crumbling faux-adobe eyesore on 11th Street, where Maggie and I had lived briefly, announced that he was tearing down the duplexes and paving the entire block to create a parking lot for downtown office workers. The bulldozing was scheduled for late August, which was when I would be leaving for California anyway, and I persuaded the landlord to let me live there dirt cheap until the wrecking ball took its first swing. All the residents had vacated the dive, except for an army of tree roaches so big and indestructible I'd seen them smoking victory cigars. I chose the largest one-bedroom "furnished" apartment, and Frank decided to move in with me and sleep in the living room on the foldout couch, which looked older than the brass cannons at the Capitol a few blocks away.

I loved my brother dearly, and I was concerned about his future. Although a soulful musician and singer who'd cut two vinyl 45s as a teenager, he was having a rough time making a living as a solo act in Austin. The bars and cafés paid him ten bucks a night and a free meal, and he passed the hat at the end of his sets. He knew he needed a day job, but his options were limited. Dishwasher, busboy, house painter, roofer in the brutal Texas weather. I was his biggest fan (tied with Beverly and Rick) and an intensely loyal supporter of his musical ambitions—sometimes with rent money, which was scarce for me too, and sometimes by helping him look for gigs. But in the summer of 1971, we were both struggling to make ends meet.

Frank Zigal performing at the Guadalupe Bar in Austin, 1970s. *Photo courtesy of Frank Zigal*

I worked at the newspaper office during the day, and at night I sat at a rickety little desk in the living room of that condemned duplex and began writing a story longhand, a method I would use for years, while Frank practiced his guitar on the couch. We wrote our ledger of debits and credits and other expenses on the sheet-rock wall. We ate a lot of mac and cheese and Rice-A-Roni mixed with hamburger meat.

Besides playing at the German beer garden called Hansel and Gretel's on West 30th Street near campus, Frank was booked as a regular at the Pink Lizard Lounge on Guadalupe and at the biker bar Sittin' Bull farther north on the same street. Rick, Beverly, and I would show up to every gig and nurse pitchers of beer with whichever housemates and other friends joined us. Rick was especially good at passing the hat because his patter was both hilarious and sharply persuasive as he cajoled the college kids and random barflies to kick in their loose change. Frank often said to the audience, "Drink up, people. The drunker you get, the better I sound." On a few occasions, usually during a late set and after we'd all knocked back gallons of weak draft beer, he would call me up to the stage to sing harmony with him on a song or two. One evening we covered the song "Wild Horses" by the Rolling Stones and blew the roof off the beer garden. Those humid, moonlit nights were long and sweet, full of magic and mischief and sexual heat, and we were all young and foolish and as romantic as Byron and Keats, certain that the good times would never end.

In July, I gave notice to Rudy Martinez that I would be leaving the newspaper biz for Stanford and the literary world, and he and Paulette were delighted for me. They praised my dull, graceless articles and said they'd miss me. A couple of years later, after LBJ had died and they lost their largest donor, they closed the office, moved to Tucson, and dedicated themselves to the "Aztec pottery business." I hope they avoided prison.

As August approached, I received an aerogramme from Maggie saying she was returning to the States and wanted to move with me to northern California. During those eight months apart, we'd both had other lovers, and I was surprised by her assumption that I would agree without question. But I'd missed her companionship, and I was happy not to make that enormous transition alone.

Two days before my departure for California, she showed up at our duplex in a bright red, brand-spanking-new Volkswagen pop-top camper that her father had bought for her in Mississippi. It was an ingenious German machine complete with closet, sink, and window screens to ward off insects while campers slept on the cushy mattress that folded out of the back seat. She'd packed the VW with all her possessions, intent on living on the West Coast for the foreseeable future, a region of the country that she and I had never laid eyes on in person. She shared my excitement to be "heading for the Frisco Bay," as Otis Redding had sung. I suspected it was the appeal of being in the hippest spot on the planet, rather than my irresistible charm, that had lured her back for our next adventure together.

On the morning we were leaving for California, I crammed all my worldly goods into her VW camper, including my Martin D-18 guitar, most of my record collection, and the Copleston philosophy books. That roach pit would be demolished in another week, and Frank had decided to move back to East 45th. I stood hugging him in the shell parking lot behind the duplex, knowing how much we'd miss each other. He was my buddy, my confidant, my inspiration. We were both aware of how far we'd come as barefoot, working-class knuckleheads from petro-stinking Texas City, a charismatic musician with a bright future ahead and a wannabe novelist on his way to a graduate creative writing program. He was very proud of his older brother and happy for my good fortune, and I promised I would bring him out to San Francisco—still the mecca for hippie life and great music in 1971—as soon as I could figure out how to do that. Maggie and I didn't even have a place to live yet.

I was a restless leaver, always searching for the Next Big Thing, always eager to escape that small stultifying hometown. At age fifteen, I'd gone away to high school in Louisiana, then to a year of college in New Mexico, then to Europe for a year of study in Switzerland. Austin had brought Frank and me together after a loose and ragged seven years hither and yon, and we'd become very close during the longest period we'd spent under the same roof since I was in the ninth grade. And now I was driving off on yet another quixotic journey without him. It was a bittersweet goodbye. Our mother had once told me, "Frank misses you when you leave. It takes him a good long while to get over that you're gone."

Maggie and I swung by to say goodbye to Rick. He and I exchanged power shakes and he hugged Maggie farewell. "Send me that story when you finish it," he said, referring to a short story I'd begun writing based loosely on him and Rod and set in a dusty West Texas hamlet not unlike Tuscola. His parting smile was filled with both sadness and hope. "It's far-fucking-out that you're going to Stanford, Tom," he said. "Knock 'em dead out there, okay? Write your ass off and make us all proud."

He handed me a small Modern Library edition of *The Selected Papers of Bertrand Russell* to take with me on my journey west. He'd signed it simply, "To Tom Zigal from Rick Roderick." I still have the book.

"I expect to hear great things about you too, Mr. Rod-rick," I said, accepting the gift and clapping him on the back. "I just hope we can make it to California, given that Zeno proved that distance and motion are illusions."

He laughed, and Maggie and I climbed aboard the pop-top camper and ventured out toward barren West Texas and the mesas and caprock of the Llano Estacado, destined for the San Francisco Peninsula. All of our lives were never the same again.

WRITING JONES

THE MEETING ROOM for the graduate creative writing seminar wasn't easy to find, almost by design, an obscure, tucked-away space located up four flights of stairs in Stanford's old main library. It was called the Jones Room, named after a Texas oil-man benefactor and brother of a Stanford English professor. Parked in the narrow hallway outside its door was a horizontal glass case that housed first editions of our forebears who'd analyzed one another's drafts behind that door. On the first day of class, I stood looking at those volumes and feeling the pressure to live up to all that impressive achievement. I'd read Ken Kesey's *One Flew Over the Cuckoo's Nest* and Larry McMurtry's *Horseman, Pass By*, but nothing else in the glass case. I had no idea who the others were: Robert Stone, Thomas McGuane, Tillie Olsen, Ernest Gaines, Wendell Berry, Peter Beagle, et al. A deep sense of dread overtook me. I knew I was just a poor boy from Texas who had a lot of catching up to do. It's a feeling that has never left me, even a half century later and seven published novels to my name.

The Jones Room had witnessed the raw emotions, declarations of admiration, and sometimes the restrained disapproval of those renowned writers as they critiqued one another's work. I was in awe of the place, but also determined to find my own space in that intimidating environment. Pulitzer recipient Wallace Stegner had retired three months earlier, and the new director was an enormously likable English professor and novelist named Richard Scowcroft. Dick had helped "Wally" establish the program in the late 1940s and had served as his assistant director for more than two decades by then.

On the first day of class, Scowcroft laid out the ground rules for the seminar: “No indiscriminate axing,” he said, calling for charity and fairness toward our classmates and their writing. He wisely warned us that there had been years when rivalries, tempers, fragile egos, and bad blood had prevailed around that table, and the chemistry had been toxic. He said that sometimes the writing students jelled and sometimes they didn’t. He wanted the very best for us. And with remarkable ease over the next nine months, our group of a dozen young fiction writers jelled.

Twice a week, we crowded around the long seminar table and listened to our classmates read what they were working on. We spoke our minds, critiqued what we heard, smiled and laughed at the right moments, asked questions, made suggestions, and sometimes civilly disagreed with one another. Our admiration and enthusiasm led us to continue our discussions at an old dive bar called Ed’s Place near campus. There were usually eight or ten of us sardined around tables pulled together in the dark recesses of what felt like a once-popular hangout for sclerotic veterans of the First World War. That beer joint became our bonding place, our shared oxytocin, a literary saloon where we let off steam and took our classmates aside, sometimes one on one, and told them a few additional thoughts about the novel chapter they’d just read aloud at the seminar. We drank pitchers of beer and shot pool and revealed the authors we were reading and our hatred for Richard Nixon and the Vietnam War, and someone would bring up the front-page stories about the occupation of Alcatraz island by Native Americans and the Zodiac Killer and a rash of other serial killings in the Bay Area, whatever suited our fancy at that heady moment in time. The older patrons sat stoop-shouldered on barstools in the garish bubbling glow of beer signs and didn’t know what to make of us, and neither did the Asian customers eating at the small Chinese restaurant accessed through the long entrance hallway off the street.

What was not to like about my new life in California? I was rubbing shoulders with real writers. Published writers. Our classmate

Alan Boatman had already published a novel with Harper & Row (*Summer's Lie*), Scott Turow had published a short story in the *Transatlantic Review*, and Michael Rogers was a regular contributor to *Rolling Stone*. Over the next two or three years, four of our classmates would publish the novels they were working on in our seminar—Robert Roth (*Sand in the Wind*), Chuck Kinder (*Snakehunter*), Michael Rogers (*Mindfogger*), and Alan Boatman again (*Comrades in Arms*). April Smith would quickly begin publishing short stories in the best places: *Atlantic Monthly, Cosmo, Redbook*. I was trying to catch up, to be their worthy peer, and their luminous talent and friendship pushed me to work harder on my craft.

By my calculation, I was only the third Texan, after Larry McMurtry and Max Crawford, to be accepted into the Stanford Writing Program. Many times I've been asked, "How the hell did you get into that program, Zigal?" My usual reply is to laugh off the insult by saying it was a clerical error. In a remote cabin in Idaho's woodsy panhandle lives a wasted old alcoholic named Tim Segal

Tom Zigal at Stanford University, 1971. *Photo courtesy of Thomas Zigal*

whose application was mixed up with mine, and he's spent the last fifty-plus years paralyzed by his rejection from Stanford. He's convinced that if he'd been accepted, he'd now be a bestselling novelist feted by the literary establishment in New York and translated into twenty-seven languages. If only.

My Stanford experience was a long time ago (1971–72), and it's not something I've spoken about very much over the past five decades. On the rare occasions when I do, I usually regret it. The resentment is palpable. I was once invited to speak to a women's book club in Austin, and I was paired with a well-known and very popular writer whose sales were enviable. One of the women asked us both, "When and how did you realize you'd been validated as a writer? That you could confidently call yourself a writer?" I thought about it and said it was when I studied with a group of exceptional young writers at Stanford. Although my skills were nowhere near the top half of the class, I felt as if I'd held my own.

Mentioning Stanford greatly annoyed my fellow writer. He asserted that he didn't have to attend a damned creative writing program to become a very successful and beloved cult figure. He'd done it the hard way, writing profusely nonstop since he was a teenager, often broke and desperate for money. He was self-taught in the various genres, mystery and science fiction and horror. He'd been translated into many languages. There were films based on his books. He was as famous as Jerry Lewis in France. Etc., etc. I liked the guy and meant no disrespect. I was sorry I'd set him off. I was just trying to answer the woman's question with honesty and accuracy.

But I'd learned my lesson. Don't say "Stanford." For god's sake, don't say "creative writing program." And so I pledged to myself that I would never speak of that experience again.

And then one year, I was on a mystery writers' panel with my former classmate April Smith, discussing our books with two other writers, and someone asked a similar question. Before I could grab April's arm and say, "Nooooo, don't say the word Stanford," she mentioned it as a seminal experience in her life.

A good-ol'-boy retired deputy sheriff was on the panel with us, and his face turned crimson. I thought he was going to pistol whip April. He'd written thirty books in a crime series featuring a deputy very much like himself, and he didn't need to attend no damn pussyfied writin' school to learn how to solve crimes in tumbleweed Arizona and chronicle them on the page. He was apoplectic. Afterwards, April and I had a couple of adult beverages at the hotel bar, and I counseled her to never again say the words "Stanford" or "creative writing program" in public.

At Stanford and later, I would discover that many of my writer friends grew up in the households of accomplished professionals—doctors, lawyers, librarians, teachers, pharmacists, business executives—with impressive book collections in their homes. Some of those homes had libraries with floor-to-ceiling shelves of hefty hardbound classics and circles of cushy armchairs for the family reading hours. Our home didn't. We had a wobbly bookcase my father built to house our encyclopedias, two dictionaries, and a book about the oil industry published by the corporation that owned the refinery where Dad worked as a pumper-gauger and later as an electrician. On one occasion when I was in my late twenties and visiting my parents in Texas City, a California writer, scion of great family wealth, was attending a convention in Houston, and I picked her up and brought her to see where I'd grown up. She later remarked to a mutual friend in Palo Alto, "I didn't notice any books in Tom's parents' house. They had no library. How did he become so well-read?"

My mother read ladies' magazines and romance novels, we kids bought and traded lots of comic books, and there were grocery store children's books stashed here and there in nooks and crannies around our home. I would ride my bike to the little house that was our town's public library and search its shelves, and I also checked out books at the small library at school and stocked up on books from the bookmobile from Galveston. Reading wasn't an obsession for me, an all-consuming passion, as it was for some of my cultured writer pals in their alienated youths. Sports was my obsession. I wanted to swing a bat like Mickey Mantle and throw passes like Johnny Unitas. But for one fleeting moment in the fifth grade, after writing a poem as a class assignment, I told my mother I was thinking about becoming a poet. She said, "They don't make any money, son. They have to find jobs they can fall back on."

Perhaps it was that lack of books on mahogany shelves in our home that led to my flights of imagination. Without any exalted volumes at my fingertips, I created my own stories. I don't know how old I was when I began to walk around in circles in the small bedroom I shared with my brother and in our garage, imagining myself as the hero of a thousand bold adventures, cowboy and soldier and football star and missionary in the darkest jungles, the tales stretching on for days and weeks in my spinning head, scene followed by vivid scene until the narrative fabric wove itself into something majestic and epic and complete, and I could finally let it go and move on to another whirling fantasy. I would slip into a kind of swoon, unaware of the sounds I was making in my high-energy circling. *Boom, zing, kerpow!* Nobody in my family made fun of me or asked me what I was doing. My mother called it "playing by himself." If I did that as a child today, I would be sent to therapy and given medication that would make me chew my lip. And if I'd done that in Salem in 1692, the town fathers would've thrown me in a pond to see if I would float. By the time I was eleven or twelve, I would inform my mom that I was going to play by myself in the garage and to please tell the booger-eating neighbor boys (who often knocked on our door looking for me to play football or wolf-across-the-river on the connected lawns) that I wasn't at home.

Walking in circles and imagining storylines that were convoluted and ongoing for weeks—that was great preparation for the writing life. And although I'd stopped circling at some point before I was in high school, I eventually turned that frenetic creative energy into writing really bad poetry and wordy songs paying homage to Bob Dylan. In my senior year of college, I took that lone short-fiction creative writing course at UT Austin and rediscovered my love of storytelling. I felt at home writing fiction, which would become the direction I would take. Constructing stories in my head and transferring them to paper was like meeting a dear friend I hadn't seen in years.

My Stanford classmates and I devoured the magazines and literary journals of our time—*Atlantic Monthly, The New Yorker, Harper's, Esquire, Playboy, Rolling Stone*—and we aspired to appear in those pages. But publishing books was the gold standard. Novels and short story collections. You weren't a real writer until you published a book. For a full decade after I'd completed my coursework at Stanford, I wrote and published a handful of short stories in literary magazines, but my greatest ambition was to publish novels. I spent most of my free time writing by hand on the blank back pages of the typed manuscripts rejected by agents and publishers and piling up like a hoarder's stash of yellowing newspapers around my desk.

My mother was right about writers needing to fall back on something to keep the lights on and food in the fridge. I learned how to balance my writing jones, mostly accomplished on weekends, with a long string of day jobs. A master's degree from Stanford gave me better choices. I graduated from those days of menial employment as a dishwasher and janitor's helper and door-to-door Great Books salesman to cushier white-collar work: proofreader, editor, college English instructor, communications director, speechwriter. Regardless of the degree of difficulty, every gig was an impediment to my writing projects, a time-consuming distraction, but I didn't have a trust fund or a devoted spouse who supported me by working as a bank executive or real estate agent while I stayed at home in my bathrobe, drinking coffee nonstop and scribbling messy drafts of the Great American Novel.

Rick and I revered books, but when we met as young undergraduates, we couldn't have imagined we would one day publish them. Reading and discussing books and sharing the ideas they engendered was deep in our DNA, and years later, when we became fathers, we didn't hesitate to pass on to our children our love of plots and characters and beautiful language and various interpretations and analyses. Sharing an appreciation of books came as natural as breathing. Rick and I and our spouses began reading and showing pictures to our children, all boys, when they were babies, and there was no doubt they would be reading by the time they were school age. Our son, Danny, read *The Hobbit* in kindergarten with one hundred percent comprehension. But then something happened that changed civilization forever. The Internet went public around 1993, and Rick and his sons became fluent in its use over the next three years. In 1996, when both of our families moved back to Austin, the Rodericks showed Danny, his mother, and me how to navigate the World Wide Web. Besides transforming every aspect of mass communications, the high-tech universe of the Internet would have a profound global impact on publishing and the book industry, an effect as monumental as Gutenberg's invention of the moveable-type printing press in 1450.

It didn't take long for us parents to question the influence of video games and the Internet and its wicked younger cousin, social media, on the millennials we were raising. Marshall McLuhan was right. The medium is both the message and the massage, and hot kinetic images and captivating videos quickly overtook the passive, softer medium of the written word on a page. Interactive engagement with computer and phone screens trumped quieter, more introspective choices. Our children embraced that change immediately. Hopscotching across toadstools, beheading ogres, and steering a car over sexy streetwalkers was far more fun and engrossing than sitting docilely and reading long gray paragraphs of type. Alarmed critics insisted that the new technology had retooled the hardwiring in our children's brains.

As the years pass, our millennial son and my stepchildren read fewer books than they used to. When they were living under my roof, they spent a disturbing amount of time on screens every day, and they often shared with the grown-ups the music and fascinating video clips and unusual stories they'd discovered on the Internet.

In fact, watching their navigations taught me how to expand my own research skills. And I was often pleasantly surprised by their interests.

Not all is lost. Recently my son drove me to an eye appointment and sat in the waiting room reading the *Histories* by Herodotus. He also enjoys the rich visual attributes of graphic novels, which are very much like the DC and Marvel comics of my childhood. What I've observed is that the younger generations switch fluidly between sites, surfing the Internet for news and information, and reading serious material on their screens. Does it matter, then, that they aren't reading longform essays and books, especially the books I read at their age? Faulkner, Hemingway, Fitzgerald, James Joyce, Thomas Wolfe, Joseph Conrad, Graham Greene, Katherine Anne Porter, Eudora Welty, Flannery O'Connor, Ken Kesey, Robert Stone. I think everyone should read these masters and many more like them, but my expectations have been tempered by this new age. I don't want to become like the grumpy older generation that told us baby boomers that rock'n'roll is trash. But I do mourn the loss of those long labyrinthine discussions about the incredible books that stirred our hearts and touched our souls.

A couple of years ago, I was shocked to hear one of my well-published writer friends declare that the format of the book as we know it is on its death bed. He predicted that ebooks will totally replace boards and paper and glossy dustjackets. If that happens in my lifetime, I will miss a book you can hold in your hands and smell. But the truth is, I read most books on an ebook reader these days because I can adjust the print to a larger size. In the final analysis, if traditional hardbacks and paperbacks go the way of hot-metal typesetting and the early word processors, so be it. What is most important, indeed essential to world culture, is that we not lose their content, the stories themselves and the remarkable storytellers, from the Greek poet Homer to Toni Morrison and Stephen King. Somewhere out there at this moment, there are children whose creative energy is propelling them to walk around in circles in their bedrooms, imagining characters and scenes and worlds far beyond their daily experiences, and they need a way to share those fantasies and ruminations with the rest of us. Long live their novels and multibook sagas and epic poems that stretch on for hundreds of pages! Long live the thousand and one weavers of mesmerizing tales!

THE MISSING YEARS

WHILE I WAS OFF at Stanford on one of my life's foundational adventures, my old Austin friends were still floating through that hazy bardo between college and what would become of them. I missed their camaraderie and the easy Austin living, but the writing life was a most worthy challenge and one I was determined to embrace.

Rick, Turner Williamson, and another Abilene friend had found a small two-bedroom house on Martin Avenue about six blocks north of East 45th Street and just as cheap because it was directly under the flight path of thunderous commercial Boeing planes landing at the airport two miles away. The house was old and the worse for wear, and except for having no refrigerator or stove, it was a perfectly acceptable roach palace for the squalor most Austin hippies preferred in those days. Turner was completing his undergraduate degree, and Rick had begun courses toward his second bachelor's degree, this time in philosophy, his future career. With poker and bridge games and cutthroat chess matches going on day and night, the toxic masculinity level was bordering on unbearable, and Elaine was wise to keep her own apartment and her job making crafts for a local hobby shop.

Sometimes Rick cooked his signature chicken cacciatore on a hot plate, and on one occasion Camel Man dropped by to treat everyone to black-eyed peas in a pressure cooker that blew up and splattered goo all over the kitchen ceiling and walls. Most of the time they ate chicken-fried steaks, burgers, and enchiladas at our favorite greasy spoons—the Stallion, King Bee, San Jacinto café—with boxes of

Mrs. Johnson's fresh melting donuts in easy reach for the stoned all-night gameplay. Nobody had a real job yet. As a group, they were only a couple of months from destitution.

One evening during that first quarter at Stanford, while I was working on the novel I'd begun to write as my thesis, I received a phone call from Rick. I was ecstatic to hear his hoarse Texas drawl. "Elaine and I are getting married in December, Tom," he said. "You've gotta come home for the wedding, man."

I was incredibly happy for him. The Fat Man had found his soulmate.

▪ ▪ ▪

I didn't make it to the wedding because I was still attending classes at Stanford in early December. Elaine had moved into Rick's bedroom at the house on Martin Avenue, and when I arrived a week or so after the wedding, they recounted the inevitable chaos of the blessed event. They were set to be married at a Methodist church in Austin's wealthy Northwest Hills neighborhood because Elaine's mother knew the minister, but the ceremony was delayed when Rick's mother, Elwynn, couldn't find the church. It must've been a nightmare trying to give directions to a little old lady driving alone into the big city from Tuscola.

Turner and Holt Williamson were the groomsmen, and Jim Bogard and several of the Abilene Boys managed to be there, no doubt hungover from the bachelor party on the previous evening. At the bride and groom's request, Frank sang two songs, including Leonard Cohen's "Bird on a Wire," and then the drunken madness ensued until the wee hours. Rod slept in his jalopy parked in the backyard at Martin Avenue, and he woke everyone at eight a.m., eager to make breakfast but wondering why the newlyweds lived in a house with no stove or refrigerator. Perhaps it was a metaphor. Or a portent. Or simply love in a time of privation.

During that holiday season, I visited their house on two or three evenings and saw that it was the same circus sideshow as East 45th Street. The all-night bridge games were as serious and complex as the scheming for a bank heist. The popularity of American master Bobby Fischer had reignited worldwide interest in the game of chess, and the matches in the Martin house were so intense you could almost smell the burnt brain-wiring in the feverish air. When Rick found himself stumped by an opponent's move, he would excuse himself to use the bathroom, where he'd stashed a chess book in the clothes hamper. *1001 Gambits and Countergambits to Humiliate Your Opponent*, or something like that. "The Two Knights Gambit? We suggest you use the Fegatello/Fried Liver Attack! e4 e5 Nf3 Nc6."

Elaine grew weary of that nonstop testosterone-driven scene. She was still working at the arts-and-crafts shop and needed a good night's sleep, but that was nearly impossible. She was also a serious artist with genuine talent who needed a quiet space to complete her paintings, but the house was too small and chaotic for reflection and concentration. As the months passed, the situation became more frustrating for her. I certainly sympathized. I'd moved into that condemned duplex to get some writing done.

Strapped for income, Rick hired on as a cook at the JCPenney coffee shop in the new Highland Mall nearby. Turner and their Abilene friend Mike Ford joined Rick on the crew as dishwashers and busboys. They were all befriended by the coffee shop's manager, an obese older alcoholic Republican whose managerial style consisted entirely of sitting at a corner table, chain smoking, and ogling the teenaged boys shuffling by. The coffee shop shut down after six months, and Rick and company happily returned to their rowdy all-nighters.

To complicate matters, Rick's boyhood friend Mickey and his girlfriend moved to Austin and homesteaded the second bedroom. It was the first time that Rick and Mickey had ever lived together. Over the next few months, the drug use intensified, mostly weed and psychedelics, and Elaine became even more unhappy. This was not the life she'd bargained for.

There were different versions of why she and Rick picked up and moved to Abilene a year later—for employment opportunities or simply to escape the Austin turmoil. They ended up crashing at a friend's apartment for a year before moving into their own house on Hickory Street, a few blocks from the Hardin-Simmons campus where Rick had launched *The Bat Report* before transferring to UT.

The years 1972 to 1977 were "the missing years" in my friendship with Rick. I lost touch with him and most of my old friends back in Austin. I'd fallen in love with the San Francisco Bay Area and told myself I would live there forever. Why would I leave? It was beautiful and *happening*, and I'd made a score of new friends who were brilliant, artistic, inspiring, enormously sophisticated. It seemed to me that all my Austin friends had settled into a listless lifestyle with dead-end jobs. Where was the passion, the vision, the cultivation of one's talent?

I was puzzled to hear that Rick and Elaine had moved to that deadly dull city in West Texas, far from any center of culture or counterculture. As Rick later observed in his autobiography, "I preferred to die from multiple rattlesnake bites rather than spend my whole life in and around Abilene, Texas. . . . No Bergman movie I ever saw exuded the kind of bedrock despair that was as common to Abilene as mesquite trees and bad drunks."

Anywhere else would've been a better choice. Houston, Dallas, San Antonio. And yet there they were, taking a step backward into that hellhole of religion and political conservatism. They lived there for two years, and I had no contact with them at all. We were in different orbits, different trajectories. Elaine took a job at the Arts and Crafts Center at Dyess Air Force Base, and Rick worked at the Abilene State School teaching shop classes and woodwork to the learning disabled. What the hell did he know about woodwork? He would drive by himself to Austin from time to time for concerts and chill out with Turner and the gang.

I imagine that those trips made him pine for *la dolce vita*. How lonely and depressing must have been the long drives back to Abilene. He couldn't have been happy living with no rowdy pals, no hippie diversions, no New Leftists, no challenging life of the mind. He and Elaine found a compatible social circle, most of them UT friends who'd graduated and moved back home. I'm sure it was comforting to spend time with a few likeminded souls in that bedrock of despair. But I suspect that his critical thinking was in a state of suspended animation, and he was feeling the same kind of compromise and brain-drain he admits to in his Teaching Company lecture entitled "Paul Ricoeur: The Masters of Suspicion" (1993), where he ruefully says that "the work of intellectuals has always been separated off from the work of ordinary people. In other words, you have to be freed from the constraints of manual labor. When I was a dishwasher, I didn't have a lot of time to do this. When I was a union organizer, I didn't have a lot of time to do this. Any time I was involved in manual labor, I didn't really have the time to do this intellectual work."[14]

I remember those nights when he and I dragged our bodies from the scullery after sweating through three hours of dishwashing at Dobie dorm, dumping wasted blobs of food into bins, hand-soaping trays, tossing sticky silverware into baskets, running everything on a conveyor belt through a Hobart machine that gushed scalding water like a car wash. Our shirts were soaked to the skin, our hands water-wrinkled and our nails grimy, our brains burned to a palmful of carbon. We struggled to read and do our class assignments. Hard manual labor was leaving us no energy or concentration. And so it must've been for Rick in Abilene, when he was teaching shop classes and woodwork at the state school. He had to have known he wasn't going to die on that hill, surrounded by rattlesnakes, mesquite trees, and bad drunks.

RETURN OF THE NATIVES

IN 1975, ELAINE became pregnant with their first child, Marshall, and they chose to raise him in Austin, where Rick longed to earn a doctorate in philosophy from the University of Texas and pursue a career as a college professor. He explained his decision in the interview with Professor Anne Buttimer: "I did what I guess is a fine revolutionary tradition: I returned to the study to rethink what had happened [in the 1960s], so part of that process was studying philosophy. But in a very broad sense I see philosophy as a conversation with economics, with history, with politics, with feminist studies, with race, and with everyday life. So I came back to philosophy in that spirit in the '70s to try to rethink what had happened in . . . the zombie-ization and the banalization of America. The study looked as good a place to be for a few years as anywhere."[15]

He and Elaine moved into a rent house on Cary Drive in Austin's Allandale neighborhood, a few blocks from the large two-story home where she'd grown up and where her parents still lived. To help with the rent, Rick invited two housemates to join them, Turner Williamson and a diminutive, slow-talking Abilene Boy known as Small Paul.

Comfortably back in his old stomping grounds, Rick and the usual suspects resumed their wicked ways, playing cards in a pandemonium of loud talk and thick smoke every evening while Elaine was tending to the new baby. Rick wasn't much help. As Elaine recalled years later, "I was left alone to try and figure out how to take care of Marshall." The nightly chaos "was hellish and I got sick of it," she said, once again desperate for peace and quiet. I don't know if she considered moving in with her parents nearby, a stoic faculty couple that our friend Tom Burditt once described as "God's frozen people." She seemed to prefer the hot-blooded Rodericks to her own family, and she succumbed to a drastic getaway plan that involved moving with her baby into Rod's cinderblock hovel on the main street of Tuscola, far from the madness of Cary Drive. I was still living in California and not privy to their thinking, but it was baffling to me that she would return to that cultural wasteland of West Texas with a baby in tow and without Rick. And sure enough, living with the cranky, eccentric Rod proved to be an absolute nightmare. Before long, he began referring to her as "Dummy," an insult reminiscent of an Archie Bunker routine, and things went downhill from there.

▪ ▪ ▪

Despite telling myself that I would never leave the glorious paradise of northern California, in November 1976 I voted for Jimmy Carter for president and Jerry Brown for governor, and the next day I boarded a plane back to Austin after more than five incredible, transformative years in the San Francisco Bay Area. My West Coast sojourn was over.

The reasons for leaving California weren't complicated. For one thing, the thrill was gone. Although I'd made many friends as an editor at a publishing company in Menlo Park and then as an English instructor at a community college twenty miles east of Berkeley, I was feeling the loss of my core Stanford pals. Most of them had moved away. Scott Turow had gone to law school and April Smith to Hollywood, and others had taken teaching jobs elsewhere—Fred Pfeil at Stephens College in Missouri, Speer Morgan at the University of Missouri, and Bill Kittredge returning to Missoula, Montana. In those last couple of years, the party had moved from Palo Alto to the Chuck Kinder residences in San Francisco, but our numbers were dwindling. Chuck and his wife, Diane, would soon be heading to the University of Pittsburgh, Max Crawford to Montana, and our recovering buddy Ray Carver, quickly making a name for himself as a short story writer, would ramble and roam into New England and the East Coast in search of a stable place to settle his typewriter and get to work in a newfound state of sobriety.

To add to my estrangement, the Me Decade was in full swing and California was its epicenter. I couldn't tolerate the navel gazing and wrongheadedness surrounding me. A handful of my friends were becoming New Age cultists like the soulless pod people in *Invasion of the Body Snatchers*, joining idiotic movements like Scientology and est (Erhard Seminars Training) and actively participating in self-absorbed "encounter sessions" in what was broadly called "the human potential movement." One attractive young couple I met at the publishing company poured most of their savings into Scientology and stopped associating with me by church decree because I was a bad influence. A couple I lived with in a massive old home in Berkeley declared themselves to be "self-actualizing therapists" who conducted "re-birthing sessions" in one of the spare rooms, until the IRS and a collection agency came looking for them and they escaped into the night with little more than the clothes on their backs. I was repulsed by all that narcissism and silly pseudo-psychoanalysis. I'd grown up in a medieval cult called Catholicism myself and I could spot flimflam a hundred cubits away.

▪ ▪ ▪

Frank and Beverly took me in. They had a spare bedroom at their house on the shabbier edge of Austin's Hyde Park neighborhood, and every morning for the rest of November and well past Christmas, Frank and I sat in the kitchen in our bathrobes, drinking coffee as the hours slipped by, catching up on my final years in San Francisco and Berkeley and his musical adventures in Austin and the million laughs and trippy scenes we'd missed out on while living apart. We were re-bonding like long lost brothers and best friends. But when Bev came home for lunch every day from her job as a typesetter for the UT printing division, what she witnessed was two unemployed hippies amped up on the caffeine fueling their frivolous small talk and scatterbrained childhood memories.

Tom and brother Frank (on the phone) in Tom's duplex in Palo Alto, mid-1970s.
Photo courtesy of Thomas Zigal

By January 1977, I'd found a one-bedroom, sparkle-popcorn-ceiling apartment in a ratty old complex in easy walking distance from their place. I remember lying on my back after eating a couple of Alice B. Toklas brownies one night and staring up at tiny astronauts negotiating the silver trails and moonlike cluster of peaks and craters on that glittering white ceiling-scape. I was convinced that long brown tree-roaches were building an impregnable fortress among the oatmeal and tea boxes in the cramped kitchen cabinets.

I soon discovered that my old buddy Rick Roderick had been living in Austin for a year, taking philosophy courses at UT, and that Elaine and Marshall were living in Tuscola "to save money." Rick and friends had moved into a small duplex only a stone's throw from the old East 45th rathole, and when I finally caught up with them, it was a joyous reunion. We were all excited to be in Austin together for the first time in years. But I also discovered that Rick and a couple of his new pals had begun to shoot up cocaine in their dirty little crash pad. It worried me. Like many of us in the counterculture, I frowned on needles and mainlining drugs. We'd seen too many of our hero musicians die of substance overdoses: Janis

Joplin, Jimi Hendrix, Jim Morrison. In all those reckless years in California, I'd consciously rejected the hard drugs—heroin, coke, crystal meth. Shooting up was heavy business, and I feared for Rick's wellbeing. When I expressed my concern, he assured me it was a temporary experiment. He just wanted to experience injected cocaine the way Freud and others had experienced it. "The rush is incredible!" he insisted. "It's night-and-day stronger than snorting the shit. I've never felt anything like it." And he noted that the coke was being administered not by him but by a medical friend who knew what they were doing with a syringe and kept an eye on him afterwards.

It didn't take long for his body to recoil dramatically from the hammer blow of mainlined coke. After the third or fourth time, his heart began to pound out of control, and it scared him so badly he rushed to a local hospital for a battery of tests. He was diagnosed with arrhythmia, the same kind of irregular heartbeat that killed Elvis, and it was clear that Rick's rapid beat, called tachycardia, was the lethal downside of cocaine. His bad reaction also scared his user buddies, who immediately dumped their two remaining ounces of white powder in the street like a baker's flour and walked away.

After his diagnosis, I didn't have to scold Rick ever again about coke or speed. He knew what the chest pain was telling him. In his earlier years, he'd struggled with allergies and various minor infirmities, but the heart was a deadly serious matter. The doctors persuaded him that arrhythmia and tachycardia would follow him for the rest of his days. It made him paranoid and obsessive about his heartbeat, and that led to occasional panic attacks and even agoraphobia a few years later. His flirtation with cocaine, however brief, may have been the beginning of his battle with hypochondria, one med chasing another to suppress the pain and anxiety.

GETTING OURSELVES BACK TO THE GARDEN

AUSTIN PROVED TO BE the perfect solace for the blues I'd been feeling in my final year in California. There was something soothing and therapeutic about returning to a place of the heart. I didn't realize how much I'd missed the Austin vibe—the laidback looseness, the easy friendships, the sly weirdness, the live bands playing country and blues in little dives tucked away in unlikely places. You could wear a T-shirt and Birkenstocks in Austin year-round and nobody noticed or cared. Women sunbathed topless at Barton Springs, and getting busted for less than four ounces of weed was only a misdemeanor. Austin was indeed a groover's paradise.

The Bay Area had been luminously beautiful, cosmopolitan, a constant lesson in refined culture, but it exacted a price: advanced planning for the simplest diversion, swarms of tourists, crime (I'd been broken into twice, once in San Francisco and once in Berkeley), heavy traffic, the ever-present tensions and hostilities of urban life. Those vexations didn't exist in the Austin of 1977. Although I hadn't lived there for nearly six years, things were very much the same as when I'd left—spontaneous, effortless, fun. There was a local proverb: "Everyone always comes back to Austin." I threw myself into everything the city offered, eagerly embracing new adventures and discoveries, new friends, unexplored terrain, and the ready pleasures of the flesh. When an Austin woman wanted you, she'd let you know.

Stanford and the Bay Area had taught me to revel in the sophistications of the literary world. Austin urged me to stay in touch with that downhome Texas boy who ran barefoot through his childhood and avoided every sign of "sivilization" like Huck Finn.

▪ ▪ ▪

The Hole in the Wall was one of the prime spots for live music in town, and it would one day become a legend because of the famous acts that played there, often after a taping at the *Austin City Limits* studio at the university across the street. Bob Dylan has rendered a fine painting of the nighttime exterior of the Hole with its marquee shining bright. Beginning in the bar's earliest days, owner Doug Cugini booked the best solo acoustic acts, giving them their own individual nights, and once they were so ordained, it took either a divine cataclysm or a trip to the Betty Ford Clinic to dislodge the performers from that coveted altar. Frank was the Wednesday-night regular, and every week Rick and I showed up early and grabbed a table near the stage and nursed pitchers of beer and chattered the night away with friends who'd slide up chairs and join us as my brother played songs for hours on end, sometimes his own remarkable compositions. By that time, he had quite a following, and listeners flocked to the Hole in the Wall to hear him.

An up-and-coming young star named Nanci Griffith reigned over Sunday evenings, which was a perfect day for her ethereal stage presence, crystalline voice, and understandable-but-ill-considered demand that the drinkers shut up and listen to her delicate lyrics. I appreciated Nanci and her songs, but I felt she needed to recognize the difference between a coffeehouse and a beer joint.

Nanci admired the older, more experienced Frank Zigal and was always there on Wednesdays to study his guitar licks, his song list, his stage mannerisms, his world-weary asides. At the end of those evenings, the musicians and a few hangers-on often ended up at a greasy-spoon diner called the King Bee on deserted Airport Boulevard, eating cheeseburgers and swapping yarns until the place closed down. I'd been back in town for only three or four months, living alone in my sparkle-ceiling apartment, and I was grateful for the companionship with Frank's posse of pickers and grinners and the young hippie women who danced along the margins of that caravan. We could usually count on Rick being there with us, entertaining everyone in the King Bee's adjoining booths with his tales of mischief and folly. Nanci was especially fond of him and his humor. She asked me for copies of my published short stories and for a list of the contemporary writers she should read. I was happy to oblige. It led to a brief romance.

A giant bearded folksinger named Mike Williams had started his own record label called B.F. Deal Records, and because he was halfway in love with Nanci—as everyone was—she persuaded him to come listen to Frank and other performers at the Hole in the Wall. Mike was impressed with my brother and two other performers, and he decided to cut a B.F. Deal sampler album that featured Nanci, Frank, John Garza "with a ten-foot voice," as Mike wrote in the liner notes, and an intense, long-narrative songwriter from southwest Louisiana "with a swamp-snake rhythm" named Will Walker. The recording sessions took place at Pecan Street Studios (formerly Odyssey Sound) on West 6th Street downtown, where celebrated records had been cut by Carole King, Jerry Jeff Walker, Doug Sahm, the 13th Floor Elevators, Joe Ely, and Asleep at the Wheel.

I sat in the studio lobby throughout Frank's sessions, listening to the various takes and admiring his original songs and the musicianship of his two sidemen, Bennet "the East Side Flash" Spielvogel on dobro and second guitar, and Spencer Starnes on bass. Accomplished local musicians and background singers traipsed in and out of the studio every evening, praising and encouraging one another as Mike worked with the artists to arrange each song. One evening he gazed through the plate glass at me listening in the waiting room and said over the speaker box, "Hey, Tom, I hear you can sing harmony. Come on in here and sing with Frank and me on Nanci's song."

It took about five minutes for the three of us to arrange our falsetto harmony on her "Texas Boy." I had learned a great deal about harmony from my own folk-singing a decade earlier and from the Gregorian Chant I'd sung in my Catholic high school music classes.

Hell, in those days I could've sung perfect harmony with the Beach Boys.

After those sessions, Mike Williams produced an LP titled *B.F. Deal Sampler vol. 1* with sketches of the four featured artists on the simple white cover. The record made only a small blip in the Austin area and received little notice elsewhere. It's now a collector's item, primarily because it was Nanci Griffith's debut. By the end of the year, she was recording her first solo album and destined for a stellar career in Nashville and beyond. The three other musicians on the sampler, including Frank, never achieved her popularity. Even after my virtuoso work singing falsetto on that track, my phone didn't light up with music industry producers hiring me for backup harmony with Linda Ronstadt or as a replacement for Art Garfunkel.

I attended the record's launch party at some rich person's plushly carpeted home. It was great to mingle with all the musicians again. I hadn't seen or spoken with Nanci in a month or so, but she was warm and friendly and she told me she was burned out on Austin, her hometown, and she was moving to Houston to explore more music opportunities. I was very sad to see her go. I didn't realize that hugging her goodbye would be our final embrace.

Frank visited her in Nashville sometime in the 1990s. They played guitars in her room at the boardinghouse where she lived, two old friends exchanging chord progressions and finger-picking techniques, jamming as they had in Austin twenty years earlier, sharing scraps of lyrics and unfinished songs, asking each other for advice on a troublesome verse they didn't have quite right yet. They were both elated to be laughing and swapping memories and singing together again. They didn't know it at the time, but it was their final playdate.

There are so many things in life I wish I could do over. So many people I should've responded to with greater attention and respect. I wish I'd stayed in touch with Nanci. Not because of her celebrity or our short-lived romance, but because she was a genuinely virtuous person with a poet's heart and a voice that could rally the archangels.

She was a seeker, an artist with exquisite taste, a kindred spirit in matters of the soul. I should've been a more thoughtful friend.

When the B.F. Deal record was released that summer, I bought a score of them with funds from my unemployment checks and gave them as gifts to family and friends, including Rick. He wore the record out, listening mostly to Frank's three cuts, and the LP survived his U-Haul moves to North Carolina and Southern California and back to Austin again. Two decades later, the vinyl album melted with a hundred others in Rick's collection after a fire destroyed the rent house where he and his sons were living. The morning after the fire, I stood holding the album's charred cover in the darkness of their scorched living room and remembered the day I knocked on his door and said, "Look what I've got!" He had held the record delicately in his hands like a precious Monet painting and yelled "All riiiiiiight!" Then he walked over and placed it on the turntable he'd stolen from god knows where, setting the needle to play Frank's song "Thieves and Fools," and he sang along at the top of his cracking voice because after all those nights at the Hole in the Wall, he already knew every word by heart.

THERE AT THE BEGINNING AND BEFORE

FOR THE ACADEMIC YEAR of 1977–78, Rick received a generous fellowship to pursue a master's degree in philosophy at Baylor University in Waco, a hundred miles north of Austin. Elaine was still living in the cinderblock hovel with their toddler Marshall and her abusive father-in-law, Rod, and she was very happy to escape Tuscola and reunite with her husband in graduate-student housing near the Baylor campus. I drove up to visit them one weekend and bunked on their sofa. Elaine shared horror tales about her exile in that damned little West Texas town. Decades later, Marshall told me, "the only thing I remember from Tuscola is Rod whacking me with his cane when I tried to cross Main Street without looking both ways." Saving money or not, it had been a mistake.

Rick had always been an avid fisherman, and on Sunday morning he dragged me to the shady banks of the Brazos River nearby, where we cast our lines into the mulchy dark water and he held forth about the conservative Baptist classmates and professors he had to endure. Baylor was a bitter cup of gall, but it was only a one-year master's program, and he was determined to persevere and get his degree on somebody else's dime.

I had caught my share of fish in Texas bays and creeks when I was growing up, but by my late twenties I'd lost patience with the sport and couldn't quite slow my over-caffeinated braincells into the zen state required to stand still quietly for hours and wait for a plastic float to tug and bob. As one comedian observed, there was a fine line between a fisherman and a moron holding a stick.

That morning, Rick caught a few undersized crappie, but I was having no luck at all and began to bitch about my conviction that a malevolent demiurge was ruling my life and, among other travails, was preventing me from hooking a single pan perch or even an old leather shoe. After listening to my whining for several minutes, Rick dropped his fishing rod and waded down into the shallow water near the bank with a net and scooped up a small perch swimming by. He grabbed my line and stuck the squirming fish on my hook, tossed it back into the water and said, "There, dammit! You've caught a fish! Ignore Gnosticism and that evil demiurge and read more Camus."

A few months later, Rick the Graduate Assistant became the editor of a student publication with the lofty title *Breviloquium Philosophicum* [A Brief Discussion of Philosophy], a collection of short papers written by him and six fellow Baylor philosophy students he'd selected for inclusion. He gave me a copy inscribed, "Dear Tom, Here is your copy of the Journal. I hope it will be good for an occasional laugh!" He signed it, "In deep appreciation of your friendship, intelligence, wit, and grit, Rick."

His paper was titled "Organicism and Marx," and its purpose was "to question the adequacy of Stephen C. Pepper's interpretive schema in regard to placing the worldview of Marx within 'organicism.'" I had no idea who and what Stephen C. Pepper and organicism were—and I still don't. (Please feel free to Google, masochistic reader.) What did concern me, however, was that Rick's essay contained sentences like "Marx views the dialectic as development that moves from stage to stage, in a spiral rather than a straight line, repeating stages already passed; development by leaps, gaps and 'interruptions of gradualness'; development by inner tendencies and their contradictions discovered in the interconnections and interdependence of all sides of a given phenomenon, relating part to part and part to whole; development towards overcomings and passings-by and retainings (*Aufhebung*)."[16]

This was clearly a cry for help to the Clarity Police and the proof I needed for an intervention. When he, Elaine, and Marshall moved back to Austin in the summer of 1978 with his master's degree in hand, Rick asked me what I thought of his essay, and we sat down to talk in the small living room of the duplex they were renting from Elaine's parents.

"It doesn't sound like *you*," I told him. "It's your view of what a philosopher should write like."

I went on to say that what was unique and impressive about him as a thinker was his ability to use comedy and references to classic movies, TV series and commercials, rock songs, nineteenth-century novels, modernist poetry, etc., to make his points about various philosophical concepts, historical movements, and schools of thought. I argued that if he used genuine Rick Roderick rhetorical techniques in his writing—the same ones he employed when spitballing and bullshitting with friends—he'd bring a fresh new dimension to the tiresome academic teaching of philosophy, and he'd make a noticeable mark in a discipline that only a small gaggle of pointy-headed scholars and grad students cared about anymore.

"Less Feuerbach and more Rick," I kept emphasizing.

We were both fans of Hunter S. Thompson. "You can easily become the Hunter Thompson of philosophy, Rick," I said, "if you write like you really think and talk. We need to hear your own voice and your gonzo sensibility, man. Not that turgid language you think the hundred members of the worldwide philosophy establishment want to read."

Rick listened and smoked, smoked and listened. I suspected that deep down inside, he knew I was right. As he said in one of his Teaching Company lectures a decade later, "If twelve people go down on the same flight, there won't be any more *Journal of Philosophy*. Because it's eleven guys writing to this other guy."

He was uncharacteristically quiet while I continued to rave on about his potential to save the discipline and how he should reveal his true self to the world the way a comedian like Richard Pryor revealed his pain and the hilarity and absurdity of life by baring his soul in his own salty language. Rick understood that I had exalted expectations for him as an intellectual force and I wouldn't stop pushing him toward the public distinction we both knew was his destiny.

Over the next eight years, while working on his book about the Frankfurt School philosopher Jürgen Habermas, Rick published essays and book reviews on such subjects as Hegel, David Hume, Jacques Derrida, Georg Lukács, Antonio Gramsci, and Herbert Marcuse. He was kind enough to inscribe three of those publications for me, and I still have them on my shelves. In one inscription, he wrote: "To Tom Zigal, There at the beginning and before—your crazy friend, Rick."[17]

Rick always issued a caveat whenever he gave me one of his publications: "I know, I know. It's dry stuff that only a philosopher's mother could love. That is, if the mother was St. Monica, the mother of Augustine."

He insisted he was playing the game required of him to establish his legitimacy in the academy. "You've got to show them you know what an omelette is before you start breaking eggs," he observed.

A couple of years earlier, a young Texas poet named Michael Anderson had launched a literary magazine called *The Pawn Review*, and after two or three issues he invited me to be his fiction editor, primarily based on a short story I'd submitted. Michael became extremely busy in his career in the world of educational textbooks, moving often—Dallas, Chicago, Kansas City, Northern California, Connecticut—so we agreed that I should take over the main responsibilities of running the magazine. One of my efforts was to increase the book reviews and literary criticism we published, which was focused mostly on Texas books and topics. We Texas writers felt snubbed by the New York and California literary establishments and needed a forum to discuss the burgeoning talent in our state.

I saw *The Pawn Review* as the perfect medium where Rick could try out his own authentic voice, and I invited him to review three novels by Texan Max Crawford, the scion of an agriculture family near the Llano Estacado who'd been a Stegner Fellow at Stanford a few years before I was in the program. I knew Max through mutual writer friends and from the many addled evenings at various bars in Palo Alto and San Francisco. Max was a Marxist like Rick, and I was correct in thinking that Rick would enjoy the novels of a fellow traveler. His essay entitled "Max Crawford: The Ambiguous Communist" was a nice riff on Max's title *The Bad Communist.* Rick rendered his literary judgment of Max's novels with appropriate nods to Georg Lukács, Habermas, and the Frankfurt School—but also to Jonathan Swift, Sinclair Lewis, and Larry McMurtry. Rick's interpretations were more measured and serious than a Hunter Thompsonesque screed and far richer than his usual academy-pleasing treatises. He called Crawford's *Waltz Across Texas* "a geared-down Oldsmobile of a novel," and he pointed out "the central dilemma of all [Crawford's] work—only politics can save us, but all politics is shit."[18] The review was a step in the right direction. Rick was very pleased that he could cut loose and be himself.

"Writing like this will set your chickens free," I assured him when the issue arrived fresh from the print shop and we stood reading it together on his front porch.

It was a dilemma he'd already faced in his life. *How far can I push this? How much can I get away with?* And it was the crux of the question he would face throughout his academic future: *How do I remain true to myself and still survive within the steep walls of this musty old museum of ideas?*

DUPLEXITIES

ELAINE'S FAMILY DUPLEX became a popular gathering place and the center of Roderick World over the next seven years. It was a small two-bedroom, orange-brick unit separated from the other unit by a junk-filled carport. A reclusive old lady had been living for a hundred years on the other side, but no one ever saw her. I suspected she was a shut-in cowering against all the chaos next door.

The duplex was located about a mile north of the university in a charming neighborhood whose handsome vintage homes and ivy-smothered Hobbit bungalows were inhabited by professors, UT senior administrators, and comfortable lawyers raising their families in walking distance of reliable Robert E. Lee Elementary, where the children wore clean blue jeans and pretty dresses and scored well above average on standardized tests. Marshall attended the school, and decades later my son and then my three stepchildren also attended Robert E. Lee, which eventually underwent a long-needed removal of the Confederate general's name.

We had our share of parties at the Roderick duplex, but the most memorable tradition was all-day-Sunday NFL television viewing, which consisted of grown men shouting at the TV set like ancient Aztecs cheering for the bloody ritual of human sacrifice. The guilty participants were Rick, myself, Frank, a very likable Abilene Boy named Tom Burditt, and the Williamson brothers, if they were in town. We were devout Houston Oilers fans, our hero Longhorn Earl Campbell, and unlike most rabid Texans, we hated "America's team," the Dallas Cowboys. As Rick always said, "I have two favorite teams—the Oilers and whoever is playing Dallas." We pulled for underdogs in almost every case, and the underachieving Oilers suited us perfectly.

Our game-watching was devoid of subtlety. We ranted and screamed, we leaped to our feet, we high-fived, we stormed in circles in the small living room, we burst outside to suck in fresh air and yell at the heavens, we kicked things, we complained about play calling and penalties, and we lectured the TV's warm tubes and coils about what *should* have happened if the coaches had sent in the right play. Each of us was capable of absurdist commentary, dubious analysis, off-the-wall literary allusions, crackpot conspiracy theories, and exaggerated memories of our own glory days on the playing fields of not-exactly-Eaton but pathetic little schools on the desolate West Texas plains and the Gulf bayshore. On one occasion, when UT history professor Ricardo Romo and his son joined us in the smoke-filled living room, little Carlos observed innocently, "Dad, you're talking to the television set. You realize they can't hear you, don't you?"

▪ ▪ ▪

Toward the end of 1979, Joe Duoto and I went to a birthday party where he met his soon-to-be girlfriend, Sandra, and I met my future wife and the mother of our son. Annette was a beautiful young Italian American woman from the Boston area in her mid-twenties, with full dark ringlets of hair and glorious greenish-blue eyes, as stylish as she was intelligent. One glance at her and one long conversation later, I realized I'd met the woman I'd been seeking for years. She'd received a degree from Brandeis University and completed grad studies in museum administration at the University of Minnesota, and she'd interned at the Walker Art Center in Minneapolis and then worked at the National Endowment for the Arts in D.C. Two months earlier, she'd moved to the cultural hinterland of Austin, Texas, for her first real adult job as the curator of contemporary art at Laguna Gloria Art Museum.

Less than a year after I met her, we moved together into a cute white bungalow on Windsor Road in Tarrytown and began to cohabitate, something I hadn't done with a girlfriend since Maggie in the Bay Area about eight light-years earlier. Annette persuaded me to buy better clothes and wash my long hair every day. I persuaded her that riding around in Austin traffic on a Moped, wearing a red cloth "helmet" that looked more like the aviator headgear for a Sopwith Camel, was a death wish and she should purchase a car. We were both sensible and good for each other.

What we shared most deeply was our working-class backgrounds. My dad worked in a refinery and her dad worked in a shipyard. My mother waited tables off and on when I was growing up, and Annette's mother sold buttons and threads in a button shop. Our parents hadn't attended college. Annette once described the two of us as "a northern and southern working-class-Catholic mirror of each other." We seemed destined to be together.

You always want your family and close friends to accept your romantic partners and like them as much as you do. You want them to see why you're in love, why you cherish this person, why they've become essential to your life. And so it was with Annette. But there was no greater challenge than introducing a new friend to Rick. In general, he had an open mind and valued fresh ideas, unique individuals and their experiences, and anyone who could teach him something. But his attitude toward newcomers joining our innermost circle rose and dipped like the Texas temperature. Because Annette was so dear to me, I prepared him in advance to meet this Yankee artsy intellectual from a culture Rick had only read about and seen in movies.

"What do you like about her?" he asked me nonchalantly.

"She subscribes to *The Village Voice*."

"Damn, she's hipper than we are," he said.

"She cooks strange Italian dishes and reads angry women's poetry."

"I've gotta meet this chick and steal her recipes," he said. "And maybe check out her bookshelves."

The amphitheater for the typical Rick Encounter of the First Kind was their small cigarette-fogged duplex living room, scene of our deranged football viewing, and that's where I introduced Annette to him and Elaine and the typical Roderick entourage. For the most part, that space was a toxic male Petri dish, but I didn't fully understand that at the time. I thought our gatherings were witty and entertaining. How could anyone *not* be charmed by our gang's scintillating verbal performances and hilarious repartee? Unfortunately for the casual visitor, the parties were less like a Parisian salon and more like a free-for-all at a sweaty boxing gym. Those get-togethers did not impress the female company as much as we hoped they would.

Decades later, Annette summoned her memories about that small crowded duplex, picturing those two chubby boys bumbling around, Marshall and their second son, Travis, and Elaine watching everything with cool detachment while smoking in the kitchen doorway. Too excited to sit down, Rick's anxious energy "propulsed him around the living room," pacing like an amphetamine junkie, and Annette recalled that when we guys were inspired or incited by the conversation, we'd leap to our feet "for emphasis, all jockeying to be the smartest and funniest. If any man scored points, Rick would try to trump him and often did."

At age twenty-six, Annette was a strong feminist who suffered no fools among the males who saw themselves as "enlightened," but the Roderick scene surprised and challenged her. She recollected that she rarely spoke, and that Rick, "the loud, assertive alpha male, brought out all my intellectual insecurities." She was kind enough to say that I didn't do that, fortunately, or our relationship wouldn't have lasted twenty-two years. "You and I could joust and talk," she said, "but I couldn't penetrate your male group. I would get lost in feminist resentment. I endured the events, but never really enjoyed them. Why go somewhere if you'd go home feeling crummy? I was so frustrated at my inability to weigh in. Or maybe I tried little bits of dry wit and just couldn't be heard. Those were still the days when I couldn't speak up very loudly," she admitted. "Rick was one of those grad students who could toss around the language with such flair. I was getting used to hearing that language and was still greatly amazed and amused at West Texas accents and colorful expressions I hadn't heard before. Minneapolis and D.C. were much more prosaic in their intellectualism."

What Annette didn't realize was that Rick was often anxious and borderline overwrought in larger gatherings, and his long screeds were a defense mechanism. Talking calmed his nerves. If he could get himself going, verbalizing the reels spinning in his head, he would find comfort and control. Situations cloaked in freewheeling anarchy did not appeal to him. At his core, Gonzo Rick had a tidy, well-ordered mind as organized as the manuscript shelves in a medieval monastery.

Annette felt that Rick's domineering behavior was often at odds with his ideology. He was philosophically sympathetic with all progressive causes, including feminism, but she was skeptical about him walking the walk. "He may have read the texts," she said, "but

Tom Zigal and Annette Carlozzi, 1980s. *Photo courtesy of Annette Carlozzi*

I never saw him apply them by extending the slightest attention to equal opportunity party jibber-jabber. The same for all you guys. And of course you were all smart and funny."

The problem was that we '60s guys considered serious discussions about music, art, literature, philosophy, and politics to be a contact sport. We took no prisoners. God help us, we were loud and confrontational and egocentric. It was the method we'd learned from the zeitgeist. A decade later, in his Teaching Company lecture "Habermas and the Fragile Dignity of Humanity" (1993), Rick explained that aggressive, sometimes obnoxious approach as a classic quest for "the better argument":

> When Socrates argues with an interlocutor, he never pulls the argument that, well, I am more powerful than you, so you are wrong. As a matter of a fact, one of the charms of Socrates is that he owns almost nothing and has almost no position, and the only force he expects you to recognize is the force that Habermas says is the only force a free human being can ever recognize, and that is that peculiar, strange, unforced force of the better argument. Habermas believes . . . that we can change our minds if we hear a better argument, and a free person can do that without being ashamed of himself or herself. You know, if you are in a free and equal situation of communication and someone convinces you through a better argument, you go, "Well, I now believe differently." But not through distortion or anything, but through just that strange force that a person feels when they become convinced. They go, "Oh gee . . . now I agree with that." That is the force that a free human can recognize, according to Habermas.[19]

Joan Muller Burditt wasn't as uncomfortable with the scene as Annette. When I spoke with Joan about her memories of Rick, she said she liked "edgy men" and that Rick was "her husband Tom multiplied by one hundred." Which was quite an assessment, because Tom Burditt was an intensely fidgety guy, constantly chewing gum

Tom Burditt and Joan Muller Burditt, 1980s.

or breath mints to avoid chain-smoking, and loud and manic in his left-wing rants, holding his own in any boisterous crowd. He was handsome and suavely bearded and bespectacled in those popular frameless John Lennon glasses, and in his spare time he was a strong, expert golfer who could drive a ball three hundred yards with little effort. Annette and I had a real soft spot for that hypochondriacal Abilene Aggie.

Joan remembered the first time she walked into the Roderick duplex. "The couch was a stain with stuffing," she said, the air heavy with cigarette smoke that would saturate your clothes in five minutes, so you'd have to throw them into the washer immediately after your visit. The bathroom door was missing its knob, leaving a round hole that made using the toilet uncomfortable with the two boys wandering around and peeking through the opening. During those get-togethers, Joan found herself drawn to Rick's "almost poetic way of expressing ideas I'd never even thought about." She compared him to the comedian Robin Williams, "but with a West Texas drawl that would make LBJ sound like a Yankee." Her intellect was tested by the scramble of topics and thinkers: Karl Marx, Aristotle, American poverty, class struggle, politics, football. She loved playing counterpoint to Rick, even though "I knew I would never win. It didn't matter. What mattered was the discourse and the belly-busting laughs."

Many years later, she still relished the vivid image of Rick's "delicate scholar's hands" carefully plucking a book from the built-in shelves in the living room when he decided to read a passage from Descartes or Voltaire to reinforce his point. As Joan put it, "I wish I'd taken notes."

What she admired about him was that despite his bluster and rough surfaces and slashing criticism of almost every aspect of the American socioeconomic and political structure, Rick always maintained a sense of hope that things could change for the better. She pointed out that he insisted we should always struggle to overthrow what was oppressive and dehumanizing to working men and women. Resistance was essential. Revolution was possible. We should never stop striving to create the best world we could imagine.

"His words would fill me with dread about the future of humankind," she said, "but then he would say something so hopeful that I felt it all may work out. Burditt and I would go home, never before midnight, and I would drop into bed and fall asleep with a smile on my face because I knew things would be okay."

One of the most notorious evenings at the duplex took place when Rick invited the Burditts, Annette, and me to play Class Struggle, a new board game he'd received as a gift. The game was more or less based on Monopoly, but instead of individuals acquiring property, it called for two teams—workers vs. capitalists—to fight it out over nuclear war and revolution. Rick insisted on being a worker, so as a lark I volunteered to be a capitalist. The game was rigged against the workers, in a reflection of real life, and I enjoyed the chance to act like a rich exploitive bastard, which I role-played with believable repugnance. When it became clear that our team of capitalists was about to win the game, Rick lumbered angrily away from the coffee table, screamed about injustices in the game's system, and kicked the screen door off its hinges. Elaine and the two other women declared the evening to be over, and we all slunk back to our homes in disbelief. The next day, a cheerful Rick phoned me to say he'd added new homemade cards to the game, to give it more balance, and he invited Annette and me to play another round. We said no thank you. The Burditts declined as well. No one wanted to experience that childish display of poor sportsmanship again.

OUT OF THE DEPTHS

IN EARLY 1979, Rick's father moved to Austin. I'm not certain what precipitated that decision, but I suspect that Rod couldn't take care of himself any longer in Tuscola. Most likely, he'd lost his cinder-block home. "The last time I saw Rod's house," said Holt Williamson, "the roof had caved in. It was an odd sensation talking to Rod as if it was normal. How do you chat with somebody when their ceiling is falling down around them? It looked like it'd been bombed. I know the place was condemned, but the city did nothing about it because they were hoping it would fall down on Rod and end their misery."

Rod took up residence in a seniors' apartment complex on Hancock Drive near a popular movie theater. I'm sure his expectation was that he would receive care and assistance from his son, although Rod was not naive enough to believe that their fractious relationship would heal itself suddenly and magically in a warm frothy chicken soup of filial love.

At about the same time, and perhaps because of his father's reappearance in his life, Rick began to experience panic attacks and slipped into the deep clutches of agoraphobia. I knocked on their door one day and found him lying on the couch, grasping his chest. He was taking short breaths, his heart was racing, and he thought he was having a heart attack. I wanted to call EMS immediately, but then he sat up, momentarily revived, and explained that he'd been having these anxiety attacks with some frequency. I thought he might've been doing cocaine again, but he insisted there were no substances involved. He said that because of his anxieties, he didn't like going out in public, where something unpredictable might happen. He left the duplex only to attend his graduate classes or to teach—he was a new assistant instructor in the philosophy department—and then he would return home as quickly as possible.

Given Rick's health concerns, Rod was not a priority for him, and as usual, the burden fell on Elaine and others. I half-wondered if Rick's attacks, consciously or unconsciously, were an excuse to avoid dealing with his difficult father. At any rate, Elaine and Rod had that contentious history of living together, and she was fed up with him and his whining and abusive tongue-lashings. So caring for Rod became a group effort. I checked in on the old boy from time to time, making sure he was fed routinely by Meals on Wheels, and Frank's wife, Beverly, was the most conscientious caretaker of us all.

Within a few months, Rod was unable to live alone in the apartment, and they moved him into a fairly cheap nursing home on Burnet Road in north Austin. It was a miserable place that smelled of urine and disinfectant, and Rod shared a small room with a poor fellow who was worse off than he was. I don't know how they got along, but Rod wasn't above trashing the guy during my visits, criticizing the roommate's habits and mental failings even while the man was lying on the bed and listening to him. It wasn't my first experience with nursing home hell, but its stench and wasted flesh and sounds of groaning desolation—and the griping of underpaid attendants who weren't well-trained and didn't much care for the work—were images that stayed with me for decades until my siblings and I had to face the same sorry considerations with our own father.

To my surprise, Rick credited me for ending his agoraphobia. As he told the story, I showed up at his doorstep one day with the latest Bruce Springsteen album, *Nebraska*, tucked under my arm. He was stretched out on the couch, eyes closed, his breathing shallow, and I said, "You've gotta hear the new Springsteen record, Rick. The lyrics are amazing."

Without a word uttered between us, we listened to the Boss wail his stark, haunting stories of homicidal drifters, lowlife mobsters, nightshift workers, used car salesmen, and a world of dead-end bleakness smothering the lives of America's dismal underclass. Songs stripped down to the basics of guitar, harmonica, and a voice echoing ghostly from a deep abyss of pain and remorse. After we'd listened to every track on both sides, Rick looked at me and said, "*Dark*, man, but I love it. I grew up with all those miscreants."

In his memory of that day, I slipped the record into its sleeve, tucked it under my arm again, and as I was leaving, I turned to him and said, "Things could be worse, Rick. You could be the guy in one of these songs. Now get up off your butt and stop feeling sorry for yourself."

And for some reason, he did.

Rick recovered and eventually started inviting his undergraduates to the duplex for parties. His students loved him. They fawned over him; they sat at his feet listening to him muse about the timeless immensities of Socrates and the Buddha; they were enthralled by his encyclopedic knowledge and wisdom and offbeat humor. Outside the classroom he was even more outrageous, riffing on everything from John Huston classics and French New Wave cinema and old *Twilight Zone* episodes to Dylan's "Desolation Row" and the romantic darkness of Blake and Baudelaire.

Rick Roderick was a man for all seasons. A man in full. At that point in his life, he'd begun to manage his debilitating anxieties and keep them at bay, at least temporarily, and he was hitting his stride in front of receptive audiences. His talent and charisma had not gone unnoticed by the most esteemed professors in both the philosophy and economics departments at the University of Texas. They recognized that a luminous new star was flaring on the horizon, and those learned eminences were beginning to believe that this young man, burning bright, was quite possibly a rare and magnificent find.

THE EARL OF DUKE

I DON'T RECALL if Rick had panic attacks on the days leading up to his defense of his dissertation on Jürgen Habermas; regardless, he impressed the committee and won their unanimous praise. His manuscript *Habermas and the Foundations of Critical Theory* was selected by the distinguished British sociologist Anthony Giddens for publication at St. Martin's Press (and Macmillan in the UK) as part of their series *Theoretical Traditions in the Social Sciences*. As its description indicates, "The series aims to create a forum for debate between different theoretical and philosophical traditions in the social sciences. The series will concentrate on the work of particular thinkers whose ideas have had a major impact on social science."

Rick and his subject, "the Hubert Humphrey of the Frankfurt School," had found their home. Even though he admired Habermas, Rick was aware of the philosopher's shortcomings, especially the charge by many Marxist scholars who criticized Habermas for what they considered his "elitist theories" confined to the academy. In Rick's Teaching Company lecture entitled "Habermas and the Fragile Dignity of Humanity" (1993), he acknowledges that "it looks like a theory that trades Marx's analysis of society as a giant factory for an analysis by Habermas of society as a giant seminar room. Have you noticed how all [of Habermas's] conditions are the ones that ought to hold in a seminar? Everybody in a seminar should be relevant, concise, sincere, and make their contributions true, and it's not lost on any of Habermas's critics that he spent his whole adult life as a professor."[20]

The book appeared in 1986, and Rick dedicated it to his wife. In his acknowledgements, he wrote, "I would like to thank those members of my generation who continue to think that 'things might be otherwise.' Several of these are my friends: Tom and Frank Zigal, Turner and Holt Williamson, Joan and Tom Burditt, and Jim Bogard. Without the lessons I have learned from them, I would not have undertaken this work."[21]

In subsequent years, the Habermas book would be translated into Chinese and German editions. A publisher at Macmillan wrote to Rick "welcoming the opportunity" to work with him on another book.

He had a number of devoted supporters in the University of Texas philosophy department, but none more loyal and admiring than his dissertation adviser, Professor Douglas Kellner, who would eventually collaborate with Rick on two or three essays published in scholarly journals like *New German Critique* and *Man and World* (now *Continental Philosophy Review*). Rick introduced me to Doug, and I hobnobbed with him at a couple of Austin parties in the 1980s before he left UT to occupy an endowed chair at UCLA. I liked Doug very much. He was a radical leftist in the academy without the usual pretentions and scholarly stuffiness and the veneer of arrogance that sometimes tainted '60s politicos. Not long after Rick's death, I emailed Doug to make sure he'd heard the sad news. "Rick was an original in every way, a True Texan, Marxist, activist, friend, husband and father, and one of the funniest and smartest guys I ever met," he replied. He recalled that Rick's "Texas accent was very pronounced and very expressive. He had very strong opinions, always radical but with humor. He always took a stand and was consistent in his values and oppositions."

With the Habermas book accepted for publication and glowing references from professors in the philosophy department, Dr. Rick Roderick, newly minted PhD, interviewed for tenure-track positions at Duke University and Dartmouth in 1985. He soon announced that he and his family would be heading for Duke in Durham, North

Carolina, his first academic gig as an assistant professor. We friends were very proud of him. We showed up to help pack their junker brown Suburban, bought for the journey, and we cheered them as they rolled away from the duplex crammed to the roof with two kids and suitcases and lugging behind them a small U-Haul trailer stuffed with more essential belongings, like the Beverly Hillbillies on their way to the big city.

Unfortunately, the Suburban dropped its transmission somewhere in Louisiana—a metaphor foreshadowing the years ahead—and the four of them spent hours sitting in a mom-and-pop café while a pair of shade-tree mechanics worked on the vehicle. It was quite possibly during that long wait that Rick revealed to Elaine that his interview with the Duke philosophy department had gone very well but they hadn't actually offered him the job yet. Elaine exploded, with good reason. *"We've given up our home and we're dragging our kids across the country and you don't know if you have a job yet, Rick?"* The two boys remember their parents arguing intensely for the next thousand miles of hard road until they reached Durham.

It was unconscionable but typical of the Artful Dodger ploys that Rick had acquired from his Fagin-like dad. When the Rodericks reached Durham, bedraggled from the long quarrelsome trip, Rick had no choice but to throw himself at the mercy of the Duke hiring committee and beg for the job. They gave it to him. It was yet another instance of Rick's power of persuasion when the chips were down and he was desperate. In the interest of historical determinism, I'm going to assume that he was their top candidate and they would've offered him the position no matter what.

Rick taught at Duke from 1985 to 1993, and for him it was the best of times, it was the worst of times. He expected to grow old, white-haired, and more rotund while teaching at that prestigious university. But over the course of those eight years, his spectacular rise and the long arc of student adulation, campus activism, and national recognition gradually bent toward disappointment and

Rick was an assistant professor of philosophy at Duke University from 1985–93.
Photo courtesy of the Roderick family

rejection. Being denied tenure, despite his enormous popularity with students and many of his peers, shook his self-confidence, triggered bouts of depression, and had a profound effect on his psyche for the rest of his life.

What is indisputable is that his students adored him. They met with him in local bars after classes to drink beer and continue their discussions of the grave matters that have survived the ages. They flocked to a Wednesday-night reading group he created. They joined him in his political activism. They gave him standing ovations at the end of semesters. On the Internet, they continue to write about him thirty years after taking his courses, crediting him for raising their awareness about issues and ideas, and they often wonder what happened to him after Duke.

Robert Tally was an undergraduate from the Durham area who took six courses with Professor Roderick, including introductions to nineteenth-century philosophy and twentieth-century Continental philosophy, a large lecture-hall course called “Marxism and Society,” a small graduate seminar on “Hegel’s *Phenomenology of Spirit*,” and an independent study of Nietzsche, which was simply Tally and Rick in one-on-one meetings in Rick’s office or over lunch. This prompted Tally to declare, “I minored in *Rick*.” By the end of his undergraduate studies, he considered Rick a friend, and he became acquainted with the Roderick family when they all lived in the same residence hall.

Rick inscribed Tally’s copy of the Habermas book, “To Rob, Thanks comrade. You can do better.” I feel confident it was a double-edged challenge.

Rob Tally went on to receive both a bachelor’s degree in philosophy and a law degree from Duke, as well as a master’s degree in literature and a doctorate in critical and cultural studies from the University of Pittsburgh. Among other works, he published a book entitled *Fredric Jameson: The Project of Dialectical Criticism* and dedicated it “In memory of Rick Roderick, who encouraged me to do better.” In the book’s acknowledgments, Tally adds, “This book is dedicated to my late advisor and friend Rick Roderick, who first recommended [Jameson’s] *Marxism and Form* as essential reading if I wished to integrate my literary and philosophical interests and who encouraged my explorations in modern critical theory. Rick was an inspiring teacher, scholar, and activist, a comrade who thoroughly embodied a commitment to the spirit of Marx’s eleventh thesis on Feuerbach.”[22]

In Karl Marx’s *Theses on Feuerbach*, which were notes unpublished in Marx’s lifetime, the eleventh thesis is his famous quotation, “The philosophers have hitherto only interpreted the world in various ways; the point, however, is to change it.” One summer when Annette and I were “letting” a flat in London, we read that quotation on Marx’s tomb in Highgate Cemetery.

Now an English professor at Texas State University in San Marcos, Rob Tally credits Rick's classroom style for having a significant influence on his own teaching. In an email to me, Tally wrote,

> I've used the term "interactive lecture" to describe how I teach a lot of my classes, and I feel like I got that—the style, not the term—from Rick. [Rick's approach] certainly wasn't straight lecture . . . because he was happy to involve others, calling on people who raised their hands, or engaging with them in other ways. (As you know, sometimes facial expressions and eye contact alone can do a lot in a classroom setting.) There's a tendency in the humanities to favor so-called "discussion-oriented" classes or, more recently, even the "flipped classroom" in which students take the lead and the professor recedes. Rick did not do this, thankfully. After all, there's one person in the room who knows a helluva lot about the subject, and nearly everyone else knows very little, so it's to the benefit of all to let the knowledgeable person take the lead. . . . [He] was quick to let students speak up and to provide valuable feedback, commentary, or conversation about what they had to say.

But even for such a nimble, charismatic, and seasoned professor, teaching wasn't always a walk in the ivy-covered woods. Rick's old nemesis, the panic attack, sometimes reared its ugly head. One of his graduate students, a young woman he'd also taught in Austin, told me he occasionally phoned her before a class and asked her to come and hold his hand to help him calm down before he ventured into the lecture hall. She assured me it wasn't a sexual ruse, and it wasn't fried nerves over a lesson plan. "Rick was just too amped up, and his heart was racing." The threats of arrhythmia and tachycardia were never far from his thoughts.

A DUAL WORLD

RICK WAS A TRUE BELIEVER in political action and became deeply involved in Duke's campus politics. But in doing so, he violated the cardinal rule for any instructor on a tenure track: Don't make waves. Don't embarrass the university administration. Don't cause their soul-crushing, bureaucratic lives to be any worse than they already are. Most assistant professors understand that rule. I've heard countless young profs say, "Well, of course I'm keeping quiet about (fill in the blank) until after I get tenure." The "blank" being "I'm a cross-dresser." "I belong to a Michigan paramilitary group." "I believe that the Reverend Moon is God." "I'm just using this pathetic gig as a springboard to a decent Ivy League school." Apparently, Rick didn't get the memo. And it's likely that even if he did, he wasn't going to suppress his anti-authoritarian impulses or deny his genuine passion for controversy and the imperatives of sociopolitical change.

Like most private universities of its kind in the 1980s, Duke had few black faculty members, only thirty-one out of fourteen hundred (two percent). In 1988, Rick began serving on Duke's Committee on Black Faculty, tasked with making recommendations on how to recruit more African American professors. The committee recommended that the university require each of its fifty-odd departments to hire one additional black faculty member by 1993. On the face of it, that doesn't seem like an unreasonable burden: five years to hire one African American professor for your department. But Duke's faculty advisory council voted down the recommendation, and that led to weeks of student and faculty protests, with Rick as a very visible presence and commanding voice near the forefront of the demonstrations. Three thousand signatures were presented to the university president, asking him to overturn the advisory council's ruling, and the president did manage to convince that rigid group to reconsider their position.

The *New York Times* covered the controversy, including the faculty advisory council's objection that the "one hire" would create a quota system. Rick was quoted in the *NYT* article: "This cannot be equated with quotas. . . . Quotas have consequences if you fail. The only consequence here is that you have to show why you have failed. Some obviously don't want to do that."[23]

In an article in the Duke student newspaper, *The Chronicle*, Rick pointed out that "while [this] university searches across the country to find great black athletes, they do not search the country and find great black faculty."[24]

His aggressive stance on racial hiring did not sit well with members of his own department and several pedants in the sciences who complained that the national competition for outstanding black PhDs was too stiff and the "one hire in five years" was virtually unattainable. But Rick didn't back down and continued to join colleagues of color in the fight for this initiative. Many observers agreed that his needling militance was a major strike against him in his quest for tenure.

A year after the Black Faculty controversy, Rick found himself embroiled in another struggle. Campus housekeepers complained about their treatment by the ominously named ServiceMaster, the private company hired by Duke to manage the housekeeping workforce. The students marched on the president's office again and presented him with a petition signed by fifteen hundred students and employees, demanding that the abusive ServiceMaster be fired. An article in the student newspaper in 1989 asserted that the company had "spoken unduly harshly to employees, increased [their] workload, and threatened them with the loss of their jobs." Rick was quoted in the same article: "Rick Roderick, assistant professor of

Rick hugging students in celebration when Duke University's Academic Council approved the Black Faculty Initiative, 1988. *Photo courtesy of the Duke Chronicle*

philosophy, said he hoped that at the least, students would leave the rally able to 'start looking around at some of the people who are invisible to them.' He advocated terminating ServiceMaster's contract and using the money the university pays ServiceMaster to fund day care, increase workers' wages, and improve campus safety."[25]

Wise, well-reasoned, generous, and humane in his intentions—but clearly the words of a godless Communist and subversive rabble-rouser. Those remarks and his participation in the confrontation were guaranteed to paint another target on his back. To everyone's surprise, however, after a second rally and several days of discussions and negotiations, Duke's President Keith Brodie terminated the ServiceMaster contract.

Rick's youngest son, Max, was only five years old when Rick was denied tenure, but Max has written a superb essay about his dad entitled "Rick Roderick and the Fragile Dignity of Humanity." In one of Max's early drafts, he said that a prevailing narrative "was that Rick had been denied tenure for helping unionize Duke's campus employees, practically sacrificing his career for the cause of workers' rights. Rick's greatest strength wasn't his activism, which he would have considered intrinsic to the actions of any man who lived with real conviction . . . it was his ability to teach that distinguished him. He was able to read and consolidate huge amounts of information and relate it concisely and understandably to a lay audience with both sincerity and respect for the intentions of the source material."

On one occasion, when Joan Muller Burditt was a consultant for Holt, Rinehart & Winston, she traveled to Durham on textbook business and met Rick at his office. She told me that it was great to see him in an intellectual setting that most suited him. As she recalled,

> He seemed happy and proud to be there as he walked me through the campus, pointing out buildings and sites. I remember the gardens. He seemed energized at that time, and of course talked incessantly. He did seem to be in a sort of dual world, and as he talked about how great Duke was, he also complained about the blue-bloodedness of the place. Finally, I said, "Then Rick, why are you here?" He said something about the best way to make change is by catching people when they're college age and exposing them to ideas that clash with what they'd come to believe, accepting the status quo. But my question might have put him on the defensive, and I imagine he had a niggling discomfort from rubbing elbows with the elites. I don't know if his protests concerning

hiring African American professors came after that or not. But I could've predicted it. We all could have.

Rick's activism may have irritated some colleagues and the administration—he was definitely a thorn in their sides—but most observers point out that what killed his tenure prospects was his lack of publications over his seven-year trial period as an assistant professor. He'd completed the Habermas book before he was hired at Duke, and he showed no progress on a second book. He talked about a book project on Hegel and another one focused on the Trinidadian Marxist scholar C. L. R. James and a third one on "the historical Marx," but in my research, I couldn't find any notes, outlines, or written pages to confirm that he'd begun those pursuits. He published only three scholarly essays and six book reviews in those seven years, and he had to know that such a slender output wasn't enough. I suspected he'd lost interest in academic scholarship and he didn't want to play the game anymore. In a Duke *Chronicle* article addressing his tenure issue, Rick succinctly expressed his feelings about scholastic research: "Roderick said that research is plagiarism and simply means 'writing books with lots of footnotes.'"[26] And in a 1991 article in the Raleigh-area newspaper *The News and Observer*, he declared that "the overwhelming majority of professors' research is not worth doing. They write articles that only three people read."[27]

He loved teaching and mentoring students, the face-to-face exchanges, the conversations in any setting, whether classroom or bar or roller rink, but it clearly bored him to do the academic grunt-work necessary to keep his job. He appeared to believe that publishing books about philosophy and its arcane fixations was a fool's errand. This wasn't the same thing I'd suggested when I read his early essays. My point wasn't that he should stop writing about philosophical matters altogether, but to write about them in his own colloquial voice and with a contemporary sensibility. Rick seemed to feel that in the late twentieth century, the field no longer lent itself to the kinds of proofs and certainties promulgated by the Hegels and Schopenhauers of an earlier time. As he said in his videotaped lecture "Derrida and the Ends of Man" (1993),

> Philosophy is not like building a house, where you start with a firm foundation and build it up and you're finished and you walk off and that's philosophy. Philosophy under the heading of deconstruction is housework, which means every day the floors have to be swept again, the dishes have to be done again, and I'll be damned, the next day is just like that again, and is just like that again, and is just like that again. . . . That is at the heart of the best of philosophy in the late twentieth century . . . the idea that it's not getting finished and it can't be.[28]

Having lived with Rick, I can confirm that he hated housework. I imagine that a similar mindset counseled him to avoid writing about a subject he considered to be tedious and repetitive and by its nature too shopworn and obscure to be analyzed in the pages of a book. At least a book he wanted to write.

While at Duke, he began writing a novel he called "On a Darkling Plain," and perhaps that endeavor became a distraction from his "real work." The title is derived from an allusion to an ancient battle in the poem "Dover Beach" by Matthew Arnold:

> And we are here as on a darkling plain
> Swept with confused alarms of struggle and flight,
> Where ignorant armies clash by night.

Toward the end of the 1980s, when I was living in Aspen and we were both visiting Austin at the same time, he gave me the first few chapters to read when we met at a bean-sprouts café for lunch. What I read was very good, a more literary roman à clef than his later *Bury Me Not*. I complimented him on its dark beauty and encouraged him to keep writing the story. As usual, he said, "If I ever finish this thing, you'll edit it for me, won't you, Tom? You'll make it acceptable." And I said of course I would. A few years later he told me that the writing had bogged down, he'd become frustrated with it, and he'd used the pages for kindling in a fireplace. It's a noble literary tradition, burning one's unsatisfactory, imperfect attempt. But what I began to understand was that after three or four years neck-deep in the academy, Rick was more interested in belletristic writing than in scholarship. There were sci-fi, cyberpunk, and even mystical elements in "On a Darkling Plain." He was looking for a more suitable outlet for his restless imagination.

RADICALLY SOCRATIC

WHEN RICK WAS APPROACHED by Tom Rollins to participate in the *Great Courses* videotape program in 1990, Rollins was in his mid-thirties, a talented and gregarious Harvard-educated lawyer who'd served as chief counsel and chief of staff for Senator Ted Kennedy and the Senate's Committee on Labor and Human Resources. Rollins had been an award-winning debater in high school and in college at Georgetown University, with a deep interest in the humanities, and he'd quit his lawyering job to found the Teaching Company, a groundbreaking enterprise focused on improving lifelong learning by using the newest technology to reach the broadest audiences worldwide. His idea was to create a VCR videotape program that featured the nation's best university professors giving lectures in their fields, everything from Shakespeare to "Modern Physics for Non-Scientists" and "The Sociology of Sexuality." Bankrolling the company himself in the early days, he maxed out his credit cards, sold all his expensive lawyer suits, and lived in an attic in Arlington, Virginia, to save money and fund his ambitious dream.

In the beginning, before he built a staff and created a rigorous process for vetting and auditioning the teachers, Rollins did all the recruiting himself. He studied student evaluations from forty highly regarded universities in America, searching for the most popular and effective classroom wizards. The youthful Tom could pass for a graduate student in those days, and on several occasions he dressed in jeans and sneakers, carried a backpack, and sat in the back of classrooms, silently observing prospective superstars.

While examining thousands of evaluations, he noticed that an assistant professor named Rick Roderick turned up on every Duke University student's top-five list. Every single student evaluation at Duke said, "You've got to take a course with Professor Roderick before you leave this place." These weren't solely philosophy majors singing Rick's praises. Rob Tally explained,

> the student make-up of Rick's classes was quite mixed. Some, like me, would've taken courses on that subject anyhow, so I really lucked out to have such a great teacher teaching courses on the subjects I was already interested in. Most, however, were there for Rick himself. He'd quickly developed a reputation for being a great teacher—and also entertaining, provocative, and wild. So I think a lot of people wanted to take a course with him just to get that experience. Some friends of mine, one pre-med and the other in electrical engineering, took his class to see what the hubbub was about.

Tom Rollins, founder of The Teaching Company. *Photo courtesy of Tom Rollins*

Those effusive tributes intrigued Tom Rollins, so he made a phone call to Rick in Durham, and on the other end of the line, Tom heard a thick accent he was familiar with from his own high school years in Texas.

He flew Rick to Washington, D.C., and put him up in a very nice hotel in Georgetown. They met in the hotel bar and spent the evening drinking and chain smoking and trading stories, discussing the Gulf War and the zeitgeist in 1990 America and what Rick intended to say in his first videotape lecture about "philosophy and human values." In his early forties by then, Rick was seven years older than Rollins and farther to the left of the liberal Ted Kennedy protégé. It made no difference. Rollins and Roderick discovered they were kindred spirits, and they were destined to become friends.

▪ ▪ ▪

The small studio in the basement of Georgetown University's medical center held fifty or sixty people, and the audience was provided by the Smithsonian Institution's adult education program, which was partnering with the Teaching Company on the project. In that very first session, Rick worked his magic behind the podium, speaking fluidly and effortlessly and seemingly without notes like a trained actor reciting a forty-five-minute soliloquy. The audience loved him: his humor, his accent, his sardonic asides, his clear descriptions of schools of philosophy and their leading minds. When the *Great Courses* hit the market, Rick's lectures skyrocketed in popularity and became their bestseller. He was quoted in a 1991 article written by Kathy Pitman in the publication *Duke Dialogue*: "There is a gap in our culture because rock stars are well-known and well-rewarded, as are politicians, comedians, and talk-show hosts. Everyone knows their names, but no one can name those who are best at teaching. The idea [of the *Great Courses*] was to find the very best so, of course, I was flattered."[29]

As an exemplar of the program, he appeared in full-page ads in the *New York Times*. He began to receive fan mail, including from "houseworkers and prisoners," he said. People in high places were beguiled by his performances—famous film directors like Steven Spielberg and George Lucas, the actor John Cleese, and politicians aplenty. Jonathan Taplin, a Princeton-educated Hollywood movie producer (*Mean Streets, The Last Waltz, Under Fire*) and former tour manager for Bob Dylan and The Band, phoned Rick to thank him for enriching Taplin's intellectual development. The president of Mitsubishi was so impressed he arranged for Rick to address a gathering of the world's Fortune 500 leaders at the University of Florence in Italy. The year prior, the speaker had been Britain's conservative prime minister Margaret Thatcher. I wish I'd been there in Florence to hear my old friend, that staunch Texo-Marxist, share his thoughts with the wealthiest capitalists on the planet.

The Teaching Company's *Great Courses* put Rick on the map, establishing him as a substantive figure in the universe of contemporary intellectual discourse. His son Max described his father's appeal in that eloquent essay "Rick Roderick and the Fragile Dignity of Humanity," written several years after Rick's death:

> Rick took on the task of boiling down western philosophy to its most significant, critical, and above all useful ideas. I found each lecture relevant in my own life and rich with ideas that pushed at the boundaries of my understanding. Perhaps more importantly, since these lectures have to compete with the hyper-real concoctions of massive entertainment brands, I also found them entertaining. Rick was a captivating speaker and writer, a skill he cultivated deliberately and with purpose. Knowledge, for him, was useless if it could not be easily shared, and his special talent was in sharing knowledge in the form of a story that was always compelling, whether it dealt with our best, worst, or dullest natures.

Tom Rollins was delighted by the attention Rick was receiving and the income he was producing for the company and for Rick himself. "Roderick definitely wins the trophy as the best irreverent [professor] around and he arouses strong feelings in everyone," he said in a Duke *Chronicle* article by Sarah Carnevale. "He's very keyed to the audience. He does whatever it takes for the light to go on in [their] eyes."[30]

As a result of the videotapes, Rick was invited to deliver papers at academic conferences, serve on panels, and moderate colloquies. He chaired sessions and presented papers at nearly thirty academic conferences and institutions, including at Harvard, Penn, and Loyola University Chicago. Dave Foley, the cofounder of the comedy troupe *Kids in the Hall* and star of their TV series, attended one of Rick's lectures at a conference in Toronto and was so impressed he used a short clip of a smiling Rick in the opening montage for the episodes.

But when it came to receiving tenure at Duke, none of that mattered. The *Great Courses* lectures didn't count for much at all. "Publish or perish" was Duke's mantra, as it is at most major universities, and Rick fell short. Tom Rollins has speculated that Rick's soaring reputation was a mark against him in the tenure process. He was considered a *popularizer*, Rollins said in one of our conversations, and Rick's purist academic peers no doubt looked down their pince-nez at that sort of thing. Professional envy, perhaps, or outright disdain. Philosophy professors are thrilled to sell six hundred copies of their unreadable tomes on Boethius and Baudrillard; Rick was reaching tens of thousands. His remarkable talent simply wasn't on the printed page.

Rick was keenly aware of the "popularizer / too commercial" criticism and addressed it in Carnevale's article: "Roderick, however, said his work is not any less intellectual just because it is a bestseller. He said it is the responsibility of intellectuals to communicate their knowledge to society. 'To think that this is not serious work because it's being put out in the public [via non-book media and VCRs] and making money seems to me to be insanity.'" He added with tongue in cheek, "'Serious work, in our society, is measured by money.'"[31]

In a post on a website dedicated to Rick after his death, Rob Tally agreed that publications were the sticking point: "Rick's occasional abrasiveness and eccentricity undoubtedly played their parts, but I can confirm that he was denied tenure for one reason mainly: lack of publications. It's true, he had published a book on Habermas, but that was basically his dissertation, so they felt it did not count. Rick was supposed to be working on a book on Hegel, but I never saw any chapter-drafts. He had only a couple of other articles published while at Duke, and that school really expected a lot more in terms of 'scholarly output.'"[32]

In a later email to me, Tally reinforced that observation: "It's clear that Rick, like Socrates, did what he did best in conversation, not through writing."

Because Rick was so popular among students, his tenure issue caused a sizable stir on campus. In May 1993, forty-five students confronted Duke's provost to demand that he explain why the university had denied tenure to a charismatic professor. The provost insisted that Rick "did not meet department standards" and added, "It's wrong [to say] that the decision was made on personal dislikes or politics."

One pair of students, Katherine Johnson and Scott Heftler, wrote a persuasive letter to the Duke *Chronicle*:

> Does anyone know why one of Duke's only nationally recognized professors has been fired? From our own conversation with Professor Roderick, we know that he has no idea—because he has never been given any specific reasons. This four-time nominee for the Alumni Undergraduate Distinguished Professor Teaching Award has been recognized by the Smithsonian Institute as the best teacher in his field. His "The Philosophy of Human Values" lecture series has been the bestselling videotape in the history of academia. He has been published in five countries. His "Habermas and the Foundations of Critical Theory" is an internationally recognized standard in the field. His work has been studied and reviewed worldwide—India, China, Denmark, Germany, etc., etc.

> No one at this university has been willing to debate with Professor Roderick, in public or private, the issue of tenure and research at Duke—either in his own case or the other controversial cases here.
>
> To further their hypocrisy, the University has time and again sent visitors to Professor Roderick's classes as an example of teaching excellence. If he is not fit to teach at Duke, why for eight years did the University continue to use him to entertain prospective freshmen? Either the University was wrong then or they are wrong now.
>
> Professor Roderick has obviously spent way too much time visiting with students, working with the Black Faculty Initiative, organizing protests (such as the one which aided the removal of the union-busting ServiceMaster from campus), working with students for gay and lesbian rights, and being involved in countless other "extracurricular" activities. Professor Roderick treated Duke students and employees as essential to the University rather than as excess baggage.
>
> Sadly, this letter cannot change anything in this specific case. However, [we] think we can learn something from this pathetic situation. We always found Professor Roderick's approach to be neither dogmatic nor crude, but radically Socratic. We have written this letter in the hopes that Duke will not sin twice against philosophy.[33]

They were implying that like Socrates, Rick was considered a corruptor of youth and had been handed a cup of hemlock. An overheated reference, yet sincere nonetheless.

But even the most persuasive student argument in the known world means next to nothing when it's aimed at faculty governance, an attack very much like blowing a paper spitball against a citadel's stone wall. Rick's journey at Duke was over, and there was no road back. He leveled a few parting shots at the culture of that esteemed "southern Ivy League" institution, quoted in the *Chronicle* article:

"My time at Duke has been like being around an old folks home for young people. . . . It is one of the most clean-cut, de-eroticized places you could ever find yourself."[34]

He must've been thinking about how different life had been in Austin.

Rick told Tom Rollins that at his final meeting with the philosophy department, he said, "I learned more philosophy in West Texas pool halls than I ever learned from you people."

And that was that. He was history. Those eight years were behind him now.

Rick finished teaching his last class at Duke in the spring of 1993. As popular and revered as he was among his students and with thousands of fans worldwide through the *Great Courses*, he had only one offer to teach elsewhere, and it wasn't at a top tier university.

HOW CAN THEY KILL ME?

DUKE AND THE WORLD OF ACADEMIA were only half of Rick's life in Durham. He was also a husband and father. In 1988, when he called to tell me he and Elaine had had a fourth child, I laughed and said, "Jesus, Rick. *Four*?"

At that point in time, environmentalists and the cognoscenti were concerned about global overpopulation, and having more than two children was considered "politically incorrect." Besides that, four kids promised to be a financial burden for someone on an assistant professor's salary, not to mention the challenges and enormous responsibility of parenting four different personalities for the next twenty-plus years. When Rick called, Annette was pregnant with our son and I was turning forty. I couldn't imagine having multiple children after such a late start.

"The way I look at having number four," Rick said over the phone—I could hear him take a long reflective drag on his cigarette—"How can they kill me when I'm already dead?"

I smiled, understanding what he meant. Having three children had already trussed that wild man in a parental straitjacket and squeezed his ailing heart. So what did it matter if he had another one?

Rob Tally remembers Rick telling him, "People say that only the rich can afford to have kids today, but I'm not going to let them win just by having the numbers. I'm going to have a bunch of kids and *arm* every one of them!"

Having four children mattered very much to Elaine, of course, who'd carried her sons through pregnancy and delivery and nourished them in their earliest months of life. She had her own ambitions as an artist and a desire for peace and quiet and enough space to work on a craft that was as important to her as Rick's teaching was to him. The saddest part was that having children did not bond the two of them permanently, and they couldn't find the love they needed from each other to sustain their marriage. They separated more than once during those eight years in North Carolina.

For their sons Marshall and Travis, ages nine and six when they arrived in Durham, the contrast to Austin was black and white. Literally. Duke University is an elite private university that caters mostly to the white children of wealth and privilege, but it's located

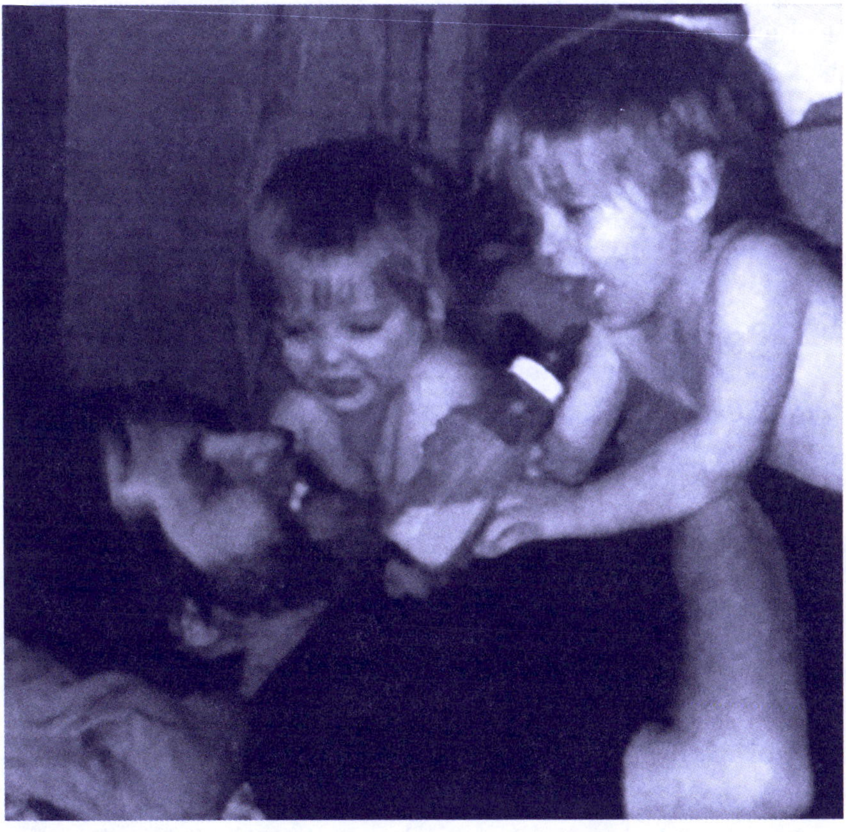

Rick wrestling with his sons Marshall and Travis, late 1970s. *Photo courtesy of the Roderick family*

in a metropolitan area that is nearly forty percent African American, with a poverty rate hovering around eighteen percent. There is a significant contrast between the campus and its environs. At the beginning, the Rodericks couldn't afford to live in the middle-class neighborhoods in which the faculty congregated, so they settled into an apartment complex where they were the only white family. The boys attended a neighborhood public school. Marshall was in the third grade, and because he was a new kid, one day when the teacher stepped out of the classroom, he had to fight a group of boys who surrounded his desk. In his earliest experience at the same school, Travis declared himself a Communist and had to fight everyone on the playground. It was a far cry from Austin's blue-ribbon Lee Elementary and its tolerant countercultural vibe.

Life improved for the boys when they eventually moved into a Duke student residence called Bassett Hall, where the Rodericks became the faculty-in-residence family. It was an older Georgian-style dormitory, red brick and stately, with dormer windows, steam radiators, hardwood floors, bunkbeds, AC window units, and a lovely green lawn out front. Bassett was located on Duke's East Campus, which had been the "women's campus" prior to 1972 and remained known for its artsy subculture because the departments of music, art and art history, literature, and philosophy were housed there. (East Campus was about a mile and a half from the West Campus and its faux-Gothic architecture and iconic Duke Chapel.) The faculty residence in Bassett was basically five dorm rooms strung together with a kitchen and extra bathrooms. Not only were the Rodericks' new accommodations cheaper and more spacious, the setting gave them easier access to a student union and campus amenities like food and recreation facilities, and Rick could walk to his classes.

Most definitely their father's sons, Marshall and Travis learned how to sneak into a sports facility to play ping-pong and foosball, and they enjoyed zooming around campus on their bicycles. Marshall recalls that on one occasion, while riding with a friend, they were harassed by a group of frat boys and knocked off their bikes. Rick took the necessary measures to send the frats to a campus disciplinary committee for their behavior, and youngster Marshall testified against them as his father sat listening in the gallery. According to Marshall, two of the frat boys were kicked out of the university and not allowed to return.

Rob Tally lived in Bassett Hall at the same time and recalls that the Rodericks' residence was a popular place for students to drop by and visit the professor and his family. Ebullient Rick was always happy to entertain his guests. Ever the sports enthusiasts, he and his sons became rabid lifelong fans of the Duke basketball team, which reached the NCAA Final Four during six of the eight years that the Rodericks were at Duke, winning the national championship twice. Tally told me that "a lot of basketball players took Rick's classes. I vividly recall sitting next to Danny Ferry, Naismith National Player of the Year and the number two overall pick in the 1989 NBA Draft. In our nineteenth-century philosophy course, Danny kept nudging me and cracking wise about Rick's mannerisms. At the time, Ferry was being compared (hyperbolically) to Larry Bird and Bill Walton as one of the best all-around college players ever, so it was pretty distracting."

Marshall remembers hoop stars Grant Hill, Bobby Hurley, Christian Laettner, and Brian Davis dropping by to hang out at the residence. His favorite player was Quin Snyder, a double major in philosophy and political science and the point guard for the team. A future NBA head coach, Snyder was a young stud riding around Durham on his motor scooter and showing up at the Rodericks' place to chill with Rick and the boys. He taught the youngsters how to dribble a basketball. One semester, Marshall talked Snyder into speaking to his elementary school class on career day. The star point guard gave one of his Final Four jackets to Rick.

Rick told me that when Bobby Hurley was seriously injured in a vehicle accident in 1993 in Sacramento, where he was playing for the Sacramento Kings, Rick was living in Southern California and contacted Grant Hill, arranging for them to visit Hurley together at the University of California, Davis, Medical Center, where Hurley was recovering in intensive care. Rick was very fond of his former students, with a sincere interest in the athletes because he viewed them as exploited labor.

In the midst of his academic responsibilities and his struggle to gain tenure, Rick's personal life was mired in the usual messy entanglements and intrigues he brought upon himself. What puzzled me and our Austin friends were Rick and Elaine's occasional reconciliations and their attempts to live together. At one point they moved to a country lane, where Elaine thought the pastoral environment would be good for everyone. At another point, by mutual agreement, Rick took the two older boys to live with him, and Elaine took the younger boys, Taylor and Max, to live with her. That didn't work because the younger pair eventually wanted to be with their older brothers and Rick, who was far more lenient about homework, sleep schedules, and hygiene. He was always willing to watch TV and play cards and board games far into the night. Rick's sense of boyhood fun never left him, and that ethic was infectious, especially among healthy growing boys who favored running wild and howling with the wolves.

▪ ▪ ▪

Rick's father, Rod, had checked out of the Austin nursing home and returned to Tuscola when the Rodericks moved to North Carolina. Rick asked Rod's cousin, a successful Tuscola banker who owed Rod a favor, to keep an eye on him. Rod died in October 1990, and Rick flew by himself to Texas to make arrangements for the memorial service. I was living with Annette and infant Danny in New Orleans and caught up in my position as director of development communications at Tulane University, and I couldn't get away to attend the funeral. Rick asked Frank to play guitar and sing at the ceremony, and Frank made the long car trip to that little town in West Texas, where he met Rick and Mickey Sansom at the local funeral home. In my phone call with Mickey a few years later, he recalled, “I was doing okay until Frank started singing Dylan’s ‘I Shall Be Released’ out at the cemetery, and I lost my shit.” Frank remembers that after the service, Rick and his old friends met at Elwynn’s beauty parlor to share Rod stories under the influence of smoke and alcohol, and the laughter and memories flowed late into the small hours.

Rod’s death was a terrible blow to Rick, far worse than if they’d enjoyed a healthy father-son relationship. Rick had never resolved his love-hate feelings for his old man, and now he never would. An only child growing up at the mercy of a cantankerous alcoholic who rode him hard and criticized him all too often, Rick was finally free from that long shadow. But it left him conflicted, nonetheless. And it must’ve raised a serious, reflective question in his own mind: *What kind of father will I be to my sons?*

HOPE

IN THE SUMMER OF 1991, the Roderick family drove through New Orleans in a hulking, well-used white Dodge Caravan on their way to visit friends and family in Texas. They spent the night with us on Arabella Street in our wonderful old rented home three blocks below the mansions on St. Charles Avenue and the streetcar tracks. I told the Roderick boys that the house was haunted by spirits from a nearby graveyard, and they stayed awake half the night camped on the floor of the living room, waiting to see ghosts.

Across the globe, 1991 was a year of transition, of flux. The Berlin Wall had come down, seventy years of Soviet Communism was quickly dissolving, and the Cold War that had dominated our lives for decades was over. The Gulf War and Operation Desert Storm against Iraq had ended, and the internal Yugoslav ethnic wars were just beginning. Rodney King was beaten by police in Los Angeles, and Michael Jordan and the Chicago Bulls won their first NBA championship and jumpstarted a new dynasty in basketball. Rap music and grunge were dominating the music markets, and Kurt Cobain and Nirvana were gaining popularity. All of our old certainties were being reexamined, and everything was changing. Rick and our two families were looking for stability but preparing ourselves for unsettling transformations on the horizon.

That first evening, Annette and Elaine chose to stay at home and bathe and babysit Taylor, Max, and Danny while I took Rick and the two teenagers, Marshall and Travis, to the French Quarter. The four of us roamed through the crowds on Bourbon Street and ended up shooting pool in one of the bars. Marshall was tall and athletic, outgoing and verbal, and at that point his younger brother resembled their grandmother Elwynn and the Reddell side of the family, short and pleasantly plump and downright reserved around so many nonstop yackers. When he was a toddler, I had nicknamed Travis "Happy Buddha" because of his tubby belly and his smiling, contented disposition, and he still possessed that zen-like tranquility.

As Rick was busy running the pool table, sinking ball after ball, he talked about his political activity at Duke and the strain and complexity of the tenure process. "It's a lot harder than I thought it would be," he said with a weary shrug. But he'd been a very popular teacher at the University of Texas and now Duke, the empirical proof being the Teaching Company's choice of him as the first philosophy professor for the *Great Courses*, and I assumed he was just expressing his usual anxieties. I expected his tenure to be a slam dunk.

With the boys listening curiously to our rambling conversation, Rick confided that his personal life with Elaine was its usual *Sturm und Drang*. But the odd thing was that when they arrived on our doorstep there in New Orleans, they seemed like composed, agreeable parents of one mind, in perfect sync, although exhausted by the long road trip cooped up in a van for twelve hours with four sons on a constant sugar high. Annette and I agreed that Rick and Elaine both appeared happier than we'd seen them in years. I thought they had a future together.

Later that night, after we'd returned from the French Quarter and the boys had settled onto couches and pallets in the living room, Rick asked me what I'd been writing lately. We hadn't seen each other in three or four years, and we were behind in our exchange of publications. I stacked a few literary magazines that contained my latest short stories on the kitchen table, along with the thick manuscript of a novel I'd completed shortly before we'd moved from Aspen to New Orleans. It was entitled "Power and Light," set in Austin in the 1970s, our wildest years together, and the story included a radical-leftist character based on Rick. To my chagrin, I hadn't been able to find an agent or publisher.

It was well past midnight, but Rick said, "Make me a strong cup of coffee, bud. I want to read all of these bad boys and catch up."

I made him a cup of coffee and went to bed, and when I woke up six hours later, he was still sitting at the kitchen table, smoking a cigarette (which we'd asked him to do outside on the patio) and smiling that mythic, world-worn smile. He hadn't gone to bed at all. "Damn, this is good stuff, Tom," he said, turning the last of the manuscript's three hundred and fifty pages. "I don't understand why you can't find a publisher."

"I've come close," I said, shuffling toward the coffee maker, "but no cigar."

The house was quiet. It was a Saturday morning and everyone else was still sleeping. He spent the next hour telling me everything he liked about the short stories and the novel. It was a welcomed salve for my ego. Our mugs filled with strong New Orleans coffee, I sat down at the table spread with loose pages and flicks of cigarette ash and asked him specific questions about the novel's various scenes and characters, what worked and what didn't. He was the perceptive critic he'd always been: incisive, nuanced, suggesting adjustments and tweaks, praising what he liked most, digging deeply into the book's politics and cultural observations, a melodramatic stage actor remembering lines of dialogue that I didn't remember myself. He was encouraging, insisting that I keep trying to get the book published, counseling me one more time what he'd always counseled: "Don't give up, Tom. Don't stop writing. Don't get discouraged. You're going to be appreciated someday. Piss on those people who don't see how good this is. Once you're established, somebody will go back and pick up these earlier books and publish them all."

And that's why Rick Roderick was my best friend. He gave me hope. He believed in me when a lot of other people didn't. And I believed in him.

A couple of hours later, when he and his family were backing out of our driveway to leave for Texas, Rick sideswiped the van's tall side-mirror against a fencepost and shattered the glass. As far as I knew, he hadn't slept a wink the night before, and I was worried he'd fall asleep at the wheel and drive them into a crawfish ditch somewhere around Rayne, Louisiana. He got out of the van, borrowed my wire cutter, snipped off the dangling cables, and threw the mirror into our trashcan. "I never use that damned thing anyway," he said, crawling back onto the driver's seat and waving goodbye. I'm pretty sure the broken side-mirror was some kind of metaphor—*Don't look back!*—or at the very least an omen promising several years of bad luck.

▪ ▪ ▪

When Rick was wrapping up his last semester at Duke in the spring of 1993, Annette, Danny, and I were packing up everything at the haunted house in New Orleans and moving to Atlanta. I'd been a trailing spouse for seven years by that point, following Annette's career in the art world, and she'd been hired to direct the public art program that would gussy up the city of Atlanta for the 1996 Summer Olympics. I was delighted that the relocation would place us within a more reasonable driving distance to the Rodericks in Durham. We could see them more often. Our sons would get to know one another. But then Rick phoned to say he'd lost his appeal for tenure and they were moving to California.

GOIN' TO CALIFORNIA, WHERE THEY SLEEP OUT EVERY NIGHT

IT BAFFLES ME that Rick couldn't land a job teaching philosophy at, say, Badlands State U. or at a small Bible college in Kentucky. Surely there were openings for a magnetic, engaging classroom teacher somewhere in Idaho or Wyoming in 1993. Was the problem that his Duke overlords wouldn't give him a positive letter of recommendation because he'd hurt their feelings? Or did Bemidji State U. and Evergreen State College also not tolerate voices calling for the hiring of more African American professors and the support of campus worker rights? I had taught English and journalism at Diablo Valley College in Pleasant Hill, California, in the mid-1970s, and they were eager to hire classroom superstars like Rick Roderick. Had the academic job market become so tight, Marx's theory of surplus labor so accurate, that Rick couldn't compete for the handful of philosophy openings nationwide that year?

In the final interview in Duke's student newspaper, reporter Katie Crocker wrote that "if students want to protest [Roderick's] departure, they can try to force the administration to reverse their decision. Otherwise, he said he will teach next year at a school in Compton in Los Angeles where he will teach adults who have lost their jobs. He did not speculate as to his future plans after that."[35]

Rick couldn't resist a few tongue-in-cheek jabs at California in his Teaching Company lecture "Marcuse and One-Dimensional Man" (1993) when he said, "I'll be moving shortly out to California where I think they have a new religion a week, a religion-of-the-week club, drive-thru religions. They worship crystals. . . . I have talked about these other forms of pseudo-pagan body worship that America now engages in. I mean, there was no concept that corresponds to the current concept of skinniness. . . . I am a little fat, and in this age, that is a mortal sin. Worse than mortal sin."[36]

The "school in Compton" was National University, whose mothership is located considerably west of Compton in the Hawthorne metro area not far from LAX. The university specializes in adult education and isn't regarded as a top tier institution of higher learning. When Rick was denied tenure, his old friend and dissertation adviser, Doug Kellner, suggested that Rick contact Carl Boggs, a distinguished and influential professor of social sciences and film studies at National who was familiar with Rick's work and willing to take a chance on him.

With four boys to feed and educate, Rick had no choice but to grab his only offer. Los Angeles beckoned. He figured there were benefits to living in the proximity of Kellner at UCLA and our old buddy Jim Bogard, who was toting movie cameras across Hollywood backlots and hanging out with Austin hippie expats who'd been floating around the edges of the Laurel Canyon scene for years.

Regardless of their marital strife, Elaine decided to move to California with the family. She was determined to be involved with raising their four sons, and California also appealed to her creative sensibility and offered better prospects for her budding career as an artist. One of her aging relatives owned a rundown house in Yucaipa, a small town seventy-two miles east of L.A. in a valley nourished by runoff from the San Bernardino Mountains. That's where the Rodericks first settled. Their son Travis told me, "It was a desert climate. I don't know if it technically qualifies as a desert, because there were some patches of vegetation, but during the summer months it would get up to a hundred and fifteen degrees during the day and in the low fifties at night. It was located at the foot of Big Bear mountain, and all of the smog from L.A. would drift over the town and just stay there trapped by the mountains."

He and his brothers didn't find the town very hospitable. "Everyone would kind of give you the stink eye," Travis said, "like they didn't take kindly to strangers. I think the main thing for me was expectations versus reality. As a middle school child, I assumed that moving from a state like North Carolina, where Jesse Helms was the US senator, to California, an infamously liberal state, that things would be very different. It turned out that Durham was a lot more liberal and sophisticated than I had given it credit for."

For Rick, it was a grueling two-hour drive, one way, to National University, but the family was short on money and the rent in Yucaipa was virtually free, the cost of living much cheaper than in the big city, and the public schools were within safe walking distance.

National University wasn't Duke, and Rick found himself teaching sociology classes to adult learners rather than the philosophy courses he'd been teaching to that elite student body in Durham. The contrast was quickly obvious to him, but I never heard him complain about the quality of his students or a need to dumb things down. He sympathized with those students. He'd grown up like them, doing manual labor as a dishwasher and short-order cook, and as he said in *Bury Me Not*, he'd "hauled hay, killed rattlesnakes for fifty cents apiece, washed cars, mowed lawns, fixed tires, and ran the pumps for John McPhail at his gas station." Rick was very familiar with the working poor.

He taught at National University from 1993 to 1996, and by all accounts, he was as popular with those older students as he was at Duke. Carl Boggs told me that Rick's students were impressed with his wide range of knowledge in social sciences and philosophy, and he won them over with his effortless references to novels, movies, current events like the Branch Davidian calamity outside Waco, and pop culture figures like the cartoon characters Beavis and Butthead. Even though Boggs liked Rick and considered him a good friend, he pointed out that Rick "didn't suffer bureaucrats" and won little favor among his colleagues and the administration. "His time at National was conflicted," Boggs said. "He made enemies at the higher level."

What were Rick's offenses? Given his personality and style, his colleagues considered him strident and theatrical and "over the top." "As much as I liked Rick," Boggs told me, "I thought he was often full of shit. Loud but superficial. A lot of sound and fury, and mostly hot air."

As I mentioned earlier, there were a few of my Austin friends who'd felt the same way about Rick. His audacious manner rubbed them the wrong way. They couldn't appreciate his substance for the smoke and mirrors.

"You know Rick. He overdid everything," Doug Kellner said in one of our phone conversations, recalling those years at National.

Kellner also detected signs of burnout. Rick sometimes didn't show up to teach his classes and made lame excuses for his absences. Boggs hinted that Rick's "lack of course structure" meant he wasn't well prepared for every class and was winging it. These were new developments, a change in behavior patterns. At the University of Texas and Duke, Rick had been consistently reliable and professional in his professorial duties.

It's tempting to blame his struggles on the long drive, the brain-numbing L.A. freeway traffic, and the grind. But I suspect he'd also begun to grapple with a more debilitating awareness growing like a tiny bleeding abscess deep in his psyche. As Tom Rollins put it best, "Rick was tired of doing Rick."

And then the strangest thing happened. Rick's *Great Courses* video lectures had captured the attention of a wealthy clinical psychologist and prolific author—let's call him Dr. Steve—who owned a sprawling, idyllic "ranch" about ninety miles north of Los Angeles near the Pacific coastline. He wanted to meet Rick and perhaps collaborate with him on a book. Dr. Steve was a generous man, and he made Rick an offer a dirt-poor West Texas boy couldn't refuse. In exchange for Rick delivering one philosophy lecture a week to the ranch residents and sundry visitors, and with a small stipend thrown in to sweeten the deal, the Roderick family could live gratis in the splendor of that edenic place and eat all the free food they could cook. Dr. Steve offered them a small house on his property, down the hill from the big house where the lectures and counseling took place, and he declared that at his own expense, the boys could choose whatever education that suited them best.

Rick was astounded that anyone—a fan, a financial backer—would be so beneficent. What was the catch? It seemed too good to be true. It was as if he'd stepped back in time to Renaissance Florence and the medieval patronage of the House of Medici.

At that point in his life, the psychologist was in his early sixties and had attained his wealth and status by treating L.A. celebrities and other Angelinos of means, and he'd convinced several parents who were struggling with troubled children to bring them to his ranch, where he would act as their parental surrogate, teacher, and shrink. One of his concepts was that unruly children should be separated from their overbearing parents and placed in a more supportive learning environment, and thus the need for a retreat off in the beautiful surfside hills far away from the temptations of the Sunset Strip and Santa Monica's Third Street Promenade. Parents were allowed to visit their children at the ranch on weekends.

When Rick told me about the setup with "Dr. Steve and the Steverinos," I was as skeptical as you are, cautious reader. I immediately suspected it was a cult like those controlled by Jim Jones, the Reverend Moon, or even Charlie Manson. But Rick was no fool, and he assured me that if he sniffed out the slightest weird kink in the arrangement, he would slap Dr. Steve upside the head and bolt with Elaine and his sons back to the smog and withering orange groves and wild jagged ravines of Yucaipa.

As it turned out, the ranch was simply a vanity project created by Dr. Steve to test some of his theories about human behavior and child rearing, and to secure an audience for his own lectures, which the Roderick boys were required to attend three times a week but never did. They were definitely Rick's sons.

The boys hated "dumb, mean, vaguely criminal" Yucaipa, as Marshall described it, so the ranch was like Shangri-La to them. They could swim in the sparkling pool, play tennis on pristine courts, drive four-wheelers like roaring dirt-bikes all over Dr.

Steve's verdant countryside and magnificent ocean overlooks, and flirt with the teenaged girls living at the compound. There were all-night poker games and softball games every Sunday. Dr. Steve flew them to watch the Los Angeles Dodgers' spring training in Florida, all expenses paid. The boys felt like they'd died and gone to heaven. Education-wise, Marshall decided to attend the public high school at a small nearby town, and Travis was transported by ranch van every couple of weeks to a tutor in faraway Venice Beach to check his homework and discuss the next assignments.

But the word *utopia* means "nowhere," and eventually there was evidence that the Steverino utopia had its share of conflicts, quirks, and suspect motivations. The girls at the ranch would occasionally ask the Roderick boys what they thought of Dr. Steve, and it was clear they were snitches fishing for anti-Steve discord and would report any subversion to their leader. Rick attended a few group therapy sessions with the psychologist and his clients, and when it became obvious that Dr. Steve was pressuring him to reveal the darkest secrets and emotional pain of his childhood, Rick refused to play the game. He would shrug and say, "My family was like a lot of poor households across this country. We were broke. Life was sometimes hard. No big deal." The very last thing he intended to do was share his life story with wealthy Californians who didn't have the slightest clue about what it was like growing up in West Texas in the 1950s and 1960s.

At that juncture in their relationship, Rick and Elaine had been through hell trying to live together, and they'd settled into what might be considered an "open marriage," although I doubt they would've called it that. It was more accurately, "You go your way and I'll go mine." Other romances and relationships were inevitable. Most couples would've agreed to divorce, but there was that inexplicable tie between them, much like the puzzling bond between Rick's incompatible parents who'd remained married but lived apart for decades. Although Rick never expressed this to me, he may have viewed Rod and Elwynn's marriage as an acceptable model for himself and Elaine. In spite of their many separations and the turmoil they both endured, Rick and Elaine stayed married on paper for the rest of his life.

Rick's drive from the ranch to National University in L.A. was even longer than the drive from Yucaipa, so the generous Dr. Steve gave him the use of an apartment in a building he owned in West Los Angeles where an attractive client named Maye resided and ran her own interior design company. Rick's apartment became a respite where he could stay for two or three weeknights while teaching. It provided him hours of relief from the endless freeways. I can imagine his joy at wandering the city streets of West L.A. in the late hours, searching for coffee and a bite to eat with his new friend Maye by his side, free from the obligations and entanglements of the ranch, free from the constant pressure of "Rick doing Rick."

As anyone could've predicted, Rick's relationship with Dr. Steve began to deteriorate after a year or so. They were two alpha males inhabiting the same pen, and when many of the Steverinos began drifting down the hill from the big house to fraternize with popular Rick and his sons at the little house, that didn't sit well with the psychologist. Nor did the fact that he and Rick were making no progress on their proposed book collaboration and Rick was refusing to participate in lectures and counseling sessions and "bonding trips" aboard the sailboat that Dr. Steve prized above all else. As Maye pointed out to me in a conversation after Rick's death, he'd started to resist Steve World because he feared that his family structure was falling apart in that environment, that he was losing control as a husband and father. In his mind, Elaine had abandoned him, emotionally and physically, and the boys were happily ensnared in the trappings of a charmed life with every sweet amenity at their fingertips. Rick felt that his influence was waning over the things that mattered most to him, and Maye sensed him retreating into a darker place. Wounded and despondent, he could think of only one way to soothe his anxieties and his sense of loss. In the summer of

1995, when Dr. Steve and several of his friends and the Steverino inner circle sailed off on a months' long voyage into the Pacific, Rick packed up all their belongings at the ranch and moved with his sons back to that shabby rent house in Yucaipa. Shangri-La was no more.

LIVING IT UP IN THE HOTEL CALIFORNIA

A YEAR LATER, after Rick and his sons returned to Austin for good, he spent long hours recounting to me what had taken place in California, including a curious sidenote—his brush with Hollywood celebrity. As I mentioned earlier, a movie producer named Jonathan Taplin, only a year older than us, discovered the *Great Courses* videotapes while Rick was still teaching at Duke and called him to say how meaningful those lectures had been for Taplin and several of his renowned friends. Rick was flattered to hear there was a buzz about him in certain L.A. circles.

The bearded, bespectacled Taplin had already lived a remarkably full and successful life by his mid-forties, when he contacted Rick. As a whip-smart, politically active Princeton student, Taplin had begun working for the legendary music manager Albert Grossman, and through that apprenticeship he'd eventually become the tour manager for superstars Judy Collins, Bob Dylan, and The Band. The Zelig-like Taplin was involved behind the scenes at several countercultural high-points of the '60s and '70s, including the controversial Newport Folk Festival when Dylan went electric, the music festivals at Woodstock and the Isle of Wight, and the unheralded three-city Transcontinental Pop Festival, which was captured in a documentary film about the Festival Express train trip across Canada with Janis Joplin, Buddy Guy, the Grateful Dead, and The Band in their most unscripted moments. At George Harrison's request, Taplin also served as production manager for the massively complex Concert for Bangladesh.

But after living in the woods near Big Pink for several years and rubbing shoulders with all those music legends, Taplin needed a change of scenery and moved to Los Angeles. He shifted gears into filmmaking, and as I mentioned earlier, he produced such movies as *Mean Streets*, *The Last Waltz*, and *Under Fire*—three films that Rick and I considered among our favorites. By the time Rick met him in person in L.A. in the mid-1990s, Taplin had also spent time as an executive at Merrill Lynch and was transitioning back to film distribution and the brave new world of video-on-demand. Rick couldn't have befriended a more plugged-in figure. Taplin had worked with the most exalted saints and sinners of pop culture in its holiest years, and he knew most of them as friends. When Bob Dylan shows up for your wedding, you have *arrived*.

Rick told me that Taplin had invited him to several dinner parties at his residence in Santa Monica, where he was introduced to Robbie Robertson, Martin Scorsese, Oliver Stone, and other heavyweights. "The thing about all those stars," Rick said to Frank and me one night, "is you expect them to be brilliant conversationalists, as witty as Oscar Wilde and as deep as Bertrand Russell, but they talk about the same old drivel that we talk about."

Jonathan Taplin: music and film producer, author, university professor. *Photo courtesy of Jonathan Taplin*

Taplin's friends and party guests were fans of Rick's videotapes and expected him to launch into long philosophical soliloquies that were both erudite and entertaining, and Rick didn't disappoint them. As we old Austin pals knew, if there was an awkward silence in any conversation, or even a pause for oxygen, Rick would fill that momentary void with concepts, anecdotes, rumors, urban legends, credible and discredited theories, and whatever flashed through his fertile imagination. I'm not sure Oscar Wilde could've kept pace with Rick when he was on a roll.

His interactions at Taplin's parties led to fascinating contacts and some freelance work in the film industry. Most notably, Oliver Stone asked him to read and give him notes on the screenplay for his upcoming movie, *Nixon*. According to Rick, he penned the famous scene of Richard Nixon (played by Anthony Hopkins) staring at a portrait of John F. Kennedy in the White House and musing, "When they look at you, they see what they want to be. When they look at me, they see what they are."

Rick maintained that George Lucas invited him to play Indiana Jones's college professor in a scene in the television series *The Young Indiana Jones Chronicles*, but the series was canceled before that episode could be filmed.

Rick also told me he'd read a pile of other scripts for various producers and directors who were looking for any semblance of philosophical or political seasoning he could sprinkle over their plots. Something to give their storylines a proper *gravitas*.

In those flashbang weeks of hyper media energy, Rick met Jay Levin, the founder and CEO of the alternative *LA Weekly* newspaper, who'd sold his enterprise in 1992 and turned his attention to the exploding galaxy of cable TV in its infancy. Levin had created a progressive cable channel called Planet Central TV and wanted to bring in intellectuals like Rick and his National University colleague Carl Boggs to add substance to the programming. One of the channel's projects was a talk show in which Rick discussed current events and environmental issues with other panelists, often

Rick with actor Edward James Olmos in Los Angeles, 1990s. *Photo courtesy of the Roderick family*

with satirical humor (a precursor of *The Daily Show*), and Marshall recalls his father coming home to Yucaipa late at night, after the long two-hour drive from Santa Monica, with his face still caked with the broadcast makeup he'd worn on the set. Travis remembers seeing the pilot episode on the air, but ultimately Levin's cable channel didn't pan out.

No chivalric adventure is worth its recounting without a beautiful woman as the Holy Grail at the end of the journey. Not long after he'd returned to Austin, Rick disclosed to me that in L.A. he'd become romantically involved with one of the legendary Bond Girls. What could be more celluloid perfect? The log line: A small-town Texas boy, who'd drooled over all those lurid Ian Fleming novels and had watched the James Bond movies in the throes of a hundred sordid teenage male fantasies, bumbles into Hollywood and fulfills his deepest desires with the real-life woman who played Holly Goodhead or Pussy Galore. Take your pick, salacious reader.

When I heard him relate these tales, sitting on his porch like an ancient mariner smoking a pipe in a rocking chair and reminiscing about his long life at sea, I wasn't convinced that the stories were true. Rick was known to exaggerate, but I could usually tell when the facts were curling loose and a finely crafted fiction was underway. And yet every time I doubted one of his Hollywood recollections—not overtly and aloud but with a suspicious smile and a grain of salt rubbing against my skeptical brain tissue—something would emerge out of the blue to give credence to what he'd said.

One day I was standing in a busy grocery line behind my cart and I noticed a photo of Rick's aging Bond Girl (*that* one!) on the cover of *People* magazine. I thumbed to her profile inside the pages and found a passage in which the interviewer asked about her many romances. The actress joked that her love life had been complicated and unusual for many years, and that the last man she'd dated was a philosophy professor with four sons. I bought the copy and drove over to show Rick, and after reading it, he glanced sidelong at me with a mischievous grin, closed his eyes, and inhaled deeply as if reliving the ecstasy of those fragrant nights in the valley of the dolls. "Ahhh, Doubting Thomas," he said, chastising me with a guttural harumph. "Would I ever lie to you?"

I was beginning to realize that everything he told me about his convoluted life in California was true.

Nearly twenty years after Rick's death, I phoned Jonathan Taplin to chat with him about our mutual friend and to examine some of the things Rick had said about his experiences in Los Angeles. At the time of my call, Taplin was in his seventies and a professor at USC's communications school, and he'd recently published a superb memoir entitled *The Magic Years: Scenes from a Rock-and-Roll Life*. He had great respect for Rick's intellect and fond memories of their friendship, and the news of Rick's early death had greatly saddened him. "He was an unsung genius," Taplin said, "a unique mind." But he felt that "the political game had escaped Rick," that knack for appeasing university administrators and academic critics, and it had cost him dearly. We talked briefly about Rick getting his toes wet in Hollywood among the moguls and dealmakers and coked-up pitch men, and Taplin was doubtful that those things had been a productive use of Rick's time. "He was a philosopher first and foremost, not a glitzy celebrity," he said, "and he should've kept going with his teaching and lecturing."

Jonathan Taplin was intimately familiar with the vicissitudes of fame and fortune in pop culture and its quicksilver allure, and when all was said and done, Rick wouldn't have disagreed with him. He knew that the Hotel California wasn't such a lovely place after all. Certainly not such a lovely place for him.

MOVING ON

THE RODERICK BOYS were unhappy about their return to Yucaipa. As Marshall observed, "Like most of California, the place was beautiful and filled with absolutely awful people." It was a strange little town. "The classier ex-Hells Angels went to Yucaipa. The others went to San Bernardino. A lot of people had garage sales every weekend, which was weird, as if they were selling bric-a-brac back and forth to each other. There was nothing to do in the town. I got arrested once because Travis and I were playing basketball on an outside court late at night. The cops really didn't want to let me go because they were sure I was on meth, because so many people there were on meth." He remembered it as a dead-end town full of high school dropouts. "There were some cool people at school, but by then I knew better than to try to make friends since we moved so often."

To make matters worse, the rent house was in need of serious repair. The old-fashioned floor heater spewed oily black smoke, irritating their lungs and staining the walls with soot, and tarantulas and black widows were creeping around the house and yard. According to the boys, vicious feral dogs roamed the ravines out back of their property, killing people's domestic cats and scattering their bloody entrails all over the neighborhood. Life in Yucaipa was a far cry from the mellow ambience and pristine landscaping at Dr. Steve's ranch.

Elaine chose to stay behind and bartend in a city near the ranch, possibly because of a romantic relationship, but she promised to drive to Yucaipa and see the boys one weekend per month. Her absence caused Rick a great deal of distress. He yearned for unity, for wholeness, for a life in which parents and their children lived at the same address.

To complicate things, Rick's girlfriend Maye was madly in love with him and made every effort to keep their relationship vital and intact. But she'd been battling chronic fatigue syndrome while trying to manage her interior design company, and the distance between her apartment in West L.A. and Yucaipa was a problem for her. Although she'd attended one of Jonathan Taplin's dinner parties with Rick, she was unaware of the Bond Girl and the extent of Rick's film and TV projects. He was adept at compartmentalizing his life into a skillfully designed maze, and he seemed to enjoy the game of making those shady paths separate and untraversable. To protect his various intrigues, the secrets and misdirections were essential.

When I spoke with Maye nearly two decades after Rick's death, she was living in the same West L.A. apartment building and still the same warm, friendly, generous person I'd come to know. In our phone conversation, she talked about those final upsetting days in Southern California. Rick had made it clear to her that he was still obsessing over his loss of Elaine and he would never get over her. "This thing with Elaine is going to kill me," he said. "I'm wearing out." Hearing that honest confession, Maye realized she couldn't measure up to Elaine, or at least to the idealized version of Elaine in Rick's head.

Maye felt there were two sides to Rick: the suave persona he showed to women and the darker, more authentic side he showed to his male friends. I suspect that most men are the same way. It's a matter of degree. But aren't women like that as well? Don't we all present the most polished version of ourselves to those we are trying to attract?

Rick told her stories about his tough upbringing and his penchant for violence as a boy and young man, and it deeply disturbed her. When she recounted those stories to me, I was certain he'd made them up. They sounded more like the ghost stories children tell around a campfire at night. I can imagine my bullshitting Texas friend having fun scaring a naïve California surfer girl with tall tales under a Malibu moon. But the real test of veracity was that he'd never told those yarns to us Texas pals. He understood his audiences.

"He owned a *gun*!" Maye exclaimed over the phone, something that didn't cause the slightest blip on my Texan radar. I'd seen Rick's flimsy .22 Saturday Night Special, its broken grip held together with duct tape. I'm not sure he could've dented a soup can with that little thing.

But one evening while they were having a long-distance phone conversation, Rick mentioned that the pistol was within easy reach and he was in such a deep chasm of depression and despair, he was considering taking his own life. Maye freaked out, hung up, and called the Yucaipa police to request a wellness check. In her understanding of what followed, four police officers showed up at Rick's house to investigate if he was endangering anyone. They asked if he needed mental health counseling.

By that point, Marshall had gone away to college at the University of Texas at El Paso, and high schooler Travis was in charge of the household and the two younger boys, ensuring they were well fed and going to school on time while Rick was hours away in Los Angeles. When I asked Travis about that incident in which the police showed up at the door, he was confident it hadn't happened. He surmised that his dad had given Maye the false impression that a dangerous, melodramatic scene had transpired with the police in order to dissuade her from making that kind of emergency call again.

I spoke with Rick by phone that summer, telling him that Annette, Danny, and I were moving back to Austin in August, the day after the closing ceremony of the 1996 Summer Olympics in Atlanta. He said he'd been considering moving back too, and we were both elated by the possibility of living in our favorite town again after so many years apart.

Travis recalled that the final decision happened quickly. Rick walked into the house one evening after the long drive from L.A. and said, "You guys hate it here and I hate it here. Let's move back to Austin."

Our mutual friend Paul Foreman, an ex-cop turned poet, small press publisher, and gold prospector, phoned Rick to tell him he'd found a great rent house for him and the boys across the street from Ramsey Park in the quaint Rosedale neighborhood of Austin. Rick fondly remembered Ramsey's swimming pool from those peaceful days when he and Elaine took young Marshall and Travis swimming there back in the late '70s and early '80s. Rick could visualize what he'd been missing for too long: a snug house, a park and pool, his old friends gathering again. He and his sons hadn't been living it up in the Hotel California, and now, as the Eagles song suggested, Rick was running for the door. It was time to drop off the key at the front desk and head on home.

RODERINGO

THE YEAR 1996 was a momentous time for our family. In early August, Annette had completed her three-year stint as visual arts producer for the Atlanta Olympics. She'd worked with artist Siah Armajani to design and construct the tower that held the Olympic cauldron, which was lit at the opening ceremony by an ailing Muhammed Ali carrying the torch. When a right-wing extremist bombed Centennial Olympic Park, killing one person and injuring more than a hundred, Annette had left the arts festival in the park and was on her way home when the pipe bomb went off in an abandoned backpack.

It was the year that Tupac Shakur was murdered in Las Vegas, and a fundamentalist group called the Taliban captured Kabul. Rupert Murdoch launched Fox News, and Hotmail was created as a web-based email service you could access from your computer. President Bill Clinton was running for a second term, and his Republican opponent was Kansas Senator Bob Dole, an army veteran seriously wounded in World War Two.

Annette and I put a down payment on a brick ranchstyle home in Austin's North Shoal Creek neighborhood, a block from Pillow Elementary School, where Danny began the second grade. Our place was only a mile from West Anderson Lane and even closer to Burnet Road, two schlocky commercial boulevards lined with junk food drive-thrus, auto parts stores and repair garages, ratty storage units hiding who-knows-what in blue barrels, and an occasional windowless lounge whose patrons were undernourished barflies prone to polyester and Wild Root Cream Oil. Decades later, the neighborhood is overrun with tall expensive condos, hipster coffee houses, and trendy bistros. Home values have quintupled. Austin has gone from a cool countercultural hideaway to a glitzy superstar destination.

Once our furniture arrived and we settled into those dog days of August, I tracked down Rick at their rent house across the street from Ramsey Park, a ten-minute drive from our new home. I reminded Danny that he'd met the Rodericks in New Orleans about five years earlier, but he had only a vague recollection of their visit. He was turning eight years old when we drove over to reconnect with my old friend and his sons, and Danny's first impressions of them remained so vivid that he wrote about them in a paper entitled "Ringo Rick Ringo Roderingo!" he composed for a class assignment when he was in middle school several years later:

> Around second grade I could easily be brainwashed by commercials and told what to think by television. I didn't have many friends, and grades dominated my priorities. All of that changed, though, thanks to three of my friends: Max, Taylor, and Rick Roderick.
>
> I remember a long time ago one summer, I was going to one of my dad's old friend from college's house, as I often had to in Austin. My parents knew half of the people in Austin! This particular friend called himself Rick. I was assured that he had children, and based on examples of other friends' children, I thought they would be rich, bratty, and boorish. When we got there, I could already see I might be wrong. The house had an overgrown lawn up to the knees and a beat-up old pickup sat in the barely distinguishable gravel driveway. A bent-over tree shaded the porch, but it showered down its evergreen needles if barely touched. A forest of obviously neglected bamboo coming from the backyard towered over the cloudy gray bungalow. We (my dad Tom and I) trudged carefully on the barely visible walkway.

When my dad and I opened the door after several unanswered knocks, I felt a hot, stuffy, and all-consuming wall of smoke hit me in the face. I soon smelled it too—whoever lived here smoked at least a pack a day. The inside of the house was shaded unusually darkly due to the smoke. Then I saw him. Lying on the couch with a cigarette in hand, an overweight man with a grizzly beard acted as the centerpiece for the room—obviously Rick, my dad's old friend.

"Ringo, Rick Ringo, Roderingo!" my dad yelled out surprisingly enthusiastically.

Rick's face lit up. "Tomski!" he yelled back in a gravelly voice.

Dad introduced me, and I shook Rick's hand. I then hurried deeper into the house, looking for the children. If they were anything like their father, I couldn't wait to meet them.

I saw them in their room, playing on some sort of game system never seen before by me. There were three of them—two who looked around my age and one who looked like he might be in college. One of the ones that looked my age was a little tubby. I walked into the room as timidly as a mouse, my shoes entirely silent on the wooden floor.

They all turned to look at me at the same time.

The skinnier little one spoke first. "Hello. My name's Taylor. You're Tom's son, right?"

"Umm . . ." I had a frog in my throat. "Uh, yes. My name is Danny. Hello."

They seemed to loosen up.

"Hi. I'm Travis. Nice to meet you," the oldest one said, grinning.

"Hello. . . . Max," the tubby one declared matter-of-factly.

I already felt a little attached to them. They all seemed to exude their own personality very distinctly. Over the day, while dad and Rick caught up with each other, I found out that they all had very unique and very funny senses of humor.

I also found out Rick was a philosophy professor, and I listened and took example from him often.

Ever since that day I would make it a point to visit them as much as possible and they gradually rubbed off on me and I became more and more like them. I didn't see Travis as much so he didn't rub off quite as much as Max and Taylor, who became my best friends.

I believe that someone is formed fifty percent by genes and fifty percent by the people around them. So, ultimately through osmosis, I absorbed their personalities and projected it slightly on myself. In effect, they've really formed who I am today, which at least in my opinion not only changed my life but also directed it away from disaster. If it weren't for them, who knows what I'd be?

Danny captured the scene perfectly, the "cloudy gray bungalow" and bamboo jungle in the backyard, the beat-to-hell Toyota pickup out front, the dense, overwhelming cigarette smog in rooms sealed tight against the Texas heat. Rick and I were very happy to see each other. That silly string of nicknames was our old greeting ritual, and like most of our interactions, it made no sense and we couldn't remember how it got started.

Rising from the couch, Rick was tan and *husky*, as my mother would've described him, but not as heavy as he'd been in earlier years, certainly not obese. I noticed gray in his beard for the first time, now that he was in his late forties, and it seemed to me that his teeth had spread with small even gaps between them, as if his head and attached jaws had expanded with age. Perhaps, I thought humorously, because his formidable brain was carrying much more knowledge and woe.

But the greatest surprise was seeing the transformation of Travis, now a senior in high school and a handsome, muscular young man who looked as if he'd been working out every day in a gym. He was no longer the chubby, awkward thirteen-year-old who'd visited us in New Orleans. His dark hair was buzzed to a half inch, a haircut we'd called a burr in the 1950s, but it wasn't a redneck bully burr but a punkish hipster look, the Clash meets Bertolt Brecht. His voice had deepened, and he was as articulate as a librarian.

How could I ever forget his birth? When the bartender announced that Rick Roderick had a phone call, he and I and a classical-pianist friend named Jacquie Helin were drinking pitchers of Wild Turkey at the Guadalupe Bar a couple of blocks from the University of Texas campus, listening to my brother Frank and his sideman, the East Side Flash, play the blues at their weekly gig. It was Elaine calling to tell Rick that her water broke and she was driving herself to the hospital. Like everyone at our table, Rick had imbibed a little too much straight whiskey, but he rushed off in his pale yellow VW Beetle in such a panic that when he arrived at the hospital, he was experiencing tachycardia, that rapid heartbeat, and he was placed on a gurney and wheeled into the ER. His gurney passed Elaine's gurney in the corridor, and Elaine said, "Hi, Rick." He said, "Hi, Elaine," and off they went in different directions. In the end, Rick's medical bill was higher than hers.

When Travis showed me around the rent house, it was touching to find that his small narrow bedroom was adorned with Buddha images—statues, candles, an incense holder, Buddha pictures of every sort. "People have been giving me Buddha stuff since I was a little kid," he said, "because for some reason, they used to call me 'Happy Buddha'."

"I remember," I said as I stared at his collection. I was the one who'd given him that nickname.

Because Elaine remained in California and Marshall was in college in El Paso, Travis continued to act as first mate of the Roderick whaler, tending to many of the grocery and cooking chores, tackling home repairs and yard maintenance, overseeing his younger brothers' schoolwork, settling minor disputes, encouraging physical exercise in the park, driving kids to video game arcades, and performing all other duties relinquished happily by Rick, who was

Max Roderick, Taylor Roderick, Danny Zigal, late 1990s. *Photo courtesy of Thomas Zigal*

relieved to resign his captainship and turn matters over to a younger and more energetic steward. Annette and I quickly discovered that if we wanted to schedule playtimes or a sleepover with Danny and the two younger boys, Travis was the one to contact and arrange details. He was in charge. An exhausted Rick appeared to be recuperating in a hammock on the poop deck of the Roderick Pequod after eleven years of chasing that white whale around Durham and Southern California.

Our first five months back in Austin were exuberant. The Rodericks and the Carlozzigals (a combo of Annette's surname and mine) got together often for meals and traipsed back and forth between homes as if we were one family. Rick and his sons were savvy about computers and the uncharted continent called the World Wide Web, and they counseled us to buy a Mac so Danny and the boys could play those early simple computer games in my study and make artwork graphics that our new printer produced in Fauvist colors.

Ever since Rick had purchased an Apple II at the end of the 1970s to use for writing his dissertation, he'd been fascinated by computer technology and its possibilities. He showed me how to search the Web for references to my name and publications, an exercise that enchanted me as if I were learning a crafty magic trick, and he explained that something called email was taking shape in the ether like a spreading nebula cloud. Soon we'd all be able to send messages to one another without paper, envelopes, and stamps. I considered Rick a conjurer in this mysterious new alchemy, and I was eager to learn every secret he knew.

The only downside to those early intense months of family friendship was that the seven of us ate too many long meals together at restaurants on way too many evenings. Sometime around Thanksgiving, Rick, Annette, and I decided we were overspending at the fine cafés of Austin and needed to slow down, cook more at home, and manage our budgets better. Our exuberant fraternity was causing us to go broke.

As I mentioned earlier, Annette had never been an adherent of the Rick mythos. Although she'd known him for sixteen years at that point, she'd always kept her distance. "My own deep-seated feminism made me skeptical of getting too close to him," she admitted. "There's a type of man of our generation who speaks like he's 'enlightened' with regard to feminism but whose ego is so grand, even narcissistic, that there's no space for the women around them. Rick was like that. Strong women know to give those men a wide berth."

But observing him in such a vulnerable state after his return to Austin—a single father struggling to keep his household together through hard economic times—she began to soften toward him. The stakes were higher now that he had four dependent children. She and I agreed that he needed our help.

"Rick was the patriarch of the family, and his sons revolved around him. He was lenient in lots of ways and really loved them. They each had their own personalities, and all were smart and self-reliant. Because you and I parented in a different way from Rick (needless to say!), I often behaved maternally to the kids."

Because our son was new to the city and didn't know anyone his age yet, she felt it was important to nurture Danny's friendship with Max and Taylor. "Danny was the fifth brother and the littlest one. Smart and funny, too. Also in awe of Rick," she said.

Her role as mother figure for the two youngest Roderick boys wasn't an easy fit. She was accustomed to parenting an only child, a sweet strawberry-blond boy who wore rimless glasses like a wizard prodigy out of a Harry Potter story. Even at eight years old, he had an acerbic wit and a precocious sense of humor and irony. He spent a lot of quiet time reading books and absorbing what was in front of him on glowing screens. By contrast, Max and Taylor were loud, quickly combative, and often in need of a bath. They didn't pick up after themselves and left a shrapnel of toys and soda cans and discarded clothes wherever they roamed. They weren't very polite to adults. When they were playing video games, Taylor took wicked delight in teasing his younger brother, the brooding Max, until he exploded and chased Taylor around the house in a screaming fury that led to brawls. Annette was surprised by such behavior and didn't know how to cope with the physical violence of boys being boys, but Rick and I had no trouble stopping their nonsense.

Years later, Annette said, "Rick and the boys' friendship was hugely impactful on Danny's ways of thinking. I sometimes objected to it, worrying that it would 'turn him into a Roderick,' but you [Tom] were more tolerant."

It may have appeared to the casual observer that I was totally absorbed in my hours-long conversations with Rick in his small living room or out on the front porch, but I always kept one eye on where Danny was at all times and what he was doing. And while I've described him as precocious and cerebral, he was no pushover and knew how to handle himself in a fistfight. So I wasn't worried about him hanging out with the slightly older Roderick boys because I felt it was time for him to get a little tougher and more independent from his parents, and I saw that Taylor and Max were going to treat him like a little brother and protect him from harm.

The three of them usually spent hours glued to video games in the boys' bedroom, but Rick would sometimes give them folding money, kick them out of the house, and tell them to go get some fresh air. So they began to explore Ramsey Park and the neighborhood, rounding up their schoolmates Owen, Willie, and Arend, who all lived nearby, and marauding the streets like a gang of Dickensian pickpockets. Sometimes they swarmed through the new Central Market a few blocks away to devour all the sample foods until the store manager banished them permanently from the premises. In the warm months, when the Ramsey pool was open, they dominated the deep end with rowdy swim games like "Sharks and Minnows," and when those violet evenings turned dark, they played "black ops" in the pitch-black park, crawling on their bellies, hiding against trees, avoiding the spotlight from a park ranger vehicle sweeping the grounds after the ten p.m. curfew.

As the youngest in that pack of scoundrels, Danny was a follower, not a leader, and when the day was over, he always recounted his adventures to his mother and me with an ironist's remove, entertained by the absurdity of everyone's behavior. We made him promise not to shoplift or destroy anything of value and to cross those busy streets using crosswalks at the stoplights. Rick had a more effective approach. He told the boys he wouldn't bail them out of juvie if they got arrested.

BRAVE NEW WORLD

IT DIDN'T TAKE RICK very long to expand his computer excursions into what would eventually be called the Internet. First he discovered the royal realm of online chess, and he worked his way up the rating ladder to a very high level of competition. During the games, he would use the message function to talk trash to his opponents, often some innocent player from Latvia or Senegal, and when Rick won, which was more often than not, he would send a short insulting message to the losers, questioning their skills. He was just psyching them out, of course, and he thought it was all in good fun, but the opponent would sometimes become upset and reply in broken English: "Why you are saying bad messages to my personage?" It wouldn't have surprised me if the Internet chess world banned Rick for life.

He also discovered a shadowy new world called online dating and showed me his computer portfolio of naked women and their soap opera poems declaring their love for him and only him. I was astonished that ordinary women would post nude photos and expose themselves to that skeevy game. I often questioned the veracity of the profiles. "Aren't these pictures from prisoners and male sex offenders messing with you?" I asked him. And when he actually started to "date" real women, I was even more astounded. He admitted that most of his early efforts were disappointing. He'd meet them in cafés, bars, and coffeehouses, and if they didn't look like their flattering photos, he'd walk out on them. He was brutally honest about his expectations, and I can imagine there were hurt feelings. I felt sorry for those desperate women and their reckless search for true romance. One of them drove all the way from Florida with her two dogs and camped out in her car on the street in front of Rick's house.

"Who is that woman in the car?" I asked him one day when I went over to visit. She looked deranged and homeless.

"She's insane and I can't make her go away," he said.

Because of incidents like that and the occasional sleazy visitor to their place, including someone eventually imprisoned for child pornography and sex with an underaged girl, Annette and I worried that something disturbing would happen when Danny was there without us. I made Rick promise to call me at my UT office if anything strange was going down. I assured him I could drive from my campus parking garage to his house in ten minutes and retrieve my son if the situation called for it.

"Don't worry about Danny," Rick insisted. "He's perfectly safe here. We all look after him."

He thought I was overprotective; I thought he was sometimes careless, oblivious. We never resolved that difference.

THE BILL HICKS OF PHILOSOPHY

AT THEIR CORE, Rick and his sons were as frugal as Depression-era farmers living through a drought, but the money he'd saved from his teaching career soon dwindled and he needed income. I was a speechwriter for the president of UT Austin and Annette was the curator of contemporary art for the university's art museum, so we both knew when campus positions were becoming available and might be compatible with Rick's talents: listings for editors, academic advisers, creative thinkers for departmental communications teams, etc. After I showed him a few of the postings and offered to arrange interviews, he spoke to me in confidence: "I appreciate what you're doing for me, Tom, but I can't do these kinds of eight-to-five jobs. I can't keep up with daily routines."

He explained that his sleep patterns were too erratic, his health too precarious. He had no stomach to become a "wage slave" and no psychological disposition for what he considered the spirit-killing drudgery of everyday work. "I'm a college teacher," he said. "In and out a few hours a week. Summers off, unless I'm desperate for money. I know I've been spoiled, but that's the life I signed up for. I've gotta find a teaching gig."

He called on the aging professors in the UT philosophy department who'd stayed in touch with him, and they suggested he apply to teach freshman seminars newly created by the provost's office.

As I was writing this chapter, I remembered that something had gone wrong between Rick and the philosophy department when they'd hired him to teach a freshman seminar for only one year and didn't renew his contract. I exchanged emails with the professor who'd been the chairman of the department at that time to ask him what had happened. He said the problem had been twofold. First, he'd been wrestling with the provost for control of who would select the teachers for the freshman seminars in philosophy, and he didn't want to be muscled into hiring Rick. "I may have agreed to [approve Rick's appointment] for one year because of a time crunch but I made it clear I wouldn't approve him beyond that." He felt that "*departments* ought to be selecting their faculty and their course offerings, not some administrative unit independent of them."

My old friend and colleague Dave Oliphant was the coordinator of those freshman seminars for the provost's office, and he said he wasn't aware of any struggle with the departments. He disputed the assertion that he and the provost's office were making heavy-handed decisions on who would teach which courses. "The professors that I worked with chose to teach the seminars themselves," Oliphant wrote to me in an email. "They were not selected by our office, and no one forced them to teach for the seminars program."

The former philosophy chairman recalled that there was a second reason he terminated Rick's appointment after one year, and in my view, it was the more revealing motive. He told me that at the time, his department was in the midst of a female grad student's federal lawsuit alleging sexual harassment and retaliation, and the department couldn't risk the slightest hint of systemic improprieties. As he put it, "Rick had a reputation—whether it had any factual basis, I don't know—for questionable behavior toward female students. The last thing the department needed, in the midst of that legal process, was one more thing the plaintiff could use as evidence of the department's [negative] environment for women students."

Those rumors of "questionable behavior" were unsubstantiated. There were no formal complaints by female students against Rick at Duke or when he'd taught at UT as a lecturer in the early 1980s.

However, when he was teaching that freshman seminar for the philosophy department in the late 1990s, an office assistant complained that Rick had addressed her as "hun" (short for "honey") one day when he rushed in to ask her to photocopy a few pages for a class hand-out. In explaining his use of the word, he couldn't convince her or her supervisors that it wasn't a sexist insult but a sweet old Texas expression of friendship and endearment. They had no idea what he was talking about. None of them had ever been served by a country waitress at a mom-and-pop café in Buffalo Gap, Texas, in the 1950s. Or by my mother, who called everyone "hun" when she was a waitress. Regardless of the cultural dissonance, once again Rick had managed to raise the ire of decision-makers in the power structure. He was Kryptonite to self-righteous moralists.

Fortunately for Rick, his friends often bailed him out. Dave Oliphant worked for our old pal Ricardo Romo, who had become the vice provost in charge of the university's freshman seminars. Dave was an accomplished poet, Spanish translator, and jazz scholar, and Ricardo was a distinguished history professor who'd moved up the ranks in the university's administration. They'd known Rick since the 1980s and appreciated his humor, intelligence, and rabid dedication to Longhorn sports. They were also aware that Rick had earned international praise for his *Great Courses* videotapes and was beloved by his students. When the philosophy department refused to renew Rick's contract after that first year, Ricardo persuaded the sociology department to sponsor him instead.

A well-known philosophy professor and I often had lunch together at a barbecue place near campus, and one day he said to me, "Tell Rick he has enemies in the philosophy department. Tell him to take"—he named a professor—"off his list of references. That guy's recommendation letter is negative and damaging."

I told Rick immediately, and he deleted the professor as a reference.

Rick taught two freshman seminars in the fall semesters from 1997 to 2000, introducing his students to courses he titled "Philosophy and Human Values (Plato, John Stuart Mill, Kant, Kierkegaard, Nietzsche, and Freud)" and "Philosophy and the Quest for Certainty (Descartes, Hume, Kant, Hegel, and Marx)." In 2000 he taught a seminar he labeled "Social Theory and Human Values (Mill, Marx, Nietzsche, and Freud)." As usual, his students adored him (including President George W. Bush's daughter, Jenna Bush), and he received the highest student evaluations of any of the freshman seminar lecturers.

He still had it—that exceptional classroom skill, an ability to entertain, educate, and challenge young minds all at the same time. His videotape devotees around the country began to refer to him as "the Bill Hicks of Philosophy," a reference to a remarkable comedian from Texas who mixed his stand-up performances with social issues, politics, and religion—a crisscross between Lenny Bruce, Richard Pryor, and George Carlin. Rick was doing Rick, and it was working again. Being back home in Austin among renegade Texans and his old hippie circle, teaching on the campus that roused memories of his early intellectual stirrings and young love, seemed to invigorate him in the classroom. He was hitting his stride the way he had at Duke. Clusters of students wanted to meet with him over coffee in the student union. Several of the Longhorn football players liked his courses so much they invited him to be a guest coach and amble around the sideline at a game in Darrell K Royal-Texas Memorial Stadium. Even the skeptical Annette had an experience with Rick that demonstrated his value as an analyst and repository of knowledge. She wrote to me in an email:

> I had an interesting visit with Rick in 1999 as I was working on my "Negotiating Small Truths" exhibition for the university's art museum. I was reading a lot of critical theory for the first time as part of a seminar I was participating in with the leading European critical art theorist/curator we brought from Paris to Austin over six months for several sessions. I had questions about the Germans, specifically the Frankfurt School thinkers and their ideas on esthetics. Rick and I had a great conversation. I admitted it was new to me, and he was an expert, but I had grasped all the subtleties and he pointed

> out ways in which my thinking about my exhibition drew from Frankfurt School ideas and also the writings of Cornel West, with whom I share an affinity, I guess, because I hadn't read him yet. I felt like Rick finally got to see the real me—the smart me—and I appreciated his advice and direction. After that, interactions with Rick were easier for me.

I continued to visit him at their home three or four times a week, often at the end of my workday at UT, when I enjoyed his company and Danny played video games with Taylor and Max. My conversations with Rick weren't always harmonious. We sometimes disagreed with each other, and the arguments could become heated. Rick despised President Bill Clinton for the Republican-coerced welfare reforms he signed into law late in the election season of 1996, and although I concurred with Rick that the new draconian measures would be devastating to poor people, single mothers, and people of color, I still supported Clinton for reelection. I wasn't going to waste my vote on a socialist or Green Party candidate like Ralph Nader. We never resolved our conflict over Bill Clinton. Rick accused me of capitulating, and I accused him of living in fantasy land. It wouldn't be the last time we locked horns over an issue or idea.

On our better days, we turned to more amenable concerns. I would sometimes explain a snag I'd run into while working on a novel and I needed a good sounding board. He was the razor-sharp reader and strategist he'd always been, listening attentively and offering options I should consider. Our method of brainstorming sometimes sounded like a police interrogation, with Rick pacing back and forth in front of his couch as he dragged on a cigarette, lost in thought.

Me: "What would the sheriff and his deputies do to a bear that had broken into a restaurant kitchen? Anesthetize it?"

Rick: "One of them would panic and shoot it dead."

Me: "Why would a wealthy New Orleans coffee baron go to such an extent to hide what happened?"

Rick: "Because the idea of spending even a single minute in the parish jail was a revolting proposition for a man of his economic class."

I found it exhilarating to be tackling a plot problem with my trusted old friend. Somewhere in our rambling exercise of give and take, back and forth, I would hear the perfect solution. We'd work through it, and I would finally have my answer. The bear. The coffee baron. Rick was delighted that I'd involved him in the puzzling out of my fictions. Whenever I declared, "Yes, that's it!" we would laugh and high-five, as proud and full of ourselves as if we were Watson and Crick deciphering the double helix. And at those moments, as his cigarette smoke settled over our ruminations, we could hear our boys cheering and laughing and jamming away in their own make-believe world in another room. Life was good. We were all euphoric together under the same roof. How could it get any better than that?

SOMETIMES I FEEL LIKE A MOTHERLESS CHILD

WHEN RICK'S MOTHER DIED in an Abilene nursing home in February 1997 at age seventy-nine, six months after he and his sons had moved back to Austin, Elwynn's doddering siblings buried her the next day in the Tuscola cemetery before telling her son she'd passed away. He was upset that he'd missed the funeral, of course, but he'd never been close to the Reddell side of the family, primarily because his aunt and uncles disliked Rod and all things Roderick. The distance had widened when the siblings sold the family home (Granny's house) that Elwynn had been living in for decades and forced her to move into her small, cramped beauty parlor, the converted Model T garage. Rick felt that their callous disregard for his feelings was revenge for his mother leaving the beauty parlor to him. There was no love lost between Elwynn's siblings and her only child. He eventually sold that little parlor for the price of a used car.

As rude and hurtful as the Reddells' manipulations had been, they were nothing compared to that ancient and heaviest of burdens. His mother was dead and a final reckoning had come. He had to face those suppressed emotions and regrets and disappointments and cringeworthy childhood memories that many of us experience when a parent dies. In Rick's case, he had to reconcile his feelings toward an absent mother who loved him very much but who'd shrunk away as the years wore on.

Her death marked a change in him. His grief diminished the joy and robust energy he'd shown when we were renewing our friendship only a few months earlier. He began to hunker on his couch for many hours at a time, drinking glass after tall glass of over-sweetened iced tea, smoking three-and-a-half packs of cigarettes a day, and dozing off between reading and watching TV and noodling around on his computer. It became harder for me to find him awake and engage him in conversations. He often appeared druggy and slow to respond, and I figured it was because he was taking medications for arrhythmia, tachycardia, and joint inflammation. What I didn't know was that he'd started seeing a shrink for anxiety and depression, and the shrink had prescribed Ativan and Diazepam. I don't know why Rick didn't disclose that to me, because we usually spilled our guts to each other, and there were very few private matters we didn't discuss. The only thing I knew was that he'd stopped drinking alcohol because it clashed with his medications, but that was an understandable decision.

In retrospect, I think it must've been our therapist friend Tom Burditt who referred Rick to a psychiatrist. Burditt couldn't prescribe meds, but he often referred his clients to shrinks and other physicians when he determined that the situation called for it. Which would explain why I sometimes overheard him and Rick quietly discussing medications like two drug dealers slyly exchanging information over a buy. Benign and generous to his friends, Burditt was no doubt checking to make sure that Rick was getting the proper medical advice and pharmaceutical help he needed to cope with his depression and other health issues.

A decade earlier, Burditt had recommended a very likable and sympathetic general practitioner to Rick and me—let's call him Dr. Greene—who'd been especially patient in his treatment of crabby Rod when he was living in an Austin nursing home. Back in town after a long absence, Rick and I had returned to Dr. Greene's care, but a few months after Elwynn's death, Rick lost faith in the good doctor's treatment of his various illnesses. The pain in his knees, lower back, and other joints was increasing, and his stress level and anxieties were mounting. On one visit, Rick insisted that he needed stronger pain medication, and Dr. Greene said, "Rick, I'm the doctor here. You need to listen to what I'm advising. We have to monitor all your meds and balance them carefully or you'll experience serious, harmful effects."

A couple of weeks later, Rick was in excruciating pain and drove to Dr. Greene's office without an appointment and caused a scene with the assistants at the front desk, demanding that the doctor see him right away. That was impossible, they told him, given the full waiting room and standard procedures. Rick became aggressive and disruptive, and the assistants threatened to call security. They reported to Dr. Greene that Rick had also insulted them persistently on the phone. The next day, the staff held a meeting in which they strongly recommended that Rick Roderick be fired as a patient.

On my next visit with Dr. Greene, he confided, "It was out of my hands, Tom. The staff voted to blackball him, and unless I wanted a full-scale rebellion and a walkout, I had to honor their decision."

I sighed and shook my head sadly. He looked concerned.

"The thing is, I like Rick," he said. "I enjoy our conversations and his humor. I want to treat him. But I have to listen to my staff. He gets very angry and sometimes out of control, and he scares them. So he isn't welcome here anymore."

Rick didn't tell me about the incident and his ouster. I think he was too embarrassed. I heard about it from Tom Burditt and then Dr. Greene himself.

Rick's banishment left him with no choice but to find a community clinic, which was all he could afford. Fortunately, there was a clinic only two blocks from his house. As I recall, he saw a new doctor every time he visited them. There was no consistency or continuity, he soon realized, no care from a physician who'd treated him for years and knew his personality and medical history. The clinicians were young and inexperienced, and he was unhappy about their indifferent demeanor and unwillingness to grant his medication requests. I don't think Rick ever found another physician with as much wisdom and expertise and the same warmth and sympathy as Dr. Greene.

Joan Muller Burditt believed that Rick's problems ran deeper than his physical ailments. She thought he'd lost something essential to his psyche. I remember sitting at a small table on Rick's front porch and listening to the two of them argue. I knew that Rick was teasing her with a straight face and his faux professorial manner, as he often did, but Joan wasn't amused. "When he returned to Austin in the late 1990s, he'd lost that sense of hope he'd always had," she wrote to me in an email. "He was bitter, hardened, caustic. He criticized me for living in Tarrytown with a swimming pool. I felt shut out."

The years were piling up on him, the struggles and disappointments, the losses and heartbreak, the dreams that had dissolved in the harsh light of day. The minor victories were fewer and farther between.

And yet even in the grip of poor health and flagging spirits, he saved a small reserve of energy for teaching the UT freshman seminars, and at some point he added classes at Austin Community College (ACC), driving that beat-up red Toyota pickup to classroom locations spread all over town. Aching and exhausted, he dragged his suffering bones down those long cold corridors of academe like a yoked Jeremiah roaming the desert lands of Judea with a heavy burning heart. But once he shuffled into a classroom and collected himself behind the podium, he blazed as bright as a wheel of fire and dazzled his students with concepts and formal arguments and Socratic dialogues in which "just the pure charm and beauty of the talk may itself contain a glimmer of truth or transcendence," as he said in one of his videotapes. A comment that may have explained the essence of Rick Roderick at his very best—the pure charm and beauty of his talk, a glimmer of truth and transcendence.

ROSEDALE

ONE DAY, DANNY AND I dropped by to visit the Rodericks and discovered a tall blonde woman making a salad for Rick in the kitchen. She was as striking as a Norse divinity, with a long braid and a friendly, confident smile and fit build, and at first I thought she was one of Rick's new online dates. But it was Maye, the Malibu surfer who'd fallen in love with him when they'd met at Dr. Steve's ranch and later lived in the same apartment building in West L.A. She told me she'd been miserable and couldn't live without him and she'd driven fourteen hundred miles to rekindle their relationship. For the next several months, she would drive back and forth to Los Angeles, staying with Rick for a few weeks and then returning to attend to her interior design company. Ultimately, she decided to shut down her shop and move in with Rick and his sons on Rosedale Avenue.

Maye was bright and genial, with an inner warmth and candor and an innocent sweetness that was surprising for an L.A. businesswoman. She credited Dr. Steve for saving her life. Her parents had divorced when she was in her teens, causing her considerable distress, and she sought professional help from the psychologist. Their sessions morphed into a friendship. She had great respect for him and his counseling abilities, and she became a regular visitor at his ranch, attending his lectures and joining his sailboat voyages into the Pacific and down the coast to Mexico.

At the Rosedale home in Austin, Rick appreciated her care and attention and her go-getter organizational skills that he hoped would help him manage the household now that Travis was working full-time and couldn't keep an eye on the two youngest boys. As Maye would confess to me later, she hadn't bargained on becoming a live-in nanny, but that was what eventually transpired, much to the displeasure of Taylor and Max, who resented all authority figures, especially anybody they suspected of trying to replace their mother.

Maye had the grace and polished manners of someone who'd grown up in a sophisticated family, and she was a lively conversationalist. Annette and I enjoyed our meals and social outings with her and Rick and the two families, and we hoped she would bring a semblance of stability to their ragged lifestyle. Having grown up on the beach in Malibu, Maye loved fresh air and summer heat, and we agreed that Taylor, Max, and Danny were spending too much time playing computer games in a smoke-filled house and needed exercise in the Texas sunshine. Our group excursions into the Austin-area greenbelts, wooded trails, and natural pools were sometimes frustrating because the outdoors were a challenge to those accomplished young indoorsmen.

The situation eventually began to overwhelm Maye. Like a Donna Reed traditional housewife and mother, she was cooking and cleaning and struggling to involve the reluctant boys in helping her with household chores. The weight of those exasperating efforts, with very little support from ailing Rick, wore her down, triggered her chronic fatigue syndrome, and made her physically ill for days at a time.

I was concerned. I didn't like the way she was being treated. Rick seemed to have lost interest in her, despite her love and hard work and her efforts to improve their lives in a hundred small ways. But Rick had fought for years to retain control of his family as the paterfamilias, and he wasn't going to let anyone interfere with his eccentric parenting. On one occasion, when Maye took him aside and suggested that he was being too harsh on one of the boys, he told her it was none of her business. On another occasion, when she was lying on a bed with Max and Taylor, innocently hugging and wrestling and giggling with them, Rick walked into the room and glared at her with silent disapproval, ending the fun. "I guess I was supposed to know my place," she told me.

The arrangement had become untenable, so she decided to move out and rent a room in the quaint Hyde Park neighborhood only a few minutes away by car, thinking it would help her maintain a relationship with Rick but relieve the pressure of living together. Strapped financially, she also secured a full-time job working at John-William Interiors, a local home furnishing and design center.

So there she was, stranded in Austin, Texas, far from her familiar comforts and stable income in California, no longer living with her boyfriend, working long hours at a job she only marginally tolerated, racked by chronic fatigue and poor health, and unsure of her future with the man she couldn't live without. She was miserable, hesitant, confused. I wasn't alone in feeling that she was being mistreated. Tom Burditt was also worried about her. Some of our friends thought that the problem was she was too soft, too fragile for Rick, not equal to the force of his personality. But what woman was equal to the force of that personality? Simone de Beauvoir on crystal meth?

Very late one night, I received a phone call from Maye, who sounded frantic and breathless. She said she'd been visiting Rick and they were making love on the couch in his living room when a strange woman burst through the front door and began beating him with doubled fists, screaming and calling him a liar and cursing him for two-timing her. She was one of Rick's online affairs. Maye panicked, afraid that the woman might be armed, and raced out of the house with only her cell phone in hand.

"Can you bring me a blanket or some of Annette's clothes?" she asked me in a hushed voice. She was in the dark park across the street, naked and hiding behind a tree, and unsure if the woman was still in the house, beating on Rick.

"Who is it?" Annette asked, half asleep under the covers. When I quickly explained what had happened, restraining my urge to laugh, she said, "I'm not getting out of bed. Take her a blanket. You'll enjoy that more than I will."

By the time I arrived at Ramsey Park with the blanket, Maye had returned to Rick's house and was dressed. He'd chased the violent woman away and offered some convoluted explanation to Maye. But the cat was out of the bag. While she'd relocated to a rented room in Hyde Park, working hard to save their relationship, Rick had resumed his old ways of dating online crazies.

The final insult came a few months later, when Maye went over to the Rosedale house the day before Thanksgiving, one of her favorite holidays, ready to join Rick in cooking a traditional meal of turkey and dressing and all the trimmings. But when she arrived, Rick's bags were packed and sitting on the living room floor, alongside the boys' backpacks, and she realized they were going somewhere. It was a terrible scene. Rick had met a wealthy woman online who lived in northern New Mexico and owned her own business, and he and his sons were planning to load up the Toyota truck and head out to her opulent home in the mountains, where she was preparing an elaborate Thanksgiving feast for them.

A distraught Maye came over to our house to talk with Annette and me. "What should I do?" she asked after disclosing what had happened. We both advised her to gather her belongings and return to Los Angeles. There was no future with Rick. He might've been my best friend, but his behavior toward her was deplorable, and I felt that no woman should endure those cruel insults.

"He'll do it again," I assured her.

"Go back home and fall in love with someone else, Maye," Annette advised. "You're a very attractive woman, and there are a thousand other guys who'd be thrilled to have a relationship with you."

She took our advice, stuffed all her belongings into her car, and moved back to L.A. It was heartbreaking to see her leave Austin under such circumstances, but leaving was the right thing to do.

I don't recall discussing her departure with Rick, probably because I knew it wouldn't do any good. He was excited about the new woman in New Mexico, but I knew that wouldn't last very long, either. And it didn't. Women were coming and going in his life, and I had no clue what he was looking for. What was his idea of the perfect partner? To be honest, it didn't matter to me anymore. I'd given up on trying to understand Rick's romantic calculations.

Maye and I spoke on the phone briefly and tearfully after Rick's death in 2002, but until I started writing this chapter, I hadn't communicated with her in two decades. We began to exchange emails and phone calls, and I enjoyed our conversations about our old friend, as painful as those discussions sometimes were. She said it took her seven years to get over him, and as we spoke, it was clear she still had very strong and loving feelings for him and memories both good and bad. She felt that "her brain was comfortable with Rick's brain," and that when she returned to L.A., she had to "dumb myself down to fit in with my old friends." She also believed that Rick suffered from a "sex addiction," a popular diagnosis for a newly designated pathology at the time, no doubt with its own twelve-step program. My unspoken response was "yes, Rick liked sex, as do most of us—but was it an addiction?" Or was it an obsessive search for validation? As I observed earlier, he never understood why attractive women would have sex with him. He didn't trust their motivations, and he kept testing his disbelief for the rest of his life.

In the final analysis, Maye remembered Rick as a man with significant limitations who "had a hard time letting women love him." It was a generous evaluation, condemning neither him nor his lovers, and possibly the most forgiving way to look at his conduct. Maye is a kind and thoughtful woman, and it's my fondest hope that she's found peace and happiness with someone special who loves and cherishes her as they stroll together, arm in arm, through those beautiful neighborhood rose gardens she values so dearly in the City of the Angels.

THE THRILL IS GONE

RICK'S PART-TIME TEACHING GIGS at UT and Austin Community College weren't enough to pay the bills and raise his sons, and he became desperate for more income. By the end of the 1990s, the royalties from the *Great Courses* videotapes had dried up, and he turned to Tom Rollins for more financial assistance, pleading with Rollins to put him on the Teaching Company payroll as a consultant so he could receive insurance benefits. But that was out of the question. Rollins was still disappointed and angry with Rick for what he considered his poor performances in his final videotaped series, *The Self Under Siege*, which had taken place six years earlier.

According to Rollins, Rick had showed up disheveled and somewhat disoriented at the tapings in 1993. Rollins had never seen him so disorganized and unprepared. On camera, Rick rambled for half an hour, not clearly focused on any single subject, and neglected the philosophy content to express his personal views about current events and pop culture. "It was clear to me that the wheels had come off and he was in some kind of personal decline," Rollins said. Everyone was surprised when Rick ended the first lecture a half hour early and walked away from the podium. An audience member confronted him, voiced her irritation, and scolded him for wasting the audience's time and the Teaching Company's money.

Rollins and his editors were able to piece together the eight lectures that became *The Self Under Siege*, he told me, "but I don't recall how that series got done. My memory may be clouded because I was so pissed off at Rick at the time. I think we made him redo some lectures, and for some issues I just gave up. In truth, his lack of preparation made me feel used and angry."

Years later, when Rick asked to be added to the company payroll, Rollins didn't hesitate to make his feelings known: "The old health marm in me came out and I counseled him to cut down on his smoking, clean up his drug-seeking behavior, and pull his life together. His physical decline was obvious, and I was worried about him. I wished he'd taken care of his body as well as he'd taken care of his mind."

Rick responded with a proposal to deliver a series of lectures on *horror*—horror and sci-fi movies and their underlying critiques of society. (I had listened to Rick enthuse about the subversive, sociopolitical messages in John Carpenter's *They Live* and other such films.) But the proposal was too far removed from what the *Great Courses* were all about, and Rollins wasn't interested. He'd lost faith in Rick, and it cost them their friendship. "I felt like I'd lost a great treasure," Rollins said.

In that period between 1997 and the end of the year 2000, I worried about Rick all the time. There were entire weeks when he couldn't rise from the couch, when the boys waited on him hand and foot, bringing him packs of cigarettes and meals he'd taught them to cook on the stove and food they'd nuked in their microwave, which always looked as if a poodle dog had actually exploded inside. Because he was a chronic smoker, which often destroys the taste buds, Rick had to douse his food with heavy doses of salt and pepper so he could taste what he was eating. In one of his low points, when he was clearly ill and only half conscious and couldn't or wouldn't tell me what was debilitating him, he said he'd lost his sense of taste entirely and didn't want to eat. For some reason I decided that he would enjoy a chocolate malt, and I made trips to EZ's diner, where Travis was the manager, to buy that drink with extra malt added. Malt turned out to be the only thing Rick could taste, and I kept bringing him those drinks until the day he appeared relatively normal again and smiled at me for the first time in two weeks. "I think I'm ready for some solid food again," he said.

I was disturbed by further signs of Rick's physical deterioration in January 2001—the beginning of his last year of life—when several of us decided to participate in the "He's Not My President" march and rally at the Texas State Capitol grounds to protest the election of George W. Bush. We were all still furious that the conservative-majority Supreme Court had shut down the election recount in Florida, thus installing George W. as president despite a highly disputed vote count and Al Gore's victory in the popular vote nationwide. Rick, Annette, and I had taken part in many rallies and marches in our time, and we were eager to introduce our sons to the grand American tradition of free speech and aggressive-but-nonviolent resistance. On George W's Inauguration Day, January 21, thousands gathered at Republic Square in downtown Austin to begin the march up Congress Avenue to the capitol. Chanting and clapping, seven of us headed out together into the raucous crowd on the parade route, including Danny, Taylor, Max, and our friend Jane Scroggs. Rick managed no more than a city block when he slowed down, stopped, and clutched his chest.

"I can't make it," he said to me. He was having difficulty breathing. It seemed like an asthma attack. I offered to drive him to the ER, but he insisted it wasn't serious, he just needed to go back to the square and sit on a bench for awhile and catch his breath. "I'm out of shape, is all. I'll find you guys a little later up at the capitol." But he walked to his truck and drove home.

A few weeks after that march, as we were sitting in his living room and discussing the autobiography he wanted to write, he revealed to me something I never thought I'd hear Rick Roderick say: He'd lost interest in sex. His libido had cratered, and he surmised it was because of all the medications he was taking, especially the anti-anxiety drugs.

"The thrill is gone," he laughed in that raspy growl, quoting one of our favorite B.B. King songs. "The thrill has gone away, Tom."

I remembered when he and I and Frank used to sit listening to that soul-wrenching blues song on the juke box while we were eating cheap chicken-fried steaks in a narrow little joint called Hank's, a couple of doors down from where the Hole in the Wall would emerge a few years later.

"It just don't do me like it used to do me," he said, making a face as if he'd tasted something bitter. "I can take it or leave it."

I was disturbed to hear him say that. He was only fifty-one years old.

We stared at each other long and hard with the inevitability of battle-weary soldiers facing surrender at the end of a forty-year war. I can't be certain, but that epiphany likely foreshadowed Rick's decision to curtail his online dating. After all, what was the point? He didn't have the energy or fascination to pursue women anymore. The mere idea exhausted him. And yet even as I understood the benefits of our aging Fat Man with a bad heart slowing down and moderating a life lived without restraint, it meant the end of something essential. Because if my good friend Rick Roderick could recognize and accept a significant change, if not a loss altogether, to that most vital element of who he was, then I too would someday have to face the cruel end of pleasure that every wrecked body must face.

THE FIRE THIS TIME

A DAY AFTER THE LAST DAY of school in the spring semester of 2001, the finale of Danny's sixth grade and his time at Lee Elementary, he and I drove to the Roderick place to celebrate the beginning of summer vacation. When we arrived, an elderly AC service man was driving the final screws into a thermostat for the central air-conditioning system he'd installed in the old house. It had taken him a week to root around in the tight attic, laying new wiring, cutting vent holes in the sheetrock ceiling, replacing an old breaker box, and hooking up a shiny outside unit that resembled *Star Wars'* R2-D2. Rick and the boys were overjoyed that their landlady had agreed to make that improvement just in time to combat the city's hottest months. It was early June and the heat was already stifling. The service man flipped a switch on the new thermostat, we could hear the AC roar to life, and the boys began to dance through the small rooms and cheer the gushing cold air like a band of desert tribesmen chanting in the downpour of a saving rain.

"Let's let the AC do its thing and cool the house down," I proposed, "while we go get something to eat. I'm buying!"

I always picked up the tab.

Rick suggested one of the oldest Mexican restaurants in town. It was owned and operated by a prominent Austin family that wasn't remotely Hispanic. They served saltine crackers instead of chips and salsa, and the last time my sister Frances and I had eaten there, twenty years earlier, we'd rushed home afterwards with bouts of diarrhea. But Rick and sons enjoyed the café's funky, old school Tex-Mex ambience, so our posse rumbled into the little place and commemorated the end of another school year, raising our saltines to salute the wild sense of freedom the three boys were feeling on the eve of summertime.

As we were returning to their home in my car, we noticed a plume of black smoke billowing above the trees in Ramsey Park. We could smell the drifting fumes. One of the boys remarked, “Wouldn’t it be crazy if that was our house?” When we veered onto their block of Rosedale Avenue, we saw two large red firetrucks and other department vehicles parked haphazardly in front of their house and a handful of firemen positioned in the front yard, hosing long arcing streams of water high onto the roof. By that time, the blaze had been somewhat contained, but the roof was a charred rubble and thick black smoke was still whirling out of the shattered windows and open front door. I jumped out of the car and raced over to the yard, where Rick’s neighbor Robert Moorhead was standing near the Toyota pickup parked in the driveway. Robert was a tall friendly cameraman and video-production specialist who lived with his wife and kids two doors up the street. His face and clothes were smudged from the smoke that had engulfed him when he tried to enter the living room as the first responder, convinced that Rick was asleep on the couch because his truck was out front.

“I couldn’t get to him!” he shouted at me through the commotion of loud motors and men issuing orders. He was slightly bent over and coughing from the harsh smoke he’d inhaled. “Rick’s in there and I couldn’t get to him! The smoke hit me like a brick wall and I couldn’t see anything! A fireman just went in there to pull him out!”

Robert was convinced that Rick had succumbed in the blaze, but before I could inform him otherwise, the young fireman jogged out of the smoking front door and pulled off his face mask respirator as he approached Robert and me. He looked like a young man right out of college. “There’s nobody in there, sir!” he said. “Nobody’s sleeping on the couch. I checked every room.”

Rick had walked from my car to his front yard and sat down on the curb in disbelief near the tires of a humming firetruck. The three of us watched him lower his face into his hands, as despondent and forlorn as the biblical Job sitting on an ash heap. He began massaging his bearded face and breathing hard, knowing they'd lost everything, what little they owned, the hand-me-down clothes and discount pots and pans and Goodwill furniture and beds and several shelves of keepsake books and records and the VCR movie collection he was proud of and one or two newish electronic devices, plus an old turntable and a used computer or two. It was all gone, like everything else in his life. His mother and father, his marriage, the teaching career he'd tried to cultivate for years, his fifteen minutes of fame with the *Great Courses*. I'd never seen him look so utterly defeated.

"Is that the owner?" the fireman asked.

Robert hurried over to hug Rick, enormously relieved that he wasn't in the burning house.

When the fireman removed his helmet and smoldering jacket, I saw that he was a well-built young Asian American man, no heavier than a hundred and seventy pounds but with muscular arms and a bodybuilder's pecs, his baggy pants held up by wide suspenders. He and I stared at the large grieving presence sitting on the curb, burying his face in his hands. Rick outweighed the fireman by nearly a hundred pounds.

"You think you could've carried that big dude out of the house?" I asked the fireman, a gentle moment of levity under such dark circumstances.

He studied Rick for a few seconds longer. "Piece of cake," he said with absolute confidence. And I believed him.

I pulled the cell phone from my pocket, sat down next to Rick on the curb, and called Annette at the university. She was upset, of course, and hurried to her car and sped over as fast as she could. For the next two hours, everything seemed suspended in a slow-motion malaise, our three boys roaming around the trucks, the firemen shutting off their hoses and securing equipment, a Red Cross woman with a clipboard kneeling down to speak with Rick, offering vouchers and coupons for food and temporary shelter. Neighbors wandered over to offer sympathy and kindness. Rick was uncharacteristically quiet. He'd retreated deep inside himself, and I couldn't imagine what he was thinking. He jabbed his chest a few times with stiff fingertips, as if trying to jumpstart his aching heart. I searched for words of comfort and practical advice, assuring him we'd find everyone a place to stay while things were sorted out. Annette and I pledged to help clean out the house and save whatever we could.

As we were sitting beside each other on that hard concrete curb, the nearly silent Rick had lit another cigarette and was pondering his fate when a late-model Oldsmobile idled along the street in front of us, an old couple gawking at the burned ruins as they slowly passed by. We glanced up and realized it was Elaine's parents, Rick's in-laws, the grandparents of his children, devout Methodists investigating the tragedy from the safety of their automobile. To us they looked like rubberneckers mesmerized by a bloody car wreck. (Robert's wife had notified them. They knew one another from church.) But the old couple didn't stop and render aid. They didn't offer to call their church's charity services. They didn't roll down a window and utter a single word of consolation to Rick. They didn't search for their grandsons left homeless by a house fire. "God's frozen people," Rick mumbled with a painful laugh, blowing a long trail of smoke toward their fleeing tail lights. As quickly and mysteriously as they'd appeared, they were gone. I don't think Rick ever heard from them again.

We took the boys to stay with us overnight, and Rick went to Frank and Bev's home because they had a spare bedroom. They asked him not to smoke in their house but offered the screened-in back porch or a comfortable lawn chair in the backyard when he needed to light one up. Exhausted by the day's events, he collapsed on the bed in their guest room and decided to indulge in secret, trying to blow smoke out an open window. He nodded off with the lit cigarette in his hand and burned a hole in their pillow. He could've set the house on fire. It was the only night Frank and Bev allowed him to stay there.

Annette and I agreed to meet Rick at the Rosedale house at daybreak the next morning to begin the cleanup. When we arrived with Taylor, Max, and Danny in tow, there was yellow DO NOT ENTER tape stretched across the front doorframe, but the door was unlocked, and we all stooped under the tape and ventured inside. The acrid odor of scorched wood and ruined sheetrock is something you'll never forget. I had smelled that odor before, when I was about twelve years old and our neighbor's house caught fire and we neighborhood boys rushed into the burning home to drag out furniture and family mementos even before the firemen arrived. For some silly reason, I was in their bathroom collecting toiletries when a fireman appeared at the door and said, "Son, get the hell out of here!" As I stepped out into the hallway with an armful of hairbrushes, toothpaste tubes, perfumes, and shampoo bottles, the ceiling collapsed in the bathroom. I would've been seriously injured had I not heeded his command.

We surveyed the rooms of the dark Rosedale house in horror and incredulity. Most of their belongings were seared and blackened and fused by the heat. Max and Taylor discovered that their PlayStation video games were destroyed, including *Metal Gear Solid,* which they'd purchased the day before with money they'd been saving for months. The TV set had warped into a large Salvador Dalí clock.

Annette was trying to organize our cleanup effort into a reasonable division of labor when an older man wearing a dark blue uniform slipped under the yellow tape and stood examining the rubble in the living room. He introduced himself as the city's fire marshal, and although I expected him to kick us out of the dangerous structure, he went about his inspection as if we were invisible. In a half hour or so, as we were gathering all of the smoky clothes from the bedrooms for washing, I noticed that the marshal was spending most of his time in the kitchen, and I asked him if he had any idea what had caused the fire.

"It started here," he said, pointing to a scorched area around a wall outlet near the kitchen sink. He'd heard that the man of the house was a chain smoker, and he speculated that Rick had left a burning cigarette in the kitchen when we went to dinner.

The previous night, I'd phoned my father, who'd been an electrician at the Marathon Oil refinery in Texas City before his retirement, and he was convinced that the new central air-conditioning was the culprit. "As soon as that AC fella hit the juice at the thermostat," my dad said, "the electricity found the weakest link in the wiring and touched off a spark."

When I told the fire marshal what my father had said, he dismissed the theory. "I don't see any evidence of that," he said, scribbling notes on a pad. "No, the fire started right here"—he gestured with his pen at the black area—"and that's what I'm writing in my report."

"Then it couldn't have been a cigarette," I said, staring at the suspect socket located about six inches above the countertop, "unless you think he taped a burning cigarette to the wall."

He was a gnarly old geezer with the kind of throwback Texas accent and country diction I'd heard all my life, probably a rank-and-file lifer who'd worked his way up to fire marshal after decades of climbing ladders into burning buildings. Nothing I said was going to change his mind.

As it turned out, the fire marshal was closer to the truth than the rest of us. Years later, Taylor told us there was a faulty thrift store toaster plugged into that outlet by the sink, and the toaster often smoked and spewed sparks when you dropped bread into the slots. You had to keep an eye on it and sometimes unplug it while you were making toast. He confessed that on the day of the fire, he'd dropped bread into the slots and forgot about it when Danny and I arrived to take everyone to dinner. We'd left the house with the bread still browning in the defective toaster, and Taylor was certain that had caused the fire. He'd held onto the secret for fifteen years before he told everyone what had happened.

After the fire marshal left, Rick showed up at the house in a slow shuffle, drained and depressed, almost sleep-walking through each room to assess the destruction in a quiet, eerie acquiescence to what the Fates had dealt him. He was still wearing that ashen mantle of defeat. I was very concerned about his ability to survive this ordeal.

Annette and I briefed him on what we were doing. The bedrooms had sustained smoke damage but their clothes hadn't caught fire. We'd bagged up all their smoky T-shirts, socks, underwear, and jeans, and we offered to soak them in our clothes washer at home. We didn't realize it would take four or five complete cycles and cup after cup of detergent to eliminate the odor. We nearly burned out our clothes dryer with all that laundry.

Frank soon appeared in his big white pickup truck, opened the tailgate, and we all teamed up and lugged out mattresses and a few lamps and a table and armchair worth salvaging. Annette and I rented a climate-controlled storage unit near our house where we unloaded their rescued possessions for safekeeping until Rick could find a suitable residence for them.

That first day, he and I went through his library, book by book, and boxed up the volumes that were only lightly singed and hadn't been soaked by the firehose water dripping from the saggy ceiling and running down the walls. I don't recall if any of his papers went unscathed—the course outlines and what might've been manuscripts or notes for future projects—but it's likely that all paper was destroyed. At one point, Rick dragged his computer and a stack of disks out of a pile of rubble, and he was excited to see they hadn't melted like the TV. Later on at our house, we inspected the computer and discovered that its hard drive was unharmed and the autobiography he'd started writing, *Bury Me Not,* had not perished in the fire. Everything he'd written about his Tuscola childhood was still intact.

"Jesus loves me, this I know," he declared, drolly proclaiming it a miracle akin to God preserving holy writ on the scrolls found in the Qumran Caves near the Dead Sea.

The house was pronounced a total loss. Their landlady was a kind soul who'd grown up in those small rooms but had moved to Waco as an adult. For sentimental reasons, she hadn't sold her childhood home and had been renting it out for years. After the fire, she phoned Rick to express her sadness and offer sympathy, and she told him that a wrecking crew would soon demolish the house. She advised him to remove anything of value before the bulldozers arrived.

The fire set off the Rodericks' homeless odyssey during the summer months of 2001. Rick was determined to keep the family together, per usual, and he used the Red Cross voucher to occupy a room free-of-charge in a sleazy motel near the interstate in north Austin. It was a high crime area with drug deals going down at all hours and sex workers milling around nearby stoplight corners and in a convenience store parking lot across the street. When I visited their motel room to make sure they were all safe and sound, Rick and his sons were camped out on two double beds and the floor. Pimps and junkies were skulking along the motel's concrete walkway outside their door, looking for trouble. Travis found a crack pipe lodged in the foam rubber of a pillow, a souvenir left behind by a previous tenant.

After a week or two of fear and loathing in lowlife motel squalor, Rick begged a prior online date to let them stay in one of her unrented apartments in the upscale complex she managed. I met her. She was a former sorority girl in her mid-thirties who looked at home in female business attire, high heels and expensive dresses, and she impressed me as too smart and attractive to have played the online dating game. She housed them in a very nice apartment with plush white wall-to-wall carpeting and shiny new furnishings, their building a honeycomb of picture windows surrounded by a bushy forest that backed into the popular Barton Creek Greenbelt hiking trail. Rick was in heaven on the large sectional sofa, holding court while smoking and eating and watching the big-screen TV. When Danny and I visited him and the boys, I wondered how long the arrangement would last. It took Rick about three days to burn a dozen holes in the virgin white carpet from the lit cigarettes he'd dropped while nodding off. When his manager friend saw the burn holes and the trashed bedrooms where the boys were staying, she pitched them out.

Rick and sons loved Ramsey Park and the encircling neighborhood, and he trolled the area for weeks in his red pickup, searching for a place to rent. Everyone was very happy when he found a comfortable two-bedroom apartment in a complex on the opposite side of the park from their demolished Rosedale Avenue house. The boys were back in their familiar environs, hanging out with neighborhood friends, driving lifeguards crazy at the Ramsey pool, and haunting the convenience stores where they'd bought (and sometimes shoplifted) bubble gum, candy bars, and Arizona Iced Tea.

Rick started swimming laps in the lap lane, and the exercise tightened his prodigious gut and tanned him like the teenager he'd been at Abilene State Park. I was relieved to see him in much better shape. But the pool closed down at the end of summer, the boys returned to school, and my old friend slipped back into his meds and inert couch life, sometimes nodding off in mid-sentence. I was in no position to help him with his struggles. I had my own to contend with. After twenty-two years together, a wonderful son, and our adventurous relocations to three other cities to support Annette's career, our marriage had fallen apart.

THE AUTUMN OF OUR DISCONTENT

WHEN THE TWIN TOWERS FELL on September 11 that year and thousands of lives were lost, Rick and I had another very animated quarrel. He expressed his usual contempt for rah-rah patriotism and quoted Malcolm X's "the chickens have come home to roost" statement the Muslim minister had made after the assassination of JFK. I adamantly disagreed and challenged my old friend in no uncertain terms. I wasn't cynical about mass murder and had no tolerance for religious zealots who killed innocent people in the name of God.

"Are you surprised that they want to destroy us?" he responded, reeling off the numerous examples in recent history in which America had committed bloody, covert, destabilizing crimes against leaders and movements unfriendly to "our interests."

I understood all of that, of course, and I'd been decrying CIA malfeasance for decades. At Stanford I'd joined a leftist group that shut down and occupied the Career Placement and Planning Center when the CIA showed up to recruit recent graduates. But I refused to accept the false equivalency that three thousand innocent civilians deserved to die because of what our government had sanctioned in Chile and the Congo thirty and forty years earlier.

In the throes of the nation's collective outrage and grief over 9/11, he and I continued to do what we'd always done together. We argued intensely about the political turmoil, we watched football games on TV and rented movies, we fed our sons the healthiest take-out food we could find, we kept an eye on them at skeevy video arcades patronized by perverts. (Rick and I loved team-shooting zombies in the game *Area 51*.) He had resumed working on his autobiography and phoning me to read passages and discuss updates, and I was putting the finishing touches on my New Orleans novel *The White League*.

The fall of 2001 turned out to be the last four months of Rick's life. I don't think he ever fully recovered from the fire. Too much trauma and dislodgment, a disruption of his routines and a serious disorder to the tidy world of concepts and constructs in his head. October was marred by his failing health and undiagnosed congestive heart condition. He didn't have health insurance or a cardiologist, and he was frustrated by the long waiting time at the free clinic. Although he continued to teach a couple of courses at Austin Community College, his energy was low and his driving was erratic, sometimes dangerous, and I cautioned Danny not to ride with him in that little Toyota truck anymore.

Elaine had returned to Austin after several years in California and moved into the duplex her parents still owned. I think she realized that the fire had damaged Rick and the boys in more destructive ways than the physical discomfort of lost possessions. She saw that Rick's life was unraveling, Max was often angry and miserable, and the older boys were indifferent toward her. These concerns made her more determined to fix what had been broken.

Her strongest criticism of Rick was that he'd tried to destroy her relationship with her sons in the same way Rod had willfully kept Elwynn away from Rick when he was growing up. But in my conversations with Marshall and Travis, they insisted that the accusation wasn't true, that Rick wanted nothing more than to reunite with Elaine and have one big happy family again. Maye had told me the same thing. Travis observed that their mother simply hadn't played a significant role in their lives while she was away in California, and he and Marshall, in particular, felt they didn't know her anymore.

In her final years in the Los Angeles area, Elaine had continued making art and had earned an MFA at the elite California Institute of the Arts (CalArts). I was impressed and proud of her for that remarkable achievement. I had always admired her artwork, no matter how bizarre and sometimes depressing the images were, and in the early 1980s I'd commissioned her to produce five illustrations and the cover art for a slim volume of my short stories. Elaine's macabre renderings perfectly captured the surreal fringe of those stories. Inscribing my personal copy, she wrote: "To Tom—Thanks for my first chance at worldwide notoriety in the art circles. Without your sick stories, I couldn't have achieved such perfection."

After her return to Austin, she'd maintained such a low profile that for two months I didn't know she was back in town. Rick and the boys didn't mention her, and that may have been the unkindest cut of all. Danny was the one who told me he'd seen her. He, Max, and Taylor had taken their PlayStation with them to visit Elaine in the old duplex.

I had no right to be judgmental about marriages. That fall, Annette and I underwent marriage counseling for weeks, but I didn't reveal the possible divorce to anyone. Not to Rick, not to Frank, Bev, or my sister Frances. I couldn't risk the word getting back to Danny, someone telling someone who told someone else, before his mother and I spoke with him first. We decided to live together until the end of the school year in June and then discuss it with him. I knew it would be the most heartbreaking moment of our lives. Our son thought we were a happy and secure family trio, and I was certain the news would devastate him. I was convinced he would never forgive us.

IN LEAGUE

I HAD EXPLAINED the entire storyline of my novel *The White League* to Rick one evening when we were eating all-you-can-eat pizza with Taylor, Max, and Danny at a pizza parlor called Cicis. Rick's beaming reaction to the various characters and subplots convinced me I had a captivating story on my hands. A couple of years later, in late October of 2001, I'd finished a solid draft and handed him a box of more than five hundred manuscript pages. He seemed delighted to begin reading them.

He was working on his autobiography, *Bury Me Not*, but he admitted to me that he'd slowed down a bit. He was a little tired and unfocused from teaching classes, and he wasn't finding the time and devotion he'd enjoyed in previous months. He was nodding off more than usual, he said, and his motivation for completing the book was waning. I continued my encouragement, assuring him that the book was very good so far and that he just needed to find his groove again and keep going. I reminded him of what he'd always said to me—"Don't give up, man. Don't stop writing. That's the only thing that'll prevent you from producing an excellent work." And I added emphatically, "This is the book you've been waiting your entire life to write."

Trying to save my marriage absorbed most of my concentration for the next few weeks, and I didn't spend much time with Rick. In retrospect, I should've paid more attention to my old friend's deteriorating health. But Rick was one of the toughest guys I'd ever met, both physically and mentally, and I couldn't imagine that I was witnessing the final telltale signs of his mortality. I wasn't alone in that regard. Other friends like Tom Burditt, Paul Foreman, and Frank spent significant time with him in those last months, and they probably felt, as I did, that Rick had been in some kind of decline but it wasn't fatal. We believed that this was merely the manifestation of advancing age, medication side effects, lack of exercise, questionable diet. He'd always had his ups and downs, but he'd bounced back every time. He was damned near indestructible. We didn't think we would lose him forever.

A month or so after I'd given him my manuscript, I realized that Rick hadn't said a word about it, which was unusual. He was a fast reader, and he'd always read my work very quickly and responded with both praise and suggestions for improvement. In early December, I asked him if he'd had a chance to read *The White League* and he said, "I'm sorry, man. I started it and kind of lost track. I don't know what's wrong with my brain. I really like it but I . . . I'm having trouble concentrating on things, Tom. I promise I'll start again tonight and get back to you as soon as I can. I'm really sorry."

Sometime between Christmas and New Year's Eve, he called to say he'd read the book and loved it. I drove over to his apartment and we had a long and inspiring discussion about the story. I asked him questions, voiced my misgivings about one scene or another, wondered if such and such was believable, the usual concerns that most writers have when they've finished a novel. Rick was remarkably generous and supportive, saying all the right things, but I could tell he wasn't himself. His mind was working, his words were thoughtful and incisive, but he looked very tired and appeared to be fighting the urge to sleep. I thought maybe he'd contracted the flu or some other malady. But he said no, he was just exhausted and needed to rest. I had no idea that his heart wasn't pumping enough blood to sustain that large and cumbersome body.

QUICK FAIR DEATH

LATE IN THE AFTERNOON on January 18, 2002, Danny and I stopped by the Roderick apartment to visit Rick and the boys. Travis greeted us at the door with tragic news. Rick's childhood friend Mickey had died of a heart attack the previous day while napping in his recliner after a long day's work in the Tuscola area, and Rick was taking the death very hard. I was shaken myself. I had survived several wild escapades with the legendary Mickey Sansom back in those far-off days of peace, love, and ten-dollar lids, and I considered him a good friend.

"Fredell asked Rick to be a pall bearer and to say a few words," Travis said. Fredell was Mickey's wife and the mother of their children. "I don't know what's gonna happen. Rick doesn't even own a suit anymore."

I gazed over at my old friend sleeping on the couch in his loose boxers. His large chest was heaving raggedly, and he was teetering on the edge of the cushions, a half turn from rolling onto the floor. Earlier that day, he'd asked Max to go with him to cancel the class he was teaching at an Austin Community College campus across town. Whether on heavy medications, sleep-deprived, or simply not getting enough oxygen to his brain, Rick knew he was in dreadful shape and didn't want his students to see him that way. Max ran inside the building to inform the students that the class wouldn't take place. He told us later that on their drive, Rick kept nodding off behind the wheel of his Toyota pickup, drifting into other lanes, and Max feared for his life.

I asked Travis if we should wake up Rick and discuss what to do about Mickey's funeral. "Let the old sleeping dog lie," Travis said with a wry smile. "He just needs a few Z's before he takes off for Tuscola tomorrow morning."

This was Rick's usual manner of repose, so we thought nothing of it. Ever since his childhood, he'd occupied couches as if they were lifeboats. He'd once confessed to me that even after sex with beautiful women under their satin sheets, he would slip away to sleep alone on their couches.

"Mickey's death has freaked him out," Travis said. "We stayed up all night talking about their adventures. The usual stories and a few I hadn't heard before. He said life doesn't make sense anymore without Mickey."

I wandered over to Rick's computer on a desk near a window and glanced at the pages of the autobiography he'd been writing for nearly a year. On top of the stack there was a passage about Mickey, and I suspected that Rick had been up all night revising it:

> As very young kids, we would walk the flat country fields for hours and invent adventures. We would stay out all night by the cattle tank and fish and talk about the days of cattle drives and gunfights and quick fair death. To us, those times were still around us in West Texas. Sometimes it even felt like they weighed on us and we would have real trouble living up to carrying that weight. We were always armed with BB guns and ready to shoot anything that moved. The air was hot even at night for much of the year and the sky was always huge. Looking at it gave you that familiar feeling of being so small that not a damn thing you ever did would matter, not that we could have said it that way. Nevertheless, it was a comfort. It helped to lift that blanket of

wild cowboy history a bit, and we indulged the comfort of it. We spent many such useless nights together. More than I can remember.

After living in Austin for a couple of years in his twenties, Mickey had returned to Tuscola and settled down while Rick continued his journey into a larger cosmopolitan world where few had experienced the boyhood thrill of wandering flat country fields with rifles tucked under their arms. Rick hadn't seen Mickey very often over the past sixteen years, while he was teaching at Duke and in California, although they would write and call each other from time to time. I had spoken to Mickey by phone the previous summer, when he was trying to track Rick down after the house fire. It was the first time we'd talked in a couple of decades. Mickey had discovered my Aspen mystery novels at his local library, and he was happy that I'd finally made something of myself. His voice was slow and whiskey deep and as wonderfully nuanced as the baritone of country singer Jim Reeves.

"Call me when Rick wakes up," I said to Travis. "I'll buy him a suit."

Less than an hour after Danny and I left Rick sleeping on the couch, Travis phoned me. I expected him to say that Rick was awake and ready to go shopping. Instead, he had difficulty speaking and there were long silences, and I thought something was wrong with the line connection. Finally he choked out the words "Rick is dead." I wasn't sure I'd heard him correctly. And then I realized he wouldn't joke about something like that. "No, Travis!" I began to repeat over and over again. "*No*, Travis, what are you saying? *No!*"

"Rick's dead, Tom. Please come over."

How was that possible? I had just seen Rick napping peacefully on the couch, resting up before facing the awful burden of burying his childhood friend.

Rick and I had talked about death many times with our usual gallows humor. We'd lost other friends our age. Rainy car wrecks, self-inflicted gunshots, cancer. We tried to be philosophical about old buddies who'd died too young. We'd coped with those tragedies with a respectful grief, but also with youthful arrogance. We were certain that would never happen to us.

That evening, as I struggled to face what Travis was telling me on the phone, I couldn't accept the cosmic absurdity of it all. How could two best friends since they were kids—who'd been as close as brothers—how could they have died one day apart? It was beyond my comprehension.

Danny heard me shouting into the phone and came running into the room. I had to find the words to tell him. He didn't believe it either and cried, "Maybe he's sick again. Or maybe he's just sleeping." He loved Rick, as did all the boys in the neighborhood. Rick was their mentor and idol, the irreverent instructor who made them laugh and made them think. He never treated them as children but as small adults who were capable of making up their own minds about the most complex human decisions. He was far more entertaining than the best video games they would ever play.

▪ ▪ ▪

When I knocked on the apartment door, breathless and squeezing Danny close to my side, a policewoman smiled through the slender opening and slipped outside into the damp concrete breezeway to ask if I was a friend of Mr. Roderick.

"For more than thirty years," I told her.

She informed us that the family had gathered in one of the small bedrooms. "The body is still on the floor in the living room," she said. "The medical examiner is with him."

Her confirmation was like an icepick shivved in my gut.

"Will you do me a favor, young man?" she said to our thirteen-year-old son, who appeared as shocked and incredulous as I. "Will you stay close to your father and turn your eyes away when you go inside?"

He said he would, and he kept his promise.

But as we walked past the kitchen toward the bedroom, I ignored her advice and glanced over to see what had happened to my old friend. His huge body lay on the cigarette-burned carpet near the couch. They had covered him with a tarp. The only exposed part of him was his right hand, the fingers curled, his skin blue, unreal. It was that small fat hand he'd used to throw out base-stealers when he was a teenaged all-star catcher in Taylor County.

I could barely contain my emotions as Danny and I knocked on the bedroom door. Elaine let us in, and the weeping began. It was a messy boys' room with too many people in too little space. Stunned mourners were sitting on the disheveled bed and crowded into every corner. I held Elaine while she cried great heaving sobs, and then I embraced their two older sons, Marshall and Travis, who grappled me like Russian sailors, their tears flowing in speechless disbelief. I made the rounds, hugging everyone, crying loudly.

Max was the only one who refused to show emotion or to leave his corner of the bedroom. Arms folded defiantly across his chest, he didn't want to be touched and turned away from me. Curiously, Danny separated from me quickly and struck the same pose in solidarity with his friend. They both seemed angry and confused and determined to avoid the demonstrations of grief around them. Later, I understood what they were feeling at that moment. Max couldn't accept that his father was dead, and Danny worried that Rick may have taken his own life. For nearly a week our son harbored that secret unfounded fear in his heart and wouldn't forgive Rick for leaving us that way.

Others began to enter the room, a trail of old friends who'd heard the terrible news. Annette had been at an art exhibition opening until she received my panicked cell-phone message, and when she arrived in the claustrophobic room, I pulled her to my chest and bawled uncontrollably. She was trembling and filled with shock and grief. A few minutes later, we heard the EMS gurney clanking out of the apartment. The policewoman appeared at the bedroom door to tell us that Rick was being transported to the morgue. The medical examiner had ordered an autopsy. We would know the cause of death in a few days.

We passed the rest of the evening in the living room of the small apartment where Rick and his sons had washed ashore after fire and firings and ill health and the many promising years of his luminous academic career had receded. The silence among those friends and loved ones was eerie and despairing.

A large phlegm-green stain blotched the carpet where Travis had tried to save his father's life. When he went to wake his dad for supper, he saw that Rick's limp body had slumped off the couch and he wasn't breathing. Travis began fighting to revive him, forcing open Rick's jaws and applying mouth-to-mouth resuscitation. Green phlegm gurgled out of Rick's windpipe, Travis told me later, and there were choking sounds from deep inside his throat. He pounded on Rick's chest, slapped his face, shook him, turned him on his side. He didn't want to alarm his two younger brothers playing video games in their bedroom, so he called 9-1-1 without telling them. He was still desperately trying to resuscitate his father ten minutes later, when the EMS team arrived with a syringe full of adrenaline they plunged into Rick's heart. There was nothing anyone could do. Rick had been dead for half an hour, and his skin was already turning blue from lack of oxygen.

▪ ▪ ▪

Annette and I sat holding hands on Rick's borrowed couch, watching Travis and Marshall cleaning the green stain on the carpet with towels and dish detergent. Divorce was still our secret. But at that moment, as we smiled wanly at each other and held hands, all I could think of was how much I loved Rick, despite his occasional infuriating behavior, and how much we were all going to miss him.

"Was it a heart attack?" asked their son Taylor. He was fifteen years old, the artist of the family, like his mother, and a budding musician with an incredible ear for music.

"I don't know, T," I said. "The autopsy will tell us, I suppose."

"He wanted a Viking funeral," said Max from a corner of the living room, his arms still folded defensively. These were the first words I'd heard him speak since Danny and I had arrived.

"A Viking funeral, like the one in that movie with Kirk Douglas," he said.

One of Rick's favorite films. I remembered hearing him request the same thing.

"Then I guess we'd better start building a ship," I said.

BLOOD BROTHERS

THE WORD OF RICK'S DEATH spread quickly that night, and more people began to appear at the apartment door in shock. It was like a scene in a Fellini movie. Boys from the neighborhood with their skateboards and baggy pants. Nearby parents who knew Rick as the eccentric guy who ranted and raved about politics in the park. Neighbors with casseroles, neighbors who felt the need to offer prayers. A female coworker from fifteen years earlier who'd often done his laundry and mowed his lawn when he had one. It was hard to breathe in all the cigarette smoke. Travis's tall, gangly childhood friend showed up with a six pack and got belligerently drunk, and around midnight he started beating his fists against the wall, cursing Rick for dying and leaving them all adrift. Everyone in that crowded room was already feeling the void in their lives.

Eventually the mourners exchanged hugs and returned to their homes, exhausted from the adrenaline rush and a profound sense of loss. Danny and Max wandered out of the apartment to watch Taylor and their buddy John sneak a cigarette in a dark parking lot. Only a few of us were left when Marshall started rummaging through the pile of pages next to Rick's computer.

"What are we going to do with his book?" he asked. "He never finished it."

Marshall was in his late twenties by then and lived with his UT graduate student girlfriend, Sarah McKinnon, a scrappy independent thinker who was fiercely competitive in board games with the Roderick boys and often challenged Rick on issues and ideas.

"Lots of great stories," Marshall said, thumbing through the printed pages. "I thought it might get published someday, if he could finish it."

I walked over to the desk and found the chapter about Rick and Mickey's boyhood adventures and finished reading it:

> One December when we were teenagers, Mickey and I borrowed a couple of Winchester saddle rifles, rounded up a week's worth of provisions, and went deer hunting. Our parents thought we were old enough not to shoot each other and that seemed to be the primary issue. Mickey's dad provided the horses, if you could call those two swaybacked nags horses, and we left for the hill country of Lemons Gap, twenty miles from town. We'd been hunting with Mickey's dad before, but this would be our first trip on our own. Rod didn't like hunting, so he usually took us fishing. Although we'd caught plenty of fish and had killed squirrels and rabbits and birds, Mickey and I hadn't shot our first deer yet.
>
> We spent two days making our way to the higher country, taking it easy on our horses, riding them slow and feeding them generously and often. We would stop at dark and camp. We built fires to keep the cold away and laid our ropes around the camp on the dubious notion that rattlesnakes would not crawl over them. We talked until late into the night and sometimes just sat and looked at the sky and said nothing for hours. I would get up in the morning and throw on a few small branches to restart the fire and then cooked scrambled eggs and salt pork and potatoes all together in our skillet. Mickey made the coffee,

strong and black. We ate enormous amounts, sat back, and smoked the Camel cigarettes Mickey had brought along. It was a great feeling.

Snow came on our third night out, and by the fourth it was white and icy cold in Lemons Gap. We were not quite prepared for the weather, so we decided it might be best to tie up the horses and start up Devil's Hill and make ourselves a deer blind. We hunched nervously in the little stand of limbs and branches and looked out for deer crossing down into the Jim Ned Valley below.

The first one came at ten o'clock that morning. Mickey couldn't get a good shot from his side of the blind, so I waited, ready. He was a beautiful animal, almost beyond description, with a tall and proud eight-point rack. I felt a dizzy sensation, which I recognized as what they call "buck fever," some primal reaction to the mere act of killing the innocent. But it was not overpowering and I shook it off and looked hard at the movement of the deer, almost still and less than eighty yards away. I leveled the rifle and used a tree branch to steady my aim. I fired and hit him heart high, killing him almost at once. The sound of the shot echoed in the hills and snow fell off the branches around us. I could hear my heartbeat. Mickey scrambled out of the blind and said, "You can shoot, son."

We dragged the deer to our camp and it took both of us to hang his carcass in a crooked mesquite tree. "You clean him. I'm going back to try and get one," Mickey said.

I cut the deer's throat with my buck knife and let him bleed out. I filled my coffee cup with

> some of the blood and set it by. Mickey's dad had showed us how to field dress a deer and I followed the routine as closely as possible. I stripped his skin, cleaned out his stomach, and packed the cold snow inside him. I used the snow to clean some of the blood off myself. It took me a long time and I remember it was late afternoon when I heard the report of Mickey's rifle, followed quickly by a second round. I went up the trail until I saw him. He had his deer. We brought the second one down and we field dressed it together. Mickey saved a cup of his blood, as I had. We finished just as it was too dark to continue. The next day we would drag the two deer down to Silver Valley, only a few hours away, on litters made Indian-style from tree limbs. Mickey's father would come to get the horses, our kills, and us. But that night, we pulled out the covered cups of deer blood, and as the snow hit our faces we drank down the spirit of the deer, if you happen to believe in such things. The blood was warm and very salty. We cut a small line in our palms with the buck knife and shook hands, blood brothers and fellow killers.

"This is as good as Hemingway," I said to Marshall. "Can you print me a copy of what's here? Let me see what I can do to find a publisher."

When your best friend dies, his voice doesn't die with him. I can still hear Rick's West Texas twang and the smoke-damaged hoarseness toward the end. I won't ever forget the million quips and witticisms and clever turns of phrase. They surface every day in my mind. I find myself using them in conversations, and every time I do, I hear him laughing along with me. As I stood there at his desk that night, staring at those pages of his unfinished book, I promised him I would see to it that his story was told. Even if it took many years and those eleven scholars at the *Journal of Philosophy* were the only ones who would read it.

VALHALLA ON THE GUADALUPE

THE AUTOPSY REPORT declared that Rick had died of congestive heart failure. I wasn't certain what that meant until I read about the condition online. I was visiting the Roderick apartment, checking on the boys, when Elaine walked in with the solemn black box of Rick's ashes. The container was about the size of my small office wastebasket.

"What's this?" Travis asked. "One kidney?" We were all expecting a huge crate, something more closely approximating Rick's fighting weight.

The consensus was that we should have a memorial ceremony in Ramsey Park, that favorite Roderick family gathering place. We invited everyone we could think of, old and new friends and kind neighbors and Rick's young admirers and academic colleagues and even a few acquaintances who weren't sure what they thought about him. On the afternoon of the memorial, a sizable crowd appeared under the shade trees. The Longhorn football team sent a flowery wreath in gratitude for Rick's friendship and support of the players in his classes.

Frank kicked things off with a couple of songs accompanied by his longtime bass player, Kelly Hope, another Texas City boy, and Turner Williamson was the first to address the gathering because he'd known Rick longer than anyone else. He told the story of how he'd met that Tuscola troublemaker at the swimming pool in Abilene State Park. I teared up and almost couldn't get through my remarks about Rick cheating St. Peter at a game of eight ball and other lighthearted reflections. Frank delivered a deep and affectionate profile of Rick that made me proud to have a brother with such profundity in his soul. It was Max's fourteenth birthday, and he read one of his poems. A friend of the older boys sang "White Rabbit" for some obscure reason. Travis read the e. e. cummings poem "my father moved through dooms of love," one of Rick's favorites, and Elaine read the lyrics to Leonard Cohen's "Bird on a Wire," which Frank had played at their wedding thirty years earlier. It was a strange brew of voices and sensibilities and unrestrained emotions, but what we all felt in common was our loss of someone who'd meant so much to us.

Fourteen hundred miles away, Maye was distraught because she couldn't make it to the memorial. "I knew I had to do something," she said, "so I held my own memorial at the beach in Pacific Palisades, next to Gladstones restaurant. I brought a boombox and played a 'missing you' song while I was standing on the rocks. As the waves crashed around me, I dropped yellow roses into the water and said goodbye."

When the speakers were finished in Ramsey Park, Elaine invited everyone for barbecue at the Roderick apartment across the street. The place soon filled with mourners standing shoulder to shoulder and eating from paper plates and sharing Rick stories while the younger boys flocked to a bedroom and played video games. And of course, no Roderick party would've been complete without a messy confrontation. When Danny and I were leaving through the complex's dark parking lot, we encountered two police officers refereeing an argument between Marshall's girlfriend, Sarah, and a gray-haired Korean War veteran who'd called 9-1-1 about the loud noise emanating from the Rodericks' apartment. I tested my privilege as an older guy wearing a nice winter jacket, buttoned-down shirt, and respectable shoes, explaining to the officers that we were celebrating the life of a dear friend and parent who'd passed away, but no one was listening. When it became clear that the quarreling would continue far longer than it needed to, and the police were still trying to sort things out, we left and drove home under a dark brooding night sky that felt as if the heaviness would never lift. I knew I would miss Rick until the end of my days.

▪ ▪ ▪

We hadn't forgotten about Rick's request for a Viking funeral. Frank and our friend Greg Valdespino went to an Austin hobby shop and bought a forty-inch model of a Viking longship, its features based on a Norse vessel excavated from a burial mound in Norway, and they began the painstaking assembly using Super Glue to ensure that the ship, set ablaze in the Viking tradition, would stay intact on its mission to carry a box of Rick's ashes southward on the Guadalupe River for hundreds of twisting miles to the Gulf of Mexico. At least that was the plan. In actuality, we all knew it was a fingers-crossed aspiration that required a very healthy imagination and a willing suspension of disbelief.

Greg was Frank's best friend and a fellow traveler who'd known Rick for decades. He was from a revered San Antonio Hispanic family, and he'd met Rick playing poker in the UT dorm in 1970. Greg was a versatile musician who could sing beautifully and for years had backed up Frank on the standup bass, banjo, and other instruments, and he'd also taught elementary school for a time and then earned a law degree at UT Austin. He never became a wealthy attorney because so many of his clients were poor Hispanic families and illegal immigrants who paid him in home-cooked meals and yardwork.

Greg and Frank labored at the longship model like medieval tinkers for several weekends, gluing and carving the balsa wood hull and adding small metal weights for balance and ballast. They attached a burnt orange Longhorn logo to a cloth mast with red and gold vertical stripes. The meticulous Greg replaced the boat's dull figurehead with an intricate dragon's head he'd carved out of wood. One weekend, Frank's Texas City buddy John Ringer showed up to visit him, and they put John to work in the guild of shipbuilders. The three of them tested the vessel in Frank and Bev's bathtub and made adjustments. Was this craft stable enough to stay afloat on a flowing river? When they set it afire, would it travel more than a few yards before capsizing, cracking to pieces against the limestone rocks, and washing downstream in a jumble of branches and other debris?

Greg owned a rustic cabin on the Guadalupe River a few miles upstream from Canyon Lake, a resort area about forty miles southwest of Austin near the quaint town of New Braunfels. When their masterpiece of Viking engineering was completed sometime that spring, Greg volunteered his cabin and the nearby river for the funeral ceremony.

Following directions scribbled on a roadmap as vague as Tolkien's runic map of Middle-earth, our caravan managed to cross cattle guards and swing open fence-gates and wheel deeper into the thick green woods until we found our bucolic destination. The party included Elaine and her four sons; Marshall's girlfriend, Sarah; the neighbor boy Owen Moorhead; Greg and his son Vincent; Frank, his daughter (also Sarah), and her boyfriend; and Annette-Danny-me. Holt Williamson drove down from his home in Roswell, New Mexico, and picked up his son, Walker, a student at Texas State University in San Marcos. We were a merry band of pointy-headed theorists and crackpot performance artists who couldn't quite believe we were pulling this off.

Lofting the longship model like a holy relic, Frank and Greg led the procession down a rocky path through the live oaks and cedar thicket to a pool of water as calm as a swimming hole. It was a spillover basin squatting alongside the gurgling river itself, its surface reflecting the wild, jungly, overhanging greenery all around us. On the way to the water, Annette continuously sang out the three notes—*bah daaaah dah! bah daaaah dah!*—that the Viking war horn sounded in the Kirk Douglas movie *The Vikings*, one of her favorite films and Rick's too. Frank set the ship on the limestone riverbank, Elaine placed a small brown box of Rick's ashes next to the mast, and everyone stooped around the vessel, filling the deck with keepsakes and mementos they'd brought to honor and remember

The model Viking ship was constructed by Frank Zigal and Greg Valdespino to carry Rick's ashes down the Guadalupe River in the Viking tradition. *Photo courtesy of Annette Carlozzi and Thomas Zigal*

Rick's friends and family members loaded mementos onto the Viking ship before it was launched, spring 2002. *Photo courtesy of Annette Carlozzi and Thomas Zigal*

Rick: a pack of his Maverick cigarettes, a deck of his well-worn playing cards, a page of poems, and other things we carried.

We packed the deck with cotton balls and pieces of cloth and a bundle of kindling that Elaine had brought, and shreds of grass the boys pulled from the ground nearby, and Frank soaked all of it in lighter fluid. He and Greg waded out into the still basin until they were chest deep in murky green water and settled the longship afloat. We didn't have a skilled archer to shoot a flaming arrow at the small striped mast, so Frank did the honors, setting the ship ablaze using Rick's tarnished Zippo cigarette lighter. It was Max who'd remembered that his father wanted a Viking funeral, and he was chosen to stand on a rock shelf and read the traditional Viking prayer:

> Lo, there do I see my father
> Lo, there do I see my mother
> and my sisters, and my brothers
> Lo, there do I see the line of my people
> Back to the beginning
> Lo, they do call to me
> They bid me take my place among them
> In the halls of Valhalla
> Where the brave may live forever!

Frank had tied a long strand of kite string to the bow and waded toward the river, guiding the burning ship out of the calm basin and

Max Roderick read the traditional Viking prayer as Frank (white T-shirt) and Greg stood in the river and set the model ship ablaze. *Photo courtesy of Annette Carlozzi and Thomas Zigal*

Frank and Greg released the burning Viking ship on its journey down the Guadalupe River. *Photo courtesy of Annette Carlozzi and Thomas Zigal*

into the Guadalupe's main stream. The river was shallow that time of year and clogged with jutting rocks and broken tree limbs and sandy shoals, and when Frank let go of the string and released the vessel to the will of nature, I thought for certain it would get lodged against the rocks or trapped in driftwood or run aground in sand or simply collapse into ashes from the fire that was consuming its mast. All of us watching from the limestone bank were astounded that the funeral ship somehow navigated without human assistance through a formidable obstacle course of stone and stumps and kept sailing into a deeper, less obstructed channel of the river that carried it downstream.

Greg's son Vincent, the same age as Max, was an outdoors boy who loved to climb trees and stalk through unfamiliar woods and fish with his dad in roaring water, and he decided to splash after the burning longship and safeguard it against mishaps as it floated farther and farther away. Not to be left out, the four other boys—Taylor, Max, Owen, and Danny—raced after Vincent in the shallows near the shoreline like a faithful band of Norse kinsmen eager to follow the ship bearing Rick's remains until they could follow it no more.

The model and the boys disappeared around a bend, and we lost sight of them. That incited the rest of us to raise our fists and cheer with shouts of joy and whistling and applause. We were all surprised and elated that our sendoff was a grand success. Rick's voyage was now in the hands of the river gods.

As Frank and Greg trudged up out of the water, our two exquisite craftsmen smiling triumphantly and soaked to the skin, we congratulated and thanked them with wet bear hugs and slaps on their shoulders. A relieved Greg invited everyone back to his cabin, where food and an ice chest full of cold beer were waiting for us as our victory mead on a sunny spring day in Texas.

A mother hen by nature, I decided to hike downriver along the shoreline to make sure those city boys hadn't been stranded in the wilds. After an eternity of fighting brush and gnarly bushes and needling branches, and struggling to keep my sneakers dry, I met them on their way back. Their clothes were as sopping wet as Frank's and Greg's. They said they'd chased after the ship for a long way but couldn't keep up with it once it hit a white-water stream. When they last saw it, the mast was still smoldering and the vessel remained upright and gliding steadily, so they waved farewell to that gallant craft and watched it vanish around another bend. And then they went swimming in the river.

"Do you think it'll make it all the way to the Gulf?" asked one of the boys.

"Rick would like that," Max said. "He loved to fish on the Gulf."

"I don't know about that ship reaching the Gulf," I said, "but I'm certain it'll enter the halls of Valhalla, where brave warriors live forever."

I assured them that one way or another, that small boxful of his dark grainy carbon would eventually spill into the river and dissolve in the silt roiling in the strong undercurrent and mix with granules of sand. It might take a thousand years for his DNA to wash into the Gulf of Mexico. But this was what Rick had wanted. The pageantry and final rites of a noble warrior who'd fought his ultimate battle.

It was both fitting and ironic that a part of him would end in water, that barefoot boy who'd wandered through the dry holes of his dusty homeland but favored the open sea.

It had been a cathartic send-off and everyone was euphoric after the ceremony, but I was still depressed about Rick's death and managing my own grief as best I could. In that moment with the boys on the riverbank, I saw the shadow pass over their faces as well. Rick was their philosopher king, their holy fool, the eccentric old coot who'd made them laugh and "pushed them to the boundaries of their understanding," as Max later observed. Rick had given these boys free rein to see and do things differently. And now they were in their teens, feisty iconoclasts aware of their teacher's wisdom but judging the world for themselves. That's what a good teacher does—introduce, challenge, listen, embrace—I told myself as we hiked back to Greg's cabin and joined the others in a communion of food and drink. And that's what my old friend had done for so many who'd known him, including myself. Was it a happy accident, or was it providential, that I'd met him at my dorm room thirty-two years earlier, that West Texas boy with all his possessions in a VW Beetle, looking for a place to lay his head? Providence is a tricky concept for an atheist to accept. All I really know is what a dull and incomplete life I would've lived without the companionship and brotherly love of my friend Rick Roderick.

FINAL WISDOM

A DOZEN YEARS AFTER Rick died, an independent filmmaker from California became infatuated with Rick's philosophy lectures on those videotapes produced by the Teaching Company, and he asked to interview me for a documentary about my old friend. The filmmaker traveled to Austin and interviewed Rick's son Marshall and Tom Burditt, and then he came to my home for a videotaped conversation as well. At one point I grew emotional when I was reminiscing about Rick, and the filmmaker said, "Don't be embarrassed. Tom Burditt teared up, too. Rick must've had quite an effect on his friends."

The filmmaker was an amiable man a few years younger than I, with a ready warmth and thoughtful demeanor. I liked him. But when he began asking questions about Rick and Elaine's marriage and their personal lives, I had to stop the interview. "You hungry?" I asked. "Let's take a break and go have lunch."

I took him to Threadgill's, a revered landmark diner that had once been a gas station and beer joint where Janis Joplin got her start as a singer. We had a few drinks over chicken-fried steaks, and I said, "Here's my advice. Don't delve into Rick's private life. It was too messy and convoluted. Stick to the lectures. His teaching. His classroom charisma and the hundreds of students who loved him. The personal stuff will divert your focus from him as an intellectual force, and you'll get lost in the weeds."

The filmmaker ultimately dropped the idea of a Rick Roderick documentary. Or perhaps he put it on hold indefinitely. I was relieved. None of Rick's old friends, and certainly not Elaine, wanted to see their marriage dissected and projected on a screen.

■ ■ ■

Faithful reader, if you've made it this far, you've read a significant portion of Rick's unfinished book. He wrote little more than a hundred pages, and he didn't get past his student years at Hardin-Simmons University. As he was reading those passages to me almost daily, sometimes in person but often by phone, I eagerly awaited what he would say about me and our friends in the Austin of the 1970s and 1980s. But that wasn't in the cards. And so I was saddled with my own faulty memories and the recollections of those who knew him. Many of our reminiscences date back five decades or more, and they're clouded by the fog of time.

At this point, you've glimpsed Rick's personality through his own words, and you've seen the world he grew up in and the many influences that shaped his life. You may be wondering precisely when and how he finally emerged as a deep thinker, an intellectual sponge who'd absorbed the entire history of Western philosophy with remarkable facility. In these pages, I couldn't pinpoint Rick's evolution as a thinker or render his mind's startling illuminations on, say, March 6, 1978, or any other date. I couldn't provide an "aha" moment or an epiphany like Saul being struck blind and falling from his horse. This is a memoir of my friendship with him, not a scholarly treatise. All I could do was tell you a few things I observed over the years and hope you'll find your way to his recorded lectures. Because those lectures are where you'll be grandly challenged and greatly entertained, I promise.

DRAMATIS PERSONAE

NOT LONG AGO, I ran into Rick's son Travis at a restaurant, and as we were hugging and saying hello, his five-year-old son, a child with the handsome Hispanic features of his mother, came up to me and said, "Hi, my name is Rick Roderick. I'm named after my grandfather." That moment was so beautiful and touching and unexpected, I had to bite my lip to keep from bawling. There is another Rick Roderick in this world, and he will outlive me.

The inhabitants of Roderick World are too numerous to account for, and their stories change almost every day, a branching vine of temporary jobs and odd professions and new partners and growing children and evolving ideologies and upsetting illnesses and passings. They are impossible to track, because as Heraclitus observed, you can never step into the same Roderick river twice. If I were to tell you where everyone lives and what they're doing today, that would change by the time you read this. So I'm contented to share a few parting thoughts from old friends and loved ones who knew Rick well.

His son Max has written the most perceptive essay about Rick to date, in which Max says, "Maybe all sons are rhyming couplets of their fathers." A fitting observation about the males I've discussed in this book. It's both an illuminating and a disturbing thought.

Tom Burditt died of cancer in 2013. His former wife, Joan Muller, and I get together sometimes over a glass of wine and reminisce about the old circle. "Rick and I had some sort of connection that I've never really explored," she said in an email. "I wanted to please him. I could see why women were attracted to his power. I loved the man, warts and all, and I'm glad I knew him. He's the only person besides my grandmother who consistently called me Joanie."

My brother Frank said, "I loved Rick because he'd give me his last dollar. If he had two dollars, he'd say, 'Hey, Frank, let's split a burger.'" Their friendship was honest and true and a thing of beauty.

Bev remembered Rick and our younger years with great affection. "Where do you start when looking back on someone who was so much a part of your early days in Austin?" she wrote in an email. "Our lives were not yet ruled by jobs and mortgages and afforded us time to drink-in the local and national politics of the day over a pitcher of beer and cheap food in the university area. Rick always had a great sense of humor, a quick wit, and an eloquent tongue that we all remember well. Those qualities made him an excellent professor of philosophy."

My son, Danny, captured how the boys felt about their mentor:

> Rick was a hero and a role model to all the young barbarians who roamed the Ramsey Park area during our early adolescent years. He was our twentieth century Socrates, full of dangerous wisdom, who taught us to question all forms of authority (including his own). I ranked him somewhere in the pantheon of subversive greatness next to Joe Strummer and Che Guevara, but instead of releasing an album or manifesto, he was able to instantiate himself and his ideas through the direct act of living. I like to think that we each carry a piece of that with us in his absence, and in this way the ethos of Rick will persist across time and geography for as long as we can remember him.

My sister Frances, ten years younger than us, knew Rick very well when she was a UT student: "I loved the man. He was like another big brother to me. Your group of pals always made me feel safe and respected, and we had a helluva lot of fun dancing and listening to live music. But if you were going to have a serious conversation with Rick, you'd better do some backup research first, or he'd clean your clock."

Turner Williamson, the linchpin for the Abilene Boys and all those friendships in the early days, remembered it as an era that "sent everyone into strange, uncharted waters. But during that interval of years, Rick and I never entertained contrary ideas or exchanged cross words. Those were the best of times. The name of the game? Respect and laughter."

His brother, Holt, remembered Rick as "a complicated character who made important contributions in the classroom, was wonderful to his friends, but left blood on the tracks." He deeply valued Rick's hunger for knowledge and social justice, but he said, "my life with Rick was not always so high-minded. As young men from West Texas now exposed to a far more exciting world, we played, we did drugs, we fished, we camped, chased girls, shared girlfriends, and on more than one occasion followed our hormones to the glaring nightlife of Boys Towns on the other side of the Mexican border. We did not go for the serapes. We were in each other's weddings and together welcomed our children into the world."

Left to right: **Danny Zigal, Esteban Gonzales (Tom Zigal's stepson), Tom Zigal, Turner Williamson, Tom Burditt, Holt Williamson, 2012.** *Photo courtesy of Thomas Zigal*

In the end, Holt rendered what I feel is the most accurate and realistic assessment of our old friend: "Still, I could see how others saw a different Rick. He was cruel, needy, arrogant, shifty, deceptive, unruly, aggressive, and completely irresponsible. He honed his dark survival skills to a razor's edge. Rick could cut your throat with a word. He'd cheat you out of your last dollar if it took all night. Essentially, Rick was a con man, a grifter with a brilliant mind and a gift of gab. Given his upbringing, he had to be, I guess, to get where he wanted to go. I'm pretty sure he didn't get there. But to me, Rick was a true friend. He could be brilliant, sincere, warm, funny, kind, and deeply loyal—if he loved you."

If he loved you.

And when he did, your world was filled with enigmas and paradoxes and ideas you hadn't yet explored, and blessed with the cleansing roar of laughter.

GRIEF AND SPLENDOR

LIKE ALL OF US in this vale of tears, Rick Roderick was an imperfect human being, and his insecurities and vulnerabilities have been amply chronicled in this book. It goes without saying that many historical figures possessed flaws that have no bearing on the words they spoke or wrote, or the art they made, or the roles they played in creating masterpieces of enlightenment and entertainment. As Rick pointed out in one of his lectures on philosopher Martin Heidegger, who was a member of the Nazi Party, "People who make terribly tragic political decisions and even very evil people can hold views that are interesting and can say things that are true."[37] As cold as this sounds, it made no difference that Karl Marx didn't know the names of his seven children, that Céline was also a Nazi pamphleteer, and that Norman Mailer stabbed one of his wives. You didn't have to like them as persons. Great thinkers and writers weren't always admirable in their daily lives. It's their work we examine, admire, remember.

Two decades after his death, Rick continues to attract new fans who've discovered his Teaching Company lectures on the Internet. He is often referred to as "the Godfather of the Online Left." He's been praised and memorialized by his former students, some of them now in their fifties, who remember him as a transformative teacher, and he's the topic of numerous podcasts hosted by scholars and critics who are fascinated by his orations. They're puzzled by his early death and wonder what happened to him. He remains a man of mystery. Other popular intellectuals have emerged, like the Slovenian philosopher Slavoj Žižek, who not only emulate Rick's eclectic style, mixing pop culture references with classic philosophy, *they also look like him.* I myself have been contacted by curious Rick Roderick admirers across the spectrum, from current university students who've written their honors theses on him to autodidacts living in rural areas who've stumbled upon him on YouTube and want to know more about him. One devotee tried to organize a weekend symposium focused on Rick's lectures. Our old friend lives on.

When Holt Williamson wrote, "I'm pretty sure he didn't get there," he raised an intriguing question: Did Rick fulfill his highest ambitions? Did he attain the goals he'd set out to reach when he was a young college student contemplating his future? In his last days and nights on this earth, when he was suffering from many physical ailments and still struggling to make a living and support his sons, was he content with how his life had unfolded? Or was he disappointed in himself?

I don't think any of us can answer those questions about Rick. The world judges us in one way, the usual measures in money and prestige and hits on the Internet, but we ourselves set our own standards, make our own bucket lists, define achievement and fulfillment in our own particular lives. In his lecture "Nietzsche: The Will to Power" (1991), Rick is conscious of his attempt at "loving the place you have found yourself in history. And sometimes that's a difficult thing to do. For me that's a quite personal remark that has to do with my own self-invention. To try to love the place I have found myself in history. Like many other people now . . . I find that difficult. Nietzsche, on the other hand, thought it might be difficult, but it was a challenge that we should attempt to meet."[38]

So it's clear that Rick was aware that he might have earned a place in history, however modest or tenuous or even insignificant, and I will leave it to future biographers to decide if he died satisfied with what he'd accomplished in his two score and twelve years.

▪ ▪ ▪

Mourners often have a "grief dream" about a loved one who has passed away. The dream can appear within a few days or even a few years after the death. Sometimes the dream is comforting and reveals the deceased person in a consoling scenario, and sometimes the dream is disturbing and sad. A grief dream can help us cope with our emotions and loss, and continue the bond we formed when they were alive.

The most vivid grief dream I've ever had was about my mother. She was sitting behind a card table under a huge spreading live oak tree across the street from her home in New Braunfels, Texas. It was a beautiful summer day, and resting on the table were drinking glasses and a dripping pitcher of iced tea, no doubt presweetened by white sugar the way Texans used to drink it when I was growing up. My two sisters and I walked out of the front door and saw her smiling at us across the street. I said, "Oh my gosh, there's Momma!" There were no houses on that side of the block, as there were in real life, only a vast green field and the magnificent oak tree. "Y'all come have a glass of tea," said my mother, filling glasses. There was no sign of my father anywhere. As we hurried across the street to share her tea, I said, "Where's Frank?" I thought he was right behind us, but when I turned, he wasn't there. "Don't worry about Frank," my mother said in a kind voice. "He always likes to hang back a little. He'll be along in a minute."

That's all I remember about the dream, which happened a few years after my mother died. The familiar elements of comfort were there—the homey Texas setting with a sheltering tree and green field, and the sweetened iced tea that was the sacramental wine of my childhood. Our mother was smiling, inviting, welcoming, and everyone was happy. Frank would show up soon, we were certain. What the dream told me was that Mom was in a warm and loving place, and her four children would forever be comforted by her watchful presence. I cherish that dream like no other.

I didn't know if I would ever have a grief dream about Rick. And when it happened, a couple of years after his death, it was a much simpler tableau.

Earlier that day I'd gone to the Ramsey Park pool to hang out with the woman I would one day marry. While she was swimming with her children, I decided to walk over to the spot where the Roderick rent house had once stood before it burned. The old place had been torn down, and the new owners were building a two-story home that looked out of scale with the quaint bungalows surrounding it. Because it was a Sunday afternoon, there were no construction workers at the site, so I ventured inside the structure, which had a newly poured concrete foundation and textured sheetrock walls that hadn't been painted yet. I stood where Rick's ratty couch had been braced against the front windows of the living room and I tried to feel the earlier ambience of that space, which had meant so much to me and our friends and Danny and a gaggle of neighborhood boys. The silence was foreign, without a trace of cigarette smoke and laughter. I tried hard to exhume the joy we'd shared in those countless days and nights, if only for a moment, but no remnant of Rick lingered on. I traipsed up the stairs to the second floor of small bedrooms and the fixtures for a bathroom, and it was inconceivable to me that a new area hovering above the old layout could exist at all. After a few minutes of shuffling around like an unhappy ghost, peering out windows, I went downstairs and left the house, heartbroken that an era had passed and there was no bringing it back.

That night, I received a telephone call in my dream. Suddenly Rick was on the line speaking to me in that singular Rick Roderick voice that everyone who ever met him can recall with absolute clarity. It was a voice you could identify among a million other voices you'd heard all your life. It was as distinctive as the voices of every famous singer and movie star and iconic politician you'd listened to in a lifetime of songs and movies and historic speeches. "Hello, Tomski," he began, addressing me by that silly name he sometimes used. He started speaking to me, and I don't recall anything he said because I stopped him as soon as I could catch my breath. "Jesus, Rick, is that really you?" He explained that I could never see him in person again, but we could talk on the phone. Those were the rules.

"Okay, how can I reach you? What's your phone number?" I asked, elated beyond words.

“I’m sorry, man,” he said, “you can’t call me. I’ll have to call you.”

He was calling from that undiscovered country from which no traveler returns. He promised he would stay in touch.

That was many years ago now, and I haven’t heard from him again.

But I want you to know this, old friend: My cellphone is usually within arm’s reach, and I will always be right here, waiting for your call.

ACKNOWLEDGMENTS

I AM A SLOW WRITER who has never mastered the art of nonfiction, which is why it took me twenty-three years, on and off, to complete this memoir about my friendship with Rick Roderick. (I also published three novels during that same period.) From the very beginning, I was fortified by the enthusiasm and encouragement from Rick's four sons, my brother, Frank, my son, Danny, and Jim Magnuson. Many others graciously shared their memories of Rick, notably Turner and Holt Williamson, Annette, Joan, Bev, Kim, Frances, Doug, Dave, Noëlle, Rob, Jonathan, and the other Tom. Fredell Sansom, Debbie Stewart, Brenda Sailing, and Jackie Vesey were most helpful in tracking down photographs, and Carlos Lowry brought his outstanding technical skills to improve the visuals. Many thanks to all!

The book has greatly benefited from the careful readings of my fellow writers Jim Kunetka, Steve Davis, Kip Stratton, and David Wilkinson. I also wish to thank Dan Williams and his staff at TCU Press for believing in this book and expertly shepherding it into print.

NOTES

1. Willie Morris, *North Toward Home: A Memoir* (Houghton Mifflin, 1967), 158.
2. Jay Jensen, *Critical-Theory* (blog), 2014.
3. Gail Caldwell, *A Strong West Wind: A Memoir* (Random House, 2006), 61.
4. Joe Nick Patoski, *Austin to ATX: The Hippies, Pickers, Slackers and Geeks Who Transformed the Capital of Texas* (Texas A&M University Press, 2019), 11.
5. Rick Roderick, interview by Anne Buttimer, 1987, posted July 21, 2011.
6. Morris, *North Toward Home*, 159.
7. Rick Roderick, "Heidegger and the Rejection of Humanism," *The Self Under Siege: Philosophy in The Twentieth Century,* Great Courses (The Teaching Company, 1993).
8. Roderick interview.
9. Gary Cartwright, "The Life and Times of Lyndon Johnson in Eight Full Stories," *The New York Times*, October 17, 1971.
10. Molly Ivins, "Oh, good grief," *The Texas Observer*, May 21, 1971.
11. Neal Spelce with Thomas Zigal, *With the Bark Off: A Journalist's Memories of LBJ and a Life in the News Media* (Dolph Briscoe Center for American History, University of Texas at Austin, 2021), 170.
12. Kaye Northcott and Jay Brakefield, "And a good time was had by most," *Texas Observer,* June 4, 1971, 4.
13. Spelce and Zigal, *With the Bark Off*, 171.
14. Rick Roderick, "Paul Ricoeur: The Masters of Suspicion," *The Self Under Siege.*
15. Roderick interview.
16. Rick Roderick, "Organicism and Marx," *Breviloquium Philosophicum,* student publication of the Philosophy Department, Baylor University.
17. "Recent Literature on Critical Theory," with Douglas Kellner, *New German Critique*, 1981.
18. Rick Roderick, "Max Crawford: The Ambiguous Communist," *Pawn Review* 5 (1981–82).
19. Rick Roderick, "Habermas and the Fragile Dignity of Humanity," *The Self Under Siege.*
20. Roderick, "Habermas."
21. Rick Roderick, *Habermas and the Foundations of Critical Theory* (St. Martin's Press, 1986).
22. Robert T. Tally, *Fredric Jameson: The Project of Dialectical Criticism* (Pluto Press, 2014), xi.

23. "Duke Requires All Departments To Hire Blacks," *New York Times*, April 22, 1988.
24. Katie Crocker, "Roderick addresses a few of his favorite topics," *(Duke) Chronicle*, April 27, 1993.
25. Chris Graham, "Brodie will decide about ServiceMaster in 10 days," *(Duke) Chronicle*, March 9, 1989.
26. Crocker, "Roderick addresses."
27. Billy Warden, "What goes on in the ivory tower," *News and Observer* (Raleigh), July 7, 1991.
28. Rick Roderick, "Derrida and the Ends of Man," *The Self Under Siege*.
29. Kathy Pitman, "Philosophy's Roderick has a hit on his hands," *Duke Dialogue*, October 18, 1991.
30. Sarah Carnevale, "Roderick's lectures return to video," *(Duke) Chronicle*, October 30, 1991.
31. Carnevale, "Roderick's lectures."
32. Robert Tally, October 18, 2019, comment on "About," *Rick Roderick*, https://rickroderick.org/.
33. Katherine Johnson and Scott Heftler, "Q: Why was Roderick denied tenure?" *(Duke) Chronicle*, April 27, 1993.
34. Crocker, "Roderick addresses."
35. Crocker, "Roderick addresses."
36. Rick Roderick, "Marcuse and One-Dimensional Man," *The Self Under Siege*.
37. Roderick, "Heidegger."
38. Rick Roderick, "Nietzsche: The Will to Power," *Nietzsche and the Post-Modern Condition*, Great Courses (The Teaching Company, 1991).

ABOUT THE AUTHOR

THOMAS ZIGAL is the author of several novels, short stories, and essays. His novels have won the Jesse Jones Award for Best Book of Fiction from the Texas Institute of Letters, the fiction award from the Philosophical Society of Texas, and the Violet Crown Award for fiction from the Writers' League of Texas. He lives in Austin, Texas.

thomaszigal.com

Photograph by Ima Leupp